Virtue and the
Making of Modern Liberalism

∗

NEW FORUM BOOKS

Robert P. George, Series Editor

A list of titles

in the series appears

at the back of

the book

Virtue and the Making of Modern Liberalism

*

PETER BERKOWITZ

PRINCETON UNIVERSITY PRESS

PRINCETON AND OXFORD

Copyright © 1999 by Princeton University Press
Published by Princeton University Press, 41 William Street,
Princeton, New Jersey 08540
In the United Kingdom: Princeton University Press,
3 Market Place, Woodstock, Oxfordshire OX20 1SY
All Rights Reserved

Third printing, and first paperback printing, 2000

Paperback ISBN 0-691-07088-1

The Library of Congress has cataloged the cloth edition of this book as follows

Berkowitz, Peter, 1959–
Virtue and the making of modern liberalism / Peter Berkowitz.
p.   cm. — (New forum books)
Includes bibliographical references and index.
ISBN 0-691-01688-7 (cloth : alk. paper)
1. Liberalism.   2. Liberalism—Moral and ethical aspects.
I. Title.   II. Series.
JC574.B47   1999
320.51'3'0973—dc21   98-34871

This book has been composed in Baskerville

The paper used in this publication meets the minimum requirements of
ANSI/NISO Z39.48-1992 (R1997) (*Permanence of Paper*)

www.pup.princeton.edu

Printed in the United States of America

3   5   7   9   10   8   6   4

TO MY PARENTS

✳

✳ *Contents* ✳

∗ *Preface* ∗

For some time now, the conviction has been growing among both politicians and professors that the fate of liberal democracy in America is bound up with the quality of citizens' character. In 1992, chastened by twelve years of Republican domination of the executive branch, Bill Clinton sought to set a new tone for his party by running for president as a New Democrat, a Democrat devoted not only to the protection of individual rights and the promotion of the social and economic bases of equality but also to the principle of personal responsibility. Clinton drew inspiration from the ideas of William Galston, a professor of political science and fellow member of the Democratic Leadership Council whose academic writings expounded "liberal virtues" and defended the propriety of a liberal state fostering qualities of mind and character that form good citizens and decent men and women.

On the other side of the aisle, sometime presidential hopeful and former Reagan secretary of education William Bennett made it to the top of the *New York Times* best-seller list in 1994 with *A Book of Virtues,* a collection of poems and short tales intended for the moral education of the young. Bennett's (and former Vice President Quayle's) onetime chief of staff, William Kristol, now editor and publisher of *The Weekly Standard,* had long argued for the importance to American politics of a "sociology of virtue." Kristol, like Galston a former professor and trained as a political theorist, envisaged a systematic study of the various intermediate or voluntary associations within civil society that foster qualities of character enabling citizens to fulfill the day-to-day demands of maintaining a liberal democracy.

As Galston's and Kristol's common academic background suggests, the rediscovery of virtue by leading Democrats and Republicans has coincided with a renaissance in virtue studies in the universities. One now finds not only liberals but also communitarians and deliberative democrats who have begun to direct their attention to questions about virtue and what can be done in a liberal democracy to cultivate it. In 1992, volume 34 of *Nomos,* the yearbook of the American Society for Political and Legal Philosophy, had virtue as its theme; major feminist thinkers champion an ethics of care that stresses the virtues of compassion and connectedness; and Aristotelians and natural law theorists have been arguing their traditional positions with a renewed vigor and self-confidence. Virtue thus has attracted the attention of leading figures inside and outside the academy.

Despite the groundswell of enthusiasm for the study and practice of virtue, the mere mention of the term still causes acute discomfort for many. To some it evokes a prudish nineteenth-century Victorian morality that equates virtue with the chastity of women. For others virtue conjures up musty metaphysical doctrines associated with Aristotle and Aquinas. For still others virtue is inseparable from the chauvinistic and martial ethic central to the classical republican tradition. Some fear that public discussion of virtue threatens the liberal principle of separation of church and state by introducing inherently religious and unavoidably divisive notions into the public sphere. And finally there are those who regard the very idea of virtue as an oppressive tool that stultifies experiments in self-creation by imposing on human affairs a degrading conformity. Although all such considerations are not equally compelling, the collective force of these one-sided characterizations weighs heavily against virtue's reputation.

Curiously, then, in current debates about the condition of liberal democracy in America one hears both an enthusiasm for, and an aversion to, virtue. And, interestingly, both the enthusiasm and the aversion derive support from the liberal tradition. The aversion to virtue is more familiar. It has roots in the liberal principles of limited government, respect for individual choice, and belief in the equality of human beings. Each citizen, it is affirmed, is the best judge of what is good for him or her; and government's job is to protect each citizen's right to frame his or her own choices about how to live while avoiding the use of state power to favor particular choices or specific forms of life. From this perspective, the very idea of a set of virtues that constitute a decent or good life can be seen as a menacing limit to individual choice, and can raise the specter of an overearnest government eager to legislate morals.

Liberalism's enthusiasm for virtue has been less well documented. The enthusiasm springs from the understanding that liberty, as a way of life, is an achievement. This achievement demands of individuals specific virtues or, to speak less formally, certain qualities of mind and character—such as reflective judgment, sympathetic imagination, self-restraint, the ability to cooperate, and toleration—that do not arise spontaneously but require education and cultivation. Liberalism's enthusiasm for virtue also has roots in the liberal state's need for citizens of a certain sort, citizens who can effectively and fairly administer liberalism's characteristic political institutions, who can keep government within limits, who can exercise their rights in a manner respectful of others and in harmony with the common good, and who can sustain the voluntary associations that compose civil society. From this perspective, it is easy to get carried away and, forgetting liberal scruples about the use of coercive state force, encourage government to take matters into its own hands in order to foster all the virtues thought necessary to the enjoyment of individual liberty and the sustenance of democratic self-government.

The aversion to, and enthusiasm for, virtue represent two opposing tendencies that arise within liberalism. Each tendency, isolated from the other, reflects a distorted image of the liberal spirit and, because of what it fails to take into account regarding government and human nature, generates cramped and rigid prescriptions for political life. The more thoughtful forms of liberalism contain both tendencies and from them weave a more supple perspective. This is not to say that any understanding of liberalism can neatly tie together all loose ends and firmly settle virtue's status. But the liberal tradition itself, I shall argue, does suggest a way, or a particular disposition of mind, to deal with the unsettled status of virtue it has bequeathed to contemporary thought. On reflection, it seems that the liberal mean between the extremes of aversion to, and enthusiasm for, virtue consists in a certain restraint in connection to virtue.

I shall emphasize that the structure of liberal thought itself guarantees that virtue will be an enduring problem for liberalism, a problem that can be neither resolved neatly by theory nor fixed once and for all by skillful institutional design or good laws. Every attempt to deny or resolve the problem of virtue within liberalism suppresses an important dimension of the liberal spirit and deprives liberal practice of flexibility and strength. To submit to the common temptation to slide toward one of the extremes is—in the effort to understand the place of virtue in liberalism, as in so many other undertakings—really a reflection of intellectual lethargy. Strange as it may sound, a certain ambivalence in regard to virtue is a mark in the liberal spirit of sobriety and vitality.

In the interest of such sobriety and vitality, this book aims to counter the extremes of aversion to, and enthusiasm for, virtue to which liberals are prone by illuminating the complex and instructive opinions about virtue and its relation to politics within the liberal tradition. I build upon the work of a diverse group of academic political theorists who, for more than a decade, have responded to the serious charge, leveled by critics on both the left and the right, that liberalism is incapable of giving an account not only of the moral and political importance of community and the common good but also of virtue. Coming at the problem from a variety of perspectives, these new liberals have articulated the contours of a substantive liberalism, one affirming that the liberal state, within bounds, ought to pursue liberal purposes and in its pursuit may, within limits, foster virtues that support liberty and self-government. But the hard-won recognition of the political importance of virtue to liberalism must not be allowed to obscure the genuine difficulties liberalism faces in giving virtue its due. One way to guard against this danger is to revisit the classic works of modern liberalism. For one finds that the stresses and strains in liberal thought are often displayed more clearly and grappled with more vigorously by earlier thinkers than by contemporary scholars.

Prompted by questions about liberalism's prospects and possibilities in the here and now, I have turned to the makers of modern liberalism to clarify the conflict between the need within liberalism to care for both public and private virtue and the hurdles liberalism puts in place to prevent government from caring for virtue too vigorously. Accordingly, this study does not offer a complete account of liberalism. Nor does it provide a comprehensive treatment of the question of virtue. Rather, its aim is to distinguish the variety of ways in which the question of virtue has arisen in the liberal tradition. It also brings into focus the considerations within liberalism that motivate as well as constrain thinking about virtue. And it identifies continuities and differences in the answers the liberal tradition has developed to the question of virtue.

The core of this book consists in an examination of the problem of virtue as it emerges in the work of four seminal thinkers in the making of modern liberalism, each original and enormously influential, none likely to be confused with the others. Through individual studies of the connections that Hobbes, Locke, Kant, and Mill establish between virtue and sound politics, I place in perspective a recurring dilemma in the liberal tradition, a dilemma which has in our own time become especially acute: liberalism depends on virtues that it does not readily summon and which it may even stunt or stifle.

This book's account of the shifting but crucial place of virtue in the liberal tradition suggests four general theses about the problem of virtue in liberalism. First, the logic of liberalism implies, and the makers of modern liberalism openly declare, that citizens and officeholders must possess a range of basic virtues in order to sustain a regime resting on the fundamental premise of liberalism, the natural freedom and equality of all human beings. Second, historically, liberalism has placed primary responsibility for cultivating those virtues on which it depends in extraliberal or nongovernmental institutions such as the family, a demanding form of private education, and the voluntary associations of civil society. Third, the tendency within—but not peculiar to—liberalism to take its principles, in practice, to an extreme weakens these extraliberal and nongovernmental sources of the virtues necessary to liberalism's preservation. And fourth, making liberalism work today requires either the renewal of these old sources for the cultivation of the necessary virtues or the creation of new ones.

Friend and foe agree that contemporary liberalism finds itself in a serious predicament. A richer and more refined account of this predicament, I believe, can be achieved if it is understood in terms of the disproportion between liberalism's need for virtue and the means readily at the disposal of today's liberalism for satisfying that need. I do not, however, take this predicament to constitute an argument against liberalism. Indeed, this book is meant to contribute to liberalism's ability to defend itself by bringing into sharper focus the contending goods that citizens must balance as they deliberate about the limited measures government may take and the steps individuals and the associations they form must take to care for the virtues that make liberal democracy work.

Virtue was a problem for the makers of modern liberalism, and it remains one for us. Our problem, however, is compounded by the fact that we often act as if we have overcome, or need not be bothered by, the difficulties and complexities that bedeviled earlier thinkers in their efforts to rein virtue in while preserving room in which it could maneuver. And yet experience attests to our ambivalence. While we praise presidents who effectively use their high office as a bully pulpit, summoning citizens to meet their responsibilities and live up to their better selves, liberal sensibilities are easily offended by the spectacle of a chief executive who dons the robes of a preacher of virtue.

Some liberals perceive the new interest in character within contemporary American political culture as an urgent response to grave social and political disorders; other liberals see such interest as the unseemly moralism of elected representatives and unelected and unrepresentative professors. In the pages to come I shall suggest that in these complex times, to feel the urgency of both responses is a mark of the liberal spirit in its fullness, because for liberalism today the care for virtue is both awkward and necessary. An exploration of the internal structure of liberal thought can explain why it must be so.

On principle, liberal regimes seek to avoid managing all things and to define and protect a private sphere where citizens can manage the most important part of their lives. This calls for restraint and responsibility from the governors as well as the governed.

Such restraint and responsibility are virtues and therefore depend on cultivation and education. The disproportion between liberalism's need for citizens and officeholders endowed with virtue and the steps that liberal regimes may take to protect and promote virtue produces a permanent instability. Yet it need not be fatal. Indeed, understanding the roots within liberalism of this permanent instability can be fruitful and even a source of virtue.

✳ *Acknowledgments* ✳

THE CONCERNS and conclusions of this book reflect important lessons I learned about liberalism and the virtues that sustain it during my early years in the Government Department at Harvard University. From Stephen Macedo I learned to appreciate the virtues that liberalism calls on citizens to exercise in public life. From Judith Shklar I acquired respect for the virtues that liberalism needs citizens to express in navigating the ordinary rigors of private life. And from Harvey C. Mansfield, Jr., I came to understand that in order to maintain the integrity of public and private life, individuals in a liberal democracy must on occasion exercise virtues that occur at the peaks of morality and politics.

I would like to thank Robert George, Professor of Politics at Princeton University, for his enthusiasm for this book, Ann Wald, Editor-in-Chief of Princeton University Press, for her long-standing interest in my work, and Lauren Lepow, Senior Manuscript Editor at Princeton Press, for her perceptive and discreet editing.

I am grateful to Martin Peretz and Leon Wieseltier for giving me the opportunity to explore in the pages of *The New Republic* a wide range of issues connected to the defense of the liberal spirit.

Adam Wolfson, Executive Editor of the *The Public Interest*, invited me to participate in a symposium on liberalism that he organized for the fall 1996 issue of *Perspectives in Political Science,* and he asked me as well to be part of a roundtable on liberalism that he put together for the 1996 American Political Science Association Convention in Washington, D.C. Thanks to these events, I was compelled to consolidate my thoughts on liberalism's virtue.

The late Joseph Hamburger, whose own work has contributed decisively to a renewed appreciation of the texture and complexity of John Stuart Mill's thought, provided to all who were fortunate enough to know him a model of the liberal spirit in action. Rogers Smith read a draft of the book and offered instructive criticism. Steven Smith has been a steady source of moral and intellectual support. Ronald Beiner, Evan Charney, Joseph Cropsey,

Jean Bethke Elshtain, Timothy Fuller, Charles Griswold, Stanley Hoffmann, Marci Kanstoroom, Jessica Korn, Robert Kraynak, James Kurth, Menachem Lorberbaum, Yehudah Mirsky, Jerry Z. Muller, Father Richard John Neuhaus, Samantha Power, Jeremy Rabkin, Paul Rosenberg, Nancy Rosenblum, Susan Shell, Bernie Steinberg, Yael Tamir, Nathan Tarcov, Steven Teles, Alan Wolfe, and James Q. Wilson have each helped me to adjust my course and nudged me in a better direction.

Barry Shain's provocations, which have not grown less outrageous over time, have continued to serve as a sharp—and much appreciated—spur to reflection. Robert Howse has set me straight on a number of crucial points concerning the intricate structure of liberal thought. Conversations stretching over several years with my new colleagues Andy Sabl and Russ Muirhead have been good fun and highly instructive. My old law school classmate Tim Lytton has been an invaluable interlocutor. And my old graduate school classmate Yossi Shain has been very kind in providing a frequent forum at the Department of Political Science of the University of Tel Aviv in which I could try out my ideas. My Tuesday night study group buddies, both from way back when—Neal Dolan, Tamar Szabó Gendler, and Zoltan Gendler Szabó—and from more recently—Robert Devigne, Malik Mufti, and Vickie Sullivan—have furnished a weekly reminder of the connection between practicing political philosophy and exercising the virtue of friendship. My sister Linda Berkowitz has once again saved me from many errors. Luke McLoughlin caught numerous inaccuracies. Stanley Kurtz has been generous with both encouragement and critique. At the last minute Jedidiah Purdy read the entire manuscript and made several incisive suggestions. Dan Choi's curiosity, criticism, and care have led to many refinements in the arguments of this book. And studying virtue and liberalism with the students in my classes at Harvard has hastened my progress, and heightened my pleasure, in understanding.

Virtue and the
Making of Modern Liberalism

✳

✳ *Introduction* ✳

> If we ask ourselves on what causes and conditions good
> government in all its senses, from the humblest to the
> most exalted, depends, we find that the principal of
> them, the one which transcends all others, is the
> qualities of the human beings composing the society
> over which the government is exercised.
> (John Stuart Mill, *Considerations on
> Representative Government*)

SINCE OPINIONS about character bear upon the one who opines, under the best of circumstances it may be embarrassing to speak about virtue. From the precarious position where one's judgments have consequences for how one ought to be judged, and suggest the standards according to which one judges others, those who wish to understand virtue are persistently tempted by two opposing tendencies. Some yield to lofty sentiments, prattling on sanctimoniously about how human beings ought to be; others, presuming to see things as they really are, resolutely search out or grimly describe the self-interested impulses that supposedly define the actual and exclusive motivations of human conduct. Yet airy idealism and narrow realism do not exhaust the range of perspectives from which virtue may be investigated. Getting down off your high horse does not condemn you to running with the pack. To be sure, the mean or middle ground from which the claims of virtue and the charges against it can be fairly evaluated is more difficult to attain and harder to hold than either of the extremes. This is partly because understanding virtue is inseparable from its exercise.

Rewarding as the study of virtue for its own sake may be, for students of politics the study of virtue is not a choice but a necessity imposed by the character of their subject matter. Not that the question of virtue has a single formulation or one right answer. Rather, like freedom, obligation, law, the regime, and justice, virtue belongs among the fundamental phenomena of political life

3

for which a respectable theory of politics must give an account and concerning which it cannot but take a stand. Silence is an option but not a solution, for, as I shall argue, a political theory that overlooks the question of virtue spawns fatal theoretical lacunae while passing by key features of the conduct for which it presumes to account.

The inescapability of virtue is more apparent in ancient and medieval political philosophy, where virtue, or the promotion of human excellence, was generally held to be the ultimate aim of politics. By contrast, modern political philosophy has tended to reject such lofty goals as impractical, delusive, and dangerous. Especially in its Enlightenment and liberal strains, modern political philosophy put forward a different fundamental goal for politics. Instead of seeking through politics to promote human perfection, the liberal tradition came to understand the goal of politics as the protection of personal freedom. The liberal tradition embraces freedom as the aim of politics on the grounds that it is both more attainable and more just than the promotion of virtue. But the repudiation of virtue as the aim of politics must not be equated with the repudiation of the very idea of virtue, or with a denial that questions of citizens' and officeholders' character are of pressing political significance. Indeed, I shall argue that the liberal tradition, through a variety of prominent spokesmen, affirms that maintenance of a political order capable of securing the personal freedom of all depends upon citizens and representatives capable of exercising a range of basic virtues. Liberalism, I shall suggest, can no more do without virtue than a person on a diet can survive without food and drink.

The liberalism to which I refer is a complex and many-sided tradtion. John Locke, Immanuel Kant, and John Stuart Mill are among this tradition's leading spokesmen. But many others—including Thomas Hobbes, Montesquieu, Adam Smith, the authors of *The Federalist*, Burke, and Tocqueville—shared its fundamental premise and in various ways elucidated its strengths and weaknesses. I shall follow Judith Shklar in understanding liberalism as a political doctrine the primary goal of which is "to secure the political conditions that are necessary for the exercise of personal freedom."[1] I add to Shklar's definition what she left implicit, namely, that even as a political doctrine liberalism rests on the fundamental premise of the natural freedom and equality of all human beings. To establish and secure the personal freedom of all, the liberal tradition has articulated a set of characteristic themes including individual rights, consent, toleration, liberty of thought and discussion, self-interest rightly understood, the separation of the private from the public, and personal autonomy or the primacy of individual choice; and it has elaborated a characteristic set of political institutions including representative democracy, separation of governmental powers, and an independent judiciary. I shall also emphasize what goes understated in Shklar's writings and is generally less well appreciated but vital to an understanding of liberalism's possibilities and prospects: notwithstanding its focus on the political conditions that support personal freedom, the liberal tradition has provided a fertile source of reflections on such nongovernmental supports of the virtues that sustain liberty as civic association, family, and religion.

The tendency within liberal thought to diminish the significance of virtue in descriptions of, and prescriptions for, political life is well known. It is less remarked that a coherent and comprehensive account of politics, liberal or otherwise, cannot succeed without giving virtue its due. To be sure, the leading theorists of liberalism adduce strong practical and theoretical reasons for, and display considerable resourcefulness in, circumscribing virtue's role. Yet the best of the liberal tradition exhibits an illuminating ambivalence and reveals a range of instructive opinions about the claims of virtue and how they can best be respected. This can be seen even and especially in that part of the tradition famous for getting along without virtue. Hobbes, for example, in his masterwork *Leviathan*, at the conclusion of his most comprehensive enumeration of the laws of nature, declares that, properly speaking, the laws of nature are not laws but moral virtues and, accordingly, that "the science of virtue and vice is moral philosophy."[2] Locke devotes an entire work, *Some Thoughts Concerning Education*, to expounding an education in virtue that begins in infancy, that extends to young adulthood, and that prepares individuals to prosper in a free society. Kant argues that ethics involves both "genuine virtue" and lesser qualities of mind and character to which he is reluctant to give the name virtue. Moreover, in the effort to accommodate the necessities of political life, Kant makes practical concessions to virtue and devises stratagems by which virtue, having been formally expelled from politics, is brought back in through the side door. And Mill understands both the exercise of individual liberty and the quality of democratic self-government to turn on the virtue of ordinary men and women and their representatives in government. The problem with much contemporary thought, I shall suggest, is not just the lack of a coherent account of the place of virtue in the political theory of liberal democracy but, more telling, the absence of embarrassment in the face of such a lack.

Over the past decade, leading liberals in the academy have contributed to the recovery of an understanding of the importance of character to liberalism. Yet the turn to "ordinary vices" and "liberal virtues" has not gone far enough.[3] Three issues deserve greater attention. First, the operation and maintenance of liberal democracy—that form of democracy in which the will of the people is grounded in and limited by individual rights—depend upon the exercise of moral and intellectual virtues that, according to liberalism's own tenets, fall outside its strict supervision, and that it not only does not always effectively summon but may even discourage or undermine. Second, the extraliberal or nongovernmental reservoirs from which liberalism has drawn in the past to foster the virtues necessary to maintain itself—in particular, the family, religion, and the array of associations in civil society—have undergone substantial transformations and can no longer be counted on in the way that the classic liberal tradition counsels. Third, liberal principles seem to spawn characteristic vices, vices that are entwined with liberal virtues and which threaten the capacity of citizens to sustain free and democratic institutions.

Oddly, some of liberalism's proponents have made common cause with its critics to insist on a fatal or at least bitter antagonism between liberalism and virtue.[4] But this is a serious mistake, one preventing liberalism from recognizing the conditions that preserve it. Contrary to much conventional wisdom, the liberal tradition not only makes room for virtue but shows that the exercise of virtue is indispensable to a political regime seeking to establish equality and protect freedom. Of course, I do not mean to say that it is a simple matter to protect or promote virtue in a liberal society; nor do I wish to deny that peculiar features of liberal thought may in the long run put the integrity of virtue at risk.[5] Rather, what I wish to suggest is that one can begin to grasp the genuine complexity of the matter and start to see the real risk by appreciating the rich and illuminating set of opinions advanced by the makers of modern liberalism about the dependence of freedom and equality on virtue.

ARISTOTLE'S ACCOUNT OF THE VIRTUES

One of the challenges confronting any exploration of the importance of virtue to liberalism consists in determining just what sort of thing is the virtue for which one is looking. The problem is pronounced because, as Hobbes and Locke are at pains to point out, the meaning of virtue is imprecise and inconstant.[6] In meeting this challenge, the classic account of virtue found in Aristotle's *Nicomachean Ethics* and *Politics* provides instruction. Not, of course, as an authoritative statement of a particular catalog of virtues, or as the last word on the ends of a truly human life, or as an entirely adequate account of the means for acquiring and promoting virtue. Rather, Aristotle's examination of the virtues serves as an advantageous point of departure for the raising of certain basic questions about virtue and its relation to politics. It also illuminates the continuity across time and culture that lies beneath the imprecision of expression and inconstancy of use surrounding the term "virtue." And it brings into better focus the advantages and limitations of the ways in which virtue in the liberal tradition has been conceived and elaborated.

The primary sense of virtue (*arete*) in ancient Greek was that of a functional excellence. The virtue of a knife is sharpness, the virtue of an eye is seeing clearly, the virtue of a judge is deciding cases impartially in accordance with law and equity, and the virtue of a human being, Aristotle thought, consisted in a certain activity of the soul in accordance with reason. What I wish to stress is that the excellence of a human being was, in Aristotle's view, not the sole type of virtue. Rather, human excellence was but an instance or species, perhaps even the most important and noble instance or species, found under the genus virtue.

In general, then, Aristotle understood virtue as a condition or state of a thing that enabled it to perform a designated task well. That task could be conventional, a result of human decision, or natural, somehow inherent in a rational order that owes nothing to the will, imagination, or activity of human beings. With regard to human beings, virtue refers to those qualities of mind and character that aid in the performance of particular tasks or in the pursuit of determinate ends. Human beings, of course, can have many ends: satisfying physical desire, cooperating for mutual advantage, acquiring wealth, winning fame and glory. And to each of these lesser ends there are corresponding virtues. Aristotle calls those qualities of mind and character that conduce to man's natural end "human virtue" or the "virtues of the soul."[7]

It is especially worth noticing that Aristotle's generic or formal definition of virtue does not entail any particular account of human nature and is as compatible with his own view that the human soul has a specific function or excellence as with, say, Hobbes's repudiation of the very idea of human perfection. In other words, the generic definition of virtue as a functional excellence can and ought to be distinguished from such controversial issues as whether human beings have a nature and, if they do, in what manner that nature can be perfected. In the absence of an overarching goal or single perfection, human beings can have or perform many functions. Human beings can be husbands and wives, citizens and store owners, investment bankers and short-order cooks, philosophers and artists, friends and foes. And each of these roles or functions requires its peculiar virtues. The distinction between human excellence and excellence at the various and sundry functions that human beings may from time to time perform, and in the diversity of tasks they may choose to pursue, is worth stressing for several reasons: the distinction is crucial to a grasp of Aristotle's moral and political philosophy on its own terms; it is vital to an appreciation of the pertinence of Aristotle's moral and political philosophy to liberalism; and it is routinely misunderstood or obscured by contemporary scholars.

Indeed, the prevailing tendency in contemporary thought is to equate virtue with the idea of human perfection—a tendency which has roots in early modern misrepresentations of Aristotle[8]—and then reject virtue on the grounds that the idea of human perfection is politically irrelevant or morally destructive or no longer intelligible. The fact is, however, that Aristotle did not understand virtue as pertaining exclusively to a human being's highest end. A human life, as Aristotle understood it, has not only a highest end but also intermediate or lesser ends, and the attainment of these intermediate or lesser ends depends on the exercise of particular virtues or qualities of mind and character.[9] Indeed, Aristotle could even refer to the virtue of the body,[10] the virtue of the nonrational element of the soul,[11] and the virtue of such (in his view) incomplete human beings as women, slaves, vulgar artisans, and children.[12] It is often overlooked—to the detriment of the understanding of Aristotle as well as liberalism—that while Aristotle's account of a human being's highest end implicates controversial opinions about human nature and metaphysical first principles, his generic definition of virtue presupposes neither a particular view of human nature nor a theoretical account of the cosmos.

What tends to be mistaken for the entirety of Aristotle's interest in the question of virtue—the question of human virtue or virtue of the soul—is, in fact, the distinctive focus of one critical part of Aristotle's political science, the part that he develops in the *Nicomachean Ethics*, and which is devoted to investigating happiness and the character of the good life.[13] In the *Ethics*, Aristotle divides human virtue into two kinds. Moral virtue, which governs feelings and actions, is a fixed disposition or character trait acquired through habituation, involving choice, and performed in accordance with right reason.[14] Intellectual virtue, which governs thought, comes mostly from teaching and is exercised in practical judgment as well as in theoretical contemplation.[15] The distinction between moral and intellectual virtue is, however, imperfect because the moral virtues involve the exercise of reason, and the perfection of reason depends upon the cultivation of the virtues of character.[16] In a kind of antiformula formula, Aristotle contends that virtue consists in doing the right thing, at the right time, in the right way, toward the right people, for the right reason.[17] This means, among other things, that what excellence in action consists in very often cannot be specified in advance and in practice always calls for the exercise of practical wisdom, or the ability to understand circumstances in context and fit one's actions to them so as to do what is right.[18] The ultimate good for a human being is happiness or flourishing, the exercise of moral and intellectual virtue in proper proportion over the course of an entire life. Virtue, however, does not guarantee happiness, since good fortune, which cannot be entirely mastered by human beings, plays an ineliminable role in securing the external goods—reputation, wealth, health, family, and friends—necessary for the effective and full exercise of the virtues.[19]

While he indicates in the *Ethics* that there is but one catalog of moral virtue—a catalog that prominently features courage, temperance, generosity, liberality, magnanimity, and justice—Aristotle observes in the *Politics* that there is a variety of forms of government or regime. Every regime depends upon citizens endowed with a specific set of virtues that are relative to the regime's particular needs and goals.[20] The excellence of citizens in a democracy, a regime in which the people, who tend to be poor, rule, and whose principles are freedom and equality, differs from the excellence of citizens in an oligarchy, a regime in which the few, who tend to be wealthy, rule. Under most regimes, the virtues of a good citizen and those of a good man will differ because actual regimes tend to exalt forms of life that are partial and incomplete, whereas the good man pursues the best life, which requires the harmonious exercise of the full range of the virtues. At best, the life of the good democrat or good oligarch involves some part of moral and intellectual virtue. Perhaps only in the best

10

regime, the regime devoted to human virtue, do the virtues of the human soul coincide with those which serve the regime's specific end.

It is common for contemporary scholars to ascribe to Aristotle, without qualification, the view that the aim of political life is to promote human excellence and perfect citizens.[21] This, however, is an unfortunate oversimplification, one that encourages many liberals in their determination to view Aristotle as irrelevant or hostile to their concerns.[22] It is true that Aristotle asserts in the *Ethics* that the "true statesman" must study virtue so as to be able to make citizens good.[23] But what he makes clear in the *Politics* is that true statesmen are at best seldom at the helm and very few actual regimes embrace virtue as their guiding principle. Given these facts of life, the primary task of politics most of the time, according to Aristotle, is not to perfect men's souls but to preserve actual imperfect regimes by fortifying citizens against the bad habits and destructive tendencies fostered by the way of life to which their regime is devoted. Aristotelian political science does not seek to transform imperfect regimes, such as democracies and oligarchies, into regimes devoted to human excellence; rather, it aims to institute measures so as to enable imperfect regimes to honor their principles and to moderate their unwise tendencies. The single greatest expedient for preserving a regime, says Aristotle, is the one most neglected by actual regimes: education in virtues that serve as a counterpoise to the characteristic bad habits and reckless desires which regimes tend to foster in their citizens.[24]

From an Aristotelian perspective, the student of politics must take into account the virtues relative to the maintenance of the specific regime in question as well as the virtues relative to a human being's final end or perfection. Particularly on Aristotle's account, inquiry into the greatest good or final end for a human being does not exhaust the inquiry into virtue because all tasks, including the political tasks of ruling and being ruled, have their associated virtues. It is true that the opinion that human perfection has a determinate form is bound to affect the assessment of

11

what must be done to preserve particular regimes. But it is also true, from Aristotle's perspective, that however the question of human perfection is decided, no regime can long survive unless qualities of mind and character that support its specific principles and purposes and counteract its unwise tendencies are deliberately cultivated and regularly exercised.

To appreciate the qualified sense in which Aristotle was a perfectionist in politics is certainly not to dispose of all the serious objections that can be raised against his account of virtue. The familiar objection remains that his catalog of virtues in the *Ethics* reflects the particular and contingent sensibilities of the ascendant class in fourth-century Athens. To this objection it is easy enough to reply that we need not follow Aristotle in every respect, that we are not bound to endorse only those or all those virtues which Aristotle discusses, and that Aristotle himself insists that in ethics and politics the truth must be indicated "roughly and in outline."[25] But even after these replies have been accorded their due weight, a thorny issue persists: by invoking the notion of a human being's characteristic activity or function and the idea of greatest good, Aristotle's account of virtue, if only at its peak, appears to depend upon a discredited metaphysical biology and a refuted speculative cosmology.

Although real, this problem poses less of an obstacle to our learning from Aristotle's practical philosophy than is commonly supposed.[26] And this is not in the first place because Aristotle's metaphysics is more defensible than has been commonly thought. It is, rather, because his overall account of virtue is less dependent upon his metaphysics than has been typically assumed. I do not mean that one can, at the end of the day, understand virtue as a human excellence without implicating controversial doctrines about human nature and the first principles of the cosmos. What I do wish to suggest is that one can begin the inquiry into the relation between virtue and politics and make considerable progress before one has firmly settled all vexing theoretical issues. At least if one takes Aristotle seriously. For Aristotle's own procedure is to consider the question of virtue as it arises in ordinary language and out of daily life, and then, by refining commonly held opinions about morality and politics and working through their implications, to move beyond them.[27]

By following Aristotle's procedure and beginning with the actual language of morality and politics rather than with final judgments about the theoretical presuppositions of such a language, contemporary students of politics can find in their world, as Aristotle found in his own, basic and pervasive claims about the moral and political significance of a range of qualities of mind and character. For in ordinary language and everyday experience we still distinguish good from bad lives, and—though our powers of discrimination, our capacity to articulate our opinions, and our confidence in our judgments may have declined—we still invoke virtues such as courage, generosity, integrity, toleration, decency, delicacy, and the capacity for love and friendship in order to characterize and evaluate both ourselves and others. This is all that one needs, from an Aristotelian perspective, to commence the investigation of virtue and take the question of the political significance of virtue seriously.

In the long run, a complete understanding of virtue does require an account of first principles and a defense of controversial opinions about human nature and the cosmos. But, especially in light of the antifoundationalist, pragmatic, and postmetaphysical perspectives that are fashionable today, it is proper to ask why virtue should be held to a more stringent standard than, say, freedom or equality or justice. If, as many contemporary liberal and postmodern political theorists believe, we can discuss freedom, equality, and justice for political purposes perfectly well without invoking foundations or appealing to first principles, then perhaps discussion about virtue can proceed some substantial distance before vexing questions about foundations and first principles receive final answers. This is not to say that the question of virtue's foundations is a small matter. It is, rather, to observe that the first principles need not be fixed firmly before an inquiry into the moral and political significance of virtue can get under way and begin to yield benefits.

I should make clear that I believe that the contemporary aversion to, or attack on, foundations is often tendentious. It confuses a strategy of avoidance appropriate to political debate with a dogmatic disavowal of the significance of metaphysics that is quite inappropriate to intellectual inquiry. And it tends to slide rapidly from a reasonable doubt about whether human beings have a nature to perfect into an invincible certainty that human beings do not. Nevertheless, it is possible to wrest an important point from the excesses characteristic of antifoundationalist, pragmatist, and postmetaphysical theorizing: in many areas of ethics and politics the foundations do not have to be secured before exploration of the key concepts can commence. Thus does the contemporary aversion to metaphysical foundations, by detaching questions about the usefulness of moral and political categories from questions about the theoretical framework that, some may suppose, renders them fully intelligible and absolutely secure, provide an opening for questions about the place of virtue in liberalism.[28]

Nevertheless, in the present climate of opinion, the very mention of human excellence is more likely to provoke patronizing smiles, cynical sneers, or outright derision than intellectual engagement. According to widespread beliefs today, tasks are not given and definite but constructed and of infinite variety, happiness is a matter of individual choice, and there exist a thousand and one acceptable styles of life. These opinions, rooted in philosophical ideas that partially constitute liberal, Enlightenment modernity, seem to remove the ground from underneath virtue understood in terms of human perfection by flatly denying that human beings have a nature to be perfected or a circumscribed range of tasks to discharge. And the contemporary critique of foundations quickly and carelessly slides from the view that philosophizing about morality and politics can proceed without perfect knowledge of foundations to the dogmatic insistence that theoretical foundations for morality and politics definitely do not exist. To understand virtue's embattled position today, one must explore the features of liberal modernity that, by encouraging a repudiation of its apparent ground, have put virtue understood as human excellence on the defensive.

LIBERAL MODERNITY AND VIRTUE

Virtue has become embattled within contemporary liberalism for reasons that go to the foundations of modern thought. Modernity is, of course, more than a way of thinking, designating a wide range of changes in cultural, economic, social, and political life that began to accelerate in Europe in the sixteenth and seventeenth centuries. Yet few would disagree that modernity crucially involves a new understanding of the human condition based on a rejection or dramatic revision of inherited ideas about nature and God. Distinctively modern thought comes into being through an explicit critique of classical Greek philosophy and biblical faith. To many medieval thinkers what was most apparent were the differences or conflict between the philosophy of Plato and Aristotle, which culminated in the idea of a self-subsistent human excellence completed in the perfection of one's rational faculty, and biblical faith, which promulgated the idea of salvation or redemption as the ultimate gift of a mysterious God. But to thinkers such as Machiavelli and Hobbes the philosophy stemming from Plato and Aristotle and the religion rooted in the Bible were alike in the most important respect. Whereas medieval thinkers grappled with the conflicting accounts of the greatest good or ultimate end taught by philosophy and faith, Machiavelli and Hobbes were more impressed by the fact that, in the teaching of both classical philosophy and biblical religion, there was a transcendent moral order, not subject to human choice or will, that established principles of right conduct, defined human happiness, and revealed the soul's perfection.

According to a standard picture of the history of the early modern world, new beliefs and changes in theoretical outlook—in particular, growing skepticism about a moral order external to and independent of human beings—placed the very notion of human excellence under powerful strain. The rise of natural science, the disenchantment of the heavenly spheres, the growth in confidence that human beings could, by focusing their minds and taking matters into their own hands, improve and perfect their condition combined to discredit the claims of theoretical reason and religious authority to guide human life. By calling into question the belief in a natural or divine order that could be known through the exercise of reason, modern philosophy, slowly but surely, seemed to reveal that the idea of human excellence was itself a human invention. And virtue, when understood as a human invention, or as a general name for qualities of mind and character that people in a particular society happened to value and praise, seemed to lose much of its splendor and become scarcely recognizable as virtue. For if human beings lacked a nature, task, or calling, then they must also lack virtue in the precise sense, for virtue, it was thought, involves the perfection of a nature.

There were also practical considerations that motivated the shift in attention away from questions about virtue. The bitter wars of religion that ravaged Europe during the sixteenth and seventeenth centuries convinced many thoughtful observers of the urgency of removing questions about ultimate salvation or the highest good from the sphere of politics. To preserve peace and order, government, it was argued, must be limited, in regard to both its legitimate end or ends and the means or powers it could use to achieve those ends. The proper aim of government was not to cultivate virtue, as, it was said, the ancient philosophers thought, but to maintain peace, protect individual rights, and promote material prosperity. To be sure, it is one thing to say that it is not *government*'s business to cultivate virtue, and quite another to assert that virtue is altogether irrelevant to the maintenance of peace, the protection of individual rights, and the promotion of material prosperity. Yet the heavy conceptual artillery and powerful rhetorical thunderbolts that the makers of modern liberalism deployed to show why government must stay out of the business of fostering human excellence suggested to many that fostering virtue of any sort was a dubious business for *all* reputable associations and self-respecting individuals.

So, according to the standard picture, while one strand of liberal thought demoted virtue on the basis of a theoretical critique of metaphysics and religion, another strand downplayed the political importance of virtue by invoking practical judgments about the dire consequences of imposing conceptions of the good life through the use of the coercive force of the state. In many cases, of course, the theoretical critique of reason was joined to the practical judgments about political necessity, with the result that opinions about human perfection were pushed into the background of moral and political thought.

This standard picture—which has been embraced by both liberals and their critics, and which, on the whole, has much to recommend it—is not in every respect adequate. It obscures an especially important matter: despite their rejection by and large of the idea that the state should be devoted to the promotion of human excellence, the makers of modern liberalism did not reject virtue as a critical category of moral and political philosophy, and never dreamed that a politics based on natural freedom and equality could achieve its goals independently of the qualities of mind and character of citizens and officeholders.

The inadequacies of the standard picture require a reconsideration of what the liberal tradition has to teach about virtue. Part of the problem, however, is that to see the inadequacies one must have already begun the reconsideration. Accordingly, I want to suggest that we can obtain valuable guidance in understanding liberalism's long-standing and fruitful entanglement with virtue by considering the writings of such formidable critics of liberal modernity as Alasdair MacIntyre, Charles Taylor, and Leo Strauss. The philosophical explorations of MacIntyre, Taylor, and Strauss shake up old habits of thought about liberalism and throw new light not only on liberalism's characteristic weaknesses and typical exaggerations but also on its internal dynamics and neglected possibilities. The suggestion that such critics estimably illuminate not only the weaknesses but also the strengths of the liberal tradition may come as a surprise to many liberals in the academy. But it should not. For it is a central liberal virtue to listen respectfully to viewpoints different from one's own, and it is a famous liberal principle that knowledge is advanced through the clash of opposing viewpoints. In this particular case, I shall show that the exercise of liberal virtue and adherence to liberal principle pay rich dividends for liberalism.[29]

Consider, for example, MacIntyre's widely discussed and controversial book *After Virtue*. MacIntyre argues that the Enlightenment project—the effort to supply a rational justification, independent of aesthetics, law, or theology, for abstract rules of right conduct[30]—has precipitated a calamitous breakdown in the language we use in speaking about virtue. On the view that the history of our concepts is an indispensable component of philosophical analysis, MacIntyre traces the transformations that the concept of virtue has undergone—from the martial qualities that characterized pre-Homeric Greek heroes to the expertise in technique and the mastery of manipulation that, MacIntyre argues, characterize exemplars within the contemporary American moral outlook: the therapist, the aesthete, and the manager. What comes to function in Aristotle's ethics as a category embracing a set of excellences of character (the virtues), traits that enabled a human being to achieve his specific excellence, deteriorated by the late nineteenth century, on MacIntyre's account, into a singular moral quality (virtue) governing the sexual conduct of women. Writing in 1981, and hence before the renaissance in virtue studies that his own work helped set in motion, MacIntyre lamented the vanishing of reflection on the virtues from contemporary academic liberal discourse and the fading of virtue as a living moral category in the lives of ordinary citizens. By demonstrating the irrationality of the theory and the emptiness of the moral life that suppressed or sought to expel virtue, MacIntyre hoped to establish the superior rationality of the Aristotelian moral tradition, in which virtue was seen as a central moral and political category.

MacIntyre's argument in *After Virtue* is vulnerable to serious criticism. It has been said that his intellectual history is one-sided; that his account of the moral decline of the contemporary world is greatly exaggerated; that his dependence on intellectual history as a causal factor, to the exclusion of political, economic, and social forces, is misguided; that he is oblivious to liberalism's achieve-

ments; and that his proposal to "men and women of good will"—
that they quietly withdraw from the political life of liberal democracy and engage in the "construction of local forms of community
within which civility and the intellectual and moral life can be
sustained through the new dark ages which are already upon
us"—is apocalyptic.[31] The truth in these criticisms, however, is
compatible with MacIntyre's central claim about the gradual im-
poverishment of our capacity to speak about virtue, and the narrow and narrowing perspective on the moral and political significance of character resulting from the internal dynamics of liberal
thought and practice.

Moreover, his critics—and MacIntyre too—overlook the opportunity for liberalism embedded in MacIntyre's interpretation of
liberal modernity's breakdown. For example, by MacIntyre's own
account, "the classical tradition of the virtues"[32] was an important
feature of English thinking about the moral life as late at least as
the first quarter of the nineteenth century.[33] It follows that virtue
was an intelligible and available concept through much of the period in which liberalism received its classic formulations. Arguably, the very conceptual transformations that MacIntyre brings
to light and which he claims have accelerated in the twentieth
century have, in distorting and diminishing our moral vocabulary,
also distorted and diminished the vocabulary necessary for exploring the role that virtue has played in the history of the making of
modern liberalism and must continue to play in any coherent defense of liberalism today. Perhaps the very breakdown of our
moral language, a breakdown that MacIntyre so effectively describes, not only inhibits us from seeing ourselves in terms of the
virtues but also has occluded the role played by opinions about
virtue in the liberal tradition.

In a more direct manner, Charles Taylor's sympathetic and
wide-ranging account of modern thought, *Sources of the Self,* also
indicates that modernity has richer resources with which to speak
about virtue than has generally been supposed.[34] In contrast to
MacIntyre, Taylor is an admirer of modern thought, but like
MacIntyre he discerns within modernity destructive tendencies.
One of these is modernity's neglect of the moral and conceptual

sources that sustain it. And one of Taylor's striking theses is that many of the achievements of which modernity is most proud have important roots in classical thought and biblical faith. Accordingly, Taylor finds that such notable achievements in the long process of the making of the modern self as the turn toward the psychological and moral depths of the individual, the affirmation of the ordinary life of work and family, and the invention of romanticism or expressive individualism were decisively prepared and crucially sustained by premodern theological categories and aspirations, categories and aspirations that modernity self-consciously rebelled against and came to pride itself on having overcome. The presumption among modern thinkers to have altogether superseded religious faith and traditional philosophy, Taylor warns, has been one cause of excesses and follies committed by modernity's champions, and is a tendency, in Taylor's view, that today threatens modernity's solid achievements. Taylor suggests that modernity has rashly weakened its position by cutting itself off from the premodern sources that have, even in its most innovative moments, inspired and nourished it. To the extent that his overall argument is sound, one would expect to find that virtue, a prominent premodern category, plays a bigger role in traditional liberalism, both visibly and behind the scenes, than received wisdom recognizes.

In the search for liberalism's neglected possibilities and untapped resources, Leo Strauss, too, can be a surprising ally. Among the most controversial and influential scholars of political philosophy in the twentieth century, Strauss may be best known for his revival of the serious study of Plato as a living source of wisdom about politics. Strauss presented his recovery of Plato's political philosophy in terms of a fundamental quarrel between ancient and modern thought. Against the prevailing scholarly consensus in the first half of the twentieth century—which saw Plato, and indeed the history of premodern Western political philosophy, as a kind of primitive protoliberalism, a necessary step on the way toward enlightenment and modern liberalism—Strauss stressed the fundamental differences separating ancient and modern philosophy. Against the scholarly consensus that came to prevail after World War II that Plato was a teacher of totalitarianism, Strauss stressed the skeptical side of Plato's thinking and the support that classical political philosophy lent to modern liberal democracy. Indeed, against contemporary self-confidence, Strauss suggestively argued with great passion and inventiveness that in the quarrel between the ancients and the moderns it was an open question as to who had the upper hand.

Owing perhaps to the practical task he set for himself, Strauss may sometimes have exaggerated the scope of the differences and disagreements between ancient and modern thought. Indeed, in the effort to awaken scholars from their dogmatic slumber, Strauss, on occasion, melodramatically emphasized the radical nature of the break with ancient and medieval thought through which modernity came into being.[35] I speak of occasional exaggeration and melodramatic emphasis because in his detailed studies of particular thinkers—as opposed to his shorter essays and brief introductions to his books—Strauss makes clear that the modern break with antiquity is frequently partial and incomplete, that important continuities mark the history of political philosophy, and that the conflict between characteristically ancient and characteristically modern ideas often plays itself out, and sometimes to fruitful effect, within the confines of modern thought.

Although his name has come to be identified with the idea that a vast gulf separates modernity from antiquity, Strauss himself, time and again in his writings, called attention to the ways in which modern thinkers, in the exposition of their moral and political ideas, had recourse to or presupposed typically ancient notions.[36] Strauss's own specific interpretations of modern political philosophers amply demonstrate that the famous quarrel between the ancients and the moderns is seldom clear-cut, and that, at its best, modern political philosophy remains fruitfully entangled with opinions characteristic of classical political philosophy. Thus, like the historical work of MacIntyre and Taylor, Strauss's critique of liberal modernity points to an important lesson about liberalism that resourceful liberals can adapt to their advantage:

gulf though there may be, there is more antiquity in modernity than is commonly supposed. Virtue is an element of this neglected antiquity within liberal modernity, and as such, I shall argue, it constitutes an important resource for liberals today.

Communitarian Criticisms and
Liberal Lessons

While one opening for the acquisition of a better understanding of virtue in liberalism has been carved out by leading critics of mainstream academic political theory, another opening arises from promising developments within the mainstream itself.[37] It is well known that a single work published in 1971, John Rawls's *A Theory of Justice*, has been largely responsible for the elevation of a particular conception of liberalism, one devoted to both the protection of individual liberty and the securing of the social and economic bases of equality, to the top of the agenda of academic political theory. A decisive measure of the impact of Rawls's work is that the family of criticisms of liberalism that sprang up in the 1980s understood liberalism—even when not explicitly addressing his work—in roughly the way Rawls did. This family of criticisms focused on liberalism's alleged indifference to conceptions of human flourishing, exclusion of the pursuit of higher goals from the domain of politics, and inattention to the ways in which a well-ordered society and a good life depend upon the exercise of virtue, the practice of citizenship, and participation in a common political life. This family of ideas came to be known as the communitarian critique of liberalism.

The communitarian critique was swiftly countered by a rejoinder from a variety of liberals, including Rawls himself. The liberal rejoinder tended to pursue two lines of argument. First, that the communitarian critics mischaracterized liberalism, attributing to it rigid theoretical dichotomies and implausible assumptions about moral psychology and social life to which liberals were not committed either by intent or by implication. And second, that many of the practicable reforms that communitarians endorsed were viable, and indeed reasonable and desirable, within a liberal framework.

The liberal rejoinder to communitarian criticism particularly emphasized the characteristically liberal concern for the moral life.[38] A new generation of liberal thinkers rejected the idea—an idea, it must be said, that derives considerable support from statements by Rawls and other eminent liberals[39]—that liberalism can be adequately grasped as a procedural political system committed to maintaining neutrality toward competing visions of the good life. The truth, according to the new liberals, is more complicated. Although it does place an emphasis on formal procedures, is primarily concerned with institutional arrangements, and does cherish the toleration of a range of practices and conceptions of the good life, liberalism is, contrary to its communitarian critics as well as some of its most influential champions, a doctrine containing a partial vision of the good and a compelling account of decent character.

The liberal rejoinder sometimes gave the impression that liberalism had weathered the storm of communitarian criticism without compromising its basic principles or backing away from its fundamental commitments. This impression, however, is misleading. In fact, the liberalism that the most prominent liberals in the academy defend today reflects a chastened understanding. The communitarian challenge spurred liberals to articulate a richer and more flexible liberalism that is less embarrassed to acknowledge its dependence on institutions, practices, and beliefs falling beyond the range of the liberal theorist's special expertise and the liberal regime's assigned jurisdiction. This more reflective and self-conscious liberalism is also better able to recognize its limitations and thus take measures to compensate for its weaknesses and disadvantages. And thanks in part to the communitarian challenge, liberal theorists have increasingly come to appreciate the capacity of a liberal framework to respect the role of moral virtue, civic association, and even religious faith in the preservation of a political society based on free and democratic institutions.[40]

The communitarian critique of Rawlsian liberalism did a great service by focusing attention on dimensions of moral and political life that academic liberalism had neglected. "Rights talk" among liberals is now better balanced by attention to responsibility and duty. Leading liberal thinkers find themselves preoccupied with the content of character. Concern for the dignity and well-being of individuals has been complemented by consideration of the role of communities in forming individuals who are capable not only of caring for themselves and cooperating for mutual advantage but also of developing enduring friendships, sustaining marriages, and rearing children. Liberal theorists have increasingly come to appreciate that the practice of limited constitutional government, the protection of basic individual rights, and the promotion of virtues such as toleration depend in part on citizens adept in the art of association. And the fact is, notwithstanding occasional reckless rhetoric to the contrary, few communitarian critics are eager to say farewell to fundamental liberal principles and virtues. The serious question that has emerged from the communitarian critique of liberalism is how well contemporary liberalism can be taught to care for those necessities which in the recent past it has been inclined to neglect: the cultivation of moral virtue, the art of association, and the practice of citizenship.

VIRTUE IN ACADEMIC LIBERALISM

In regard to virtue, at least, the challenge consists in making explicit and refining an appreciation that is already present in the seminal text of contemporary liberal political theory. For it has frequently been overlooked that an instructive account of liberalism's dependence on certain necessary virtues was already available a decade before the communitarian critique of liberalism arose. And this instructive account could be found in the very place that the communitarian critique implied it was least likely to appear, in Rawls's *A Theory of Justice*.[41]

In the neglected third part of *A Theory of Justice*, Rawls defines the virtues as "sentiments, that is, related families of dispositions and propensities regulated by a higher-order desire, in this case a desire to act from the corresponding moral principles."[42] Much

could be said about Rawls's redefinition of virtue in terms of sentiment, desire, and moral principle and his exclusion of habit, consequences, and practical wisdom from virtue's definition. But
what I wish to call attention to is Rawls's recognition of virtue's
necessity. In particular, political stability in a well-ordered liberal
society, Rawls holds, depends upon citizens with grounds for
mutual trust, a capacity for friendship, and a shared sense of justice.[43] Such virtues as Rawls believes a liberal state depends upon,
however, do not, according to him, develop naturally or easily.
They are, in Rawls's account, in part the happy by-product of life
under just institutions. But they must also, Rawls argues, be actively cultivated.

In an ideal or well-ordered liberal state, Rawls explains, the necessary moral virtues begin to emerge in the private sphere. It is in
the family that the child first develops the capacity for love and
trust.[44] Subsequently, the rich array of voluntary or secondary associations that flourish in a well-ordered liberal society foster the
"cooperative virtues," which include "justice and fairness, fidelity
and trust, integrity and impartiality."[45] Finally, through fulfilling
the offices of citizenship, individuals develop an allegiance to the
principles of justice such that they learn to treat fellow citizens as
the free and equal beings they are.[46] What must be stressed in
connection with Rawls's account of how the virtues are acquired is
that the private virtues, the cooperative virtues, and the virtue of
justice are, in his view, not luxuries but necessities for liberal citizens. In the absence of citizens endowed with the requisite virtues,
a liberal state, Rawls indicates, would suffer political instability
and would be unable to maintain its essential institutions.[47]

Rawls's sketch of the sources of the necessary virtues in a well-
ordered liberal society is an explicitly idealized account.[48] This,
however, does not justify his dubious claim that the salutary effect
of life under liberal institutions is to dissolve "men's propensity to
injustice,"[49] a claim that is a contemporary manifestation of the
old Enlightenment illusion of inevitable progress, the conceit that
reason and history are cooperating to bring about the moral improvement of humankind. But the larger point is that if even in
a well-ordered society liberal institutions depend upon citizens

endowed with moral virtue, would not the importance of virtue be greater still in an imperfect liberal democracy where citizens would find it necessary to negotiate mutual distrust, formal inequities, and structural defects in basic political institutions? That is, doesn't the logic of Rawls's own account imply the critical importance of virtue to the sort of imperfect liberal democracy in which we live? And doesn't his idealized account also imply that since ordered institutional life is one key source for the formation of moral virtue, in an imperfectly ordered liberal society virtue would be not only more important but harder to come by? Having argued that the public good in a liberal state depends upon moral virtue, and that the sources of moral virtue in such a state are intact, two-parent families, a vibrant civil society, and active citizen participation, Rawls leaves the reader to wonder what steps a liberal regime and its citizens may or must take in nonideal circumstances—circumstances, for example, in which families are in disarray, civil society is moribund, and political participation is anemic—to promote the private and public virtues on which stability in a liberal democracy depends.[50]

A growing discrepancy between liberal democracy's need for virtue and its supply of it is, of course, no idle hypothetical scenario but, rather, an increasingly common description of the actual condition in which American liberal democracy finds itself today. It is for this reason that the complicated interrelation of liberalism, virtue, and what Tocqueville called "the art of association" has become a subject of growing investigation.[51] What needs to be emphasized at this juncture is that it is from within the very confines of Rawlsian liberalism that questions arise about the connection between the virtues necessary to the maintenance of liberalism and the range of sources that sustain them. Although it is certainly not the only perspective that makes virtue an issue, and despite the fact that it has not had much noticeable effect on the interest in virtue exhibited by Rawls's most devoted readers, a Rawlsian perspective directs students of liberal democracy in America to ask what means, consistent with liberal principles, a liberal regime such as America and the individuals whose lives it frames ought to adopt to support the family, to revivify intermediate associations, and to encourage participation in democratic political processes.[52]

Rawlsian liberalism is not alone in articulating a connection between liberal hopes and the need for virtue. Like Rawls, Joseph Raz insists that liberalism needs virtue, but unlike Rawls, Raz believes that the liberal state should be directed toward the perfection of the individual. Raz observes—and Rawls would no doubt agree—that the moral ideal of personal autonomy, which he finds at the heart of liberalism, presupposes particular "inner capacities" and "character traits." But Raz parts ways with Rawls when he argues that it is one of the tasks of liberal government to promote the qualities of mind and character that support autonomy.[53] Raz does not say very much about what this promotion would look like. Concerned as he is with the ground and scope of principles, Raz does not investigate the beliefs, practices, and institutions that support the virtues of autonomy. Nor does he explore in any detail the extent of the education required to foster the "cognitive capacities," "emotional and imaginative make-up," and "character traits" necessary to the leading of an autonomous life.[54] Thus, like Rawls, Raz develops a theory that raises questions which he does not pursue and implicates issues whose significance he does not fully acknowledge about the institutional sources that might sustain the virtues supporting liberalism.

Stephen Macedo and William Galston have each argued that liberalism calls forth and depends upon a specific set of virtues they call liberal virtues.[55] The liberal virtues, according to Macedo, include "broad sympathies, self-critical reflectiveness, a willingness to experiment, to try and to accept new things, self-control and active, autonomous self-development, an appreciation of inherited social ideals, an attachment and even an altruistic regard for one's fellow liberal citizens."[56] These virtues, according to Macedo, are relative to liberal regimes in two senses: they are fostered by beliefs, practices, and institutions typical of liberalism; and the stability of liberal regimes depends upon citizens endowed with them. But Macedo reluctantly acknowledges that a liberal regime cannot always be counted on to generate consistently and in ample supply the virtues its citizens need to preserve it. Although he remains optimistic, he allows, in the final lines of his book, the possibility that liberal regimes may depend for their vitality on the lingering effects of a pre- or extraliberal ethic.[57]

Galston, in his state-of-the-art study, makes thematic what Macedo only touched upon: political liberalism today derives support from a variety of perspectives and schools of thought that are by no means exhaustively defined by the liberal tradition. And Galston takes more seriously the possibility that liberal regimes do not automatically produce the virtue necessary to their own preservation.[58] Together, the self-critical liberalisms of Macedo and Galston suggest that one of the internal resources liberalism can call on to meet the challenges it faces today is its capacity to recognize its dependence on external or extraliberal and nongovernmental sources of virtue. Of course, the capacity to recognize a need must be distinguished from the ability to satisfy it.

Like Macedo and Galston, Judith Shklar believed that if they wish to defend liberalism effectively and understand it fully, liberals cannot avoid speaking about character. But in contrast to Macedo and Galston, Shklar doubted that the defense of liberalism required a search for insight beyond the framework of liberal thought. She saw no particular need for liberalism to seek nourishment from forms of life and schools of thought not essentially liberal.

In *Ordinary Vices*, perhaps her most original and best-known book, Shklar adopts an intriguing strategy for speaking about character in a liberal register.[59] The strategy consists in providing an account of the character or moral psychology of a good liberal that avoids mention of virtue and the good by dwelling on the vices and what is evil. Shklar is, of course, prepared to acknowledge that here and there one may encounter citizens with good characters, but what is really worth mentioning and resisting, she holds, is the propensity to cruelty, a propensity exhibited in such common qualities as hypocrisy, snobbery, betrayal, and misanthropy.[60]

In fact, Shklar's avoidance of virtue in her account of liberal character is more an achievement of rhetoric than a real achievement. Nor could it be otherwise, since vices are conceptually related to virtues. One need not understand virtue, as did Aristotle, as a mean between two vicious or defective extremes to recognize that a vice—a blameworthy disposition or form of conduct—becomes intelligible only in the context of a range of dispositions, actions, and ends that can be seen as fitting or good.

On inspection Shklar can be seen to presuppose opinions about the good and virtue despite her reluctance to use the terms. For example, although it concentrates on what is bad and should be avoided, Shklar's delightful exploration of the psychology of the snob is grounded in the suppressed presupposition that snobbery is bad because people are entitled to a minimum of respect and dignity.[61] The critique of snobbery, moreover, implies that the disposition to recognize the equality of your fellow human beings and the ability to treat them accordingly are deserving of praise but, like many fine things, do not come naturally and instead require education and effort. A determination, however resolute, to speak only of vice and evil does not erase a theoretical dependence on virtue and the good.

Speaking more generally, the establishment of cruelty as the greatest evil is, in fact, itself motivated by opinions about the good and what people ought to do however they may be inclined. Furthermore, the view that human beings are pained not only by experiencing cruelty but by observing it has serious limitations as a descriptive statement; it must be qualified by the common observation that people can experience delight in witnessing a rival squirm, and the well-attested fact that for many behaving cruelly and observing cruel actions give pleasure. If the avoidance of causing or contributing to cruelty is meant by Shklar as a prescription or norm, then it must derive its force from a conception of the good that explains why the taste for cruelty should be curbed and the infliction of pain be avoided. An account, however elegant and subtle, that puts to one side the question of what is to be pursued and instead focuses on what must be avoided cannot avoid raising the question (though it can, of course, refuse to provide answers or to acknowledge the question it has raised) of why the pursuit of such avoidance is good. Unlike an unwanted visitor at the door, virtue and opinions about the good cannot be made to go away by our ignoring them.[62]

As for the question of where the qualities on which liberalism depends will come from, Shklar, surprisingly for a thinker who scorned viewing politics through the lens of speculative theory and prided herself on emancipating liberalism from the grip of illusion, casually asserts that life in a liberal regime will indirectly have a salutary effect on the character of citizens. Indeed, Shklar goes beyond Rawls in her optimistic assessment of the power of life under liberal institutions to provide citizens with a kind of spontaneous moral education. But she does so with even less justification, since Rawls's explicit purpose was to sketch a well-ordered or idealized society. With scarcely a shred of empirical evidence or theoretical analysis of passion and interest to support her, Shklar declares that living under the sway of liberal institutions and procedures will encourage "habits of patience, self-restraint, respect for the claims of others, and caution."[63] Even this heroic assumption, Shklar implicitly acknowledges, will not supply liberal regimes with all the necessary virtues. And she indicates that some of the moral virtues in citizens that sustain liberalism—"moral courage, self-reliance, and stubbornness to assert themselves effectively"—are not automatically generated by liberal institutions and procedures.[64]

Shklar sees nothing wrong with the indirect shaping of character by the day-to-day operations of the political institutions of the liberal state. Indeed, she sees such shaping as not only an inevitable but a beneficial part of the liberal state's internal dynamic. But she does deny that creating "specific kinds of character" can be part of the liberal state's deliberate educative mission.[65] And she fails to consider whether all the effects of liberal institutions on citizens' character are favorable to liberalism.

Shklar thus bequeaths a riddle to those who would follow her. On the one hand, she holds that "liberal politics depend for their success" on specific virtues.[66] On the other hand, she denies that liberal regimes can ever take direct action to cultivate the virtues they require: "All it [liberal politics] can claim is that if we want to promote political freedom, then this is appropriate behavior."[67]

What happens, though, if the political institutions that Shklar believes are responsible for fostering the moral virtues she deems necessary to the well-being of the liberal regime do not have the effect she ascribes to them, or, when running well, have that effect but cease to work properly? And what if, in addition to the sources which she does discuss, civic association, family, and religion grow embattled but prove indispensable to the cultivation of the virtues, both those promoted by liberal institutions and those not, that sustain the liberal state?

One problem with Shklar's account of liberalism is that she presents what is in significant measure an empirical and sociological claim—that is, that public life in a liberal state fosters the necessary citizens' virtues—as if it were a theoretical truth. By doing so, Shklar's analysis shifts attention away from systematic empirical investigation of whether and to what extent public life actually does educate citizens for liberty. Moreover, the theory she favors overlooks, for no good reason, the role of private life and intermediate associations in the fostering of the necessary virtues. And it fails to raise the question of whether liberal institutions also produce bad effects, generating attitudes and vices inimical to the liberal spirit. Finally, presenting as an inflexible conclusion of theory what is better conceived as a flexible dictate of prudence, Shklar removes from the agenda questions about even limited measures the state may take to foster basic moral virtues. If Shklar's view were accepted, then in hard times, when public life in a liberal state becomes stagnant or rancorous, civil society lethargic, and the family embattled, the state would be obliged to sit idly by and watch helplessly from the sidelines as the wellsprings of the virtues necessary for order and liberty slowly evaporated.

The efforts of Rawls, Raz, Macedo, Galston, and Shklar to establish that character is a critical dimension of liberal political philosophy are highly instructive. But they have not yet gone far enough in clarifying, especially in hard times, the disproportion between liberalism's need for virtue and the means liberalism can muster to foster the virtues it needs its citizens to possess. Nor have they taken full advantage of the resources within the liberal tradition for illuminating the connections between virtue and a politics based on the natural freedom and equality of all. And they have not given sufficient attention to the vices that liberal principles can engender. It is my aim to show in the ensuing chapters that the old or classic liberalism has much to say to the new liberalism about the sources, scope, and susceptibilities of the virtues on which liberalism depends.

Virtue and the Making of Modern Liberalism

By exploring the transformations that virtue undergoes in the works of four seminal figures in the making of the modern liberal tradition, I shall bring to light in the coming chapters the often subtle appreciation of virtue woven into the fabric of modern liberal thought. In studies of Hobbes, Locke, Kant, and Mill, I show that each advances distinctive and instructive opinions about virtue and its relation to a politics based on liberalism's fundamental premise, the natural freedom and equality of all. At the same time I shall emphasize the practical and theoretical obstacles each thinker faces in the attempt to provide virtue the breathing room it needs to perform its function well.

In various ways the makers of modern liberalism derive the necessity of virtue from the logic of politics and derive from the logic of a state based on natural freedom and equality the conclusion that government has at most a very limited role to play in protecting or promoting virtue. This limitation was less of a liability when liberalism could confidently rely upon extraliberal or nongovernmental sources of virtue. The weakening or exhaustion of these sources does not bring about a weakening of liberalism's need for virtue; it only weakens liberalism's capacity to satisfy its need.

While the thinkers examined in this book certainly do not exhaust the range of opinions about virtue within the liberal tradition, they are preeminent and do constitute a broad spectrum. Moreover, since among the makers of modern liberalism they are least commonly associated with the idea that a well-ordered state requires citizens capable of exercising a range of basic virtues, they represent excellent test cases for the thesis that virtue is a critical component of any reasonable liberal theory of politics. There is, after all, no serious dispute that reflection on the qualities of mind and character that support liberty is critical to the principles expounded by Montesquieu, Hume, Smith, or Tocqueville. But there is comparatively little recognition that virtue is a crucial category in the political theories of Hobbes, Locke, Kant, and Mill. Perhaps pinpointing the roles that virtue, according to these thinkers, must play in politics does not prove once and for all that virtue is absolutely essential for liberalism or that it must always remain a problem for which only contingent and changing remedies will avail. Nevertheless, through the establishment of both the importance and the problematic character of virtue among the theorists in the liberal tradition best reputed for getting along without it, the burden of proof at least is shifted. Those who believe that liberalism is obliged to do without virtue, or those who hold that liberalism can make do with whatever supply of virtue happens to be at its disposal, must take up the matter not only with liberalism's critics but with liberalism's founding fathers and classic authors.

In the book's conclusion, I shall return to contemporary concerns about the prospects for liberal democracy in America. In particular, I shall suggest that lacunae or incoherence in such leading contemporary schools as deliberative democracy, feminism, and postmodernism are in crucial cases rooted in the contortions theorists undertake to keep virtue out of theory and politics, or in the ruses they devise to bring it back in under wraps and without pronouncing its name. I shall go on to connect the results of the investigation of the place of virtue in liberalism to contemporary debate about the family and associational life. I shall suggest that one of the key criteria for determining where government should intervene in civil society and where it should abstain from intervention is the manner and extent to which the practice or association in question supports the virtues necessary to the preservation of liberal political society.

In sum, liberal democracy rests on an unstable equilibrium between the healthy liberal impulse to economize on virtue and the inescapable demand for some minimum of good character in citizens and officeholders. A certain restraint in liberals in connection to virtue reflects a sound insight, because within the intellectual framework of liberalism virtue is vulnerable to persuasive theoretical and practical criticism yet remains indispensable to a complete account of free and democratic politics. Compared to the ambivalences that distinguish earlier liberal political theory, the failure to be embarrassed by the problem of virtue that marks much contemporary thought betrays a loss of understanding and balance. Liberalism has good reasons for seeking to diminish the significance to politics of virtue but betrays a tendency to take this economizing to an extreme by denying or forgetting virtue. The recognition that the real tension is not between liberalism and virtue but, rather, one that arises within liberalism about how to sustain the necessary virtues should provoke among liberals a tinge of embarrassment. Such embarrassment, however, is no disgrace. It may even provide an auspicious point of departure for the understanding of liberalism's virtue.

Hobbes: Politics and
the Virtues of a Lesser Order

I N MANY CASES, academic liberals and their leading critics treat the political theory of Thomas Hobbes as if it were the secret power behind the throne in the other's camp. Each side is only too happy to convict the other of Hobbism and at pains to deny traces of Hobbes's thought within its own ranks. Hobbism remains, as it was in Hobbes's own time, a grave accusation.[1]

Critics of liberalism tend to be the more aggressive, eager to portray Hobbes as a paradigmatic liberal theorist whose geometric method, materialist metaphysics, mechanistic psychology, and atomistic vision of society exemplify the poverty of the liberal spirit.[2] Meanwhile, when confronted with the image of Hobbes as one of their own, liberals often react sharply; pointing to Hobbes's theory of indivisible and inseparable sovereign power and insistence on state supervision of university curriculum and church teaching, they emphatically declare that Hobbes cannot be understood to be a liberal in any meaningful sense.[3]

As often happens when passions flare and partisans draw sharp lines in the sand, the truth in its complexity and fine-grained texture becomes the first casualty. In the debate over Hobbes's relation to liberalism, each side errs not so much in what it points to as in what it fails to acknowledge in Hobbes's political theory. In their efforts to present Hobbes as liberalism's torchbearer, liberalism's critics abstract from the fact that Hobbes's political science does little to insure the protection of traditional liberal freedoms and rejects the need, made thematic by the liberal tradition, to limit government power through careful institutional design. At the same time, liberals who wish to deny any relation whatsoever to Hobbes overlook the fact that Hobbes's doctrine of absolute sovereignty is explicitly established for the limited purpose of securing and maintaining peace, while subjects' obligation to obey the civil law is limited, according to Hobbes's theory, by the natural and inalienable right to self-preservation.[4] In short, the effort by both liberals and their critics to place Hobbes in the other's camp has, among other things, obscured certain family resemblances that Hobbes's thought bears to liberalism.

While Hobbes is not a liberal in the classic sense of the term, he should be seen as a major figure in the laying of the foundations of the liberal theory of the state.[5] Indeed, the affinities or family resemblance between Hobbes's political theory and liberalism are numerous and striking. Hobbes argued that human beings are fundamentally equal and endowed with certain natural and inalienable rights;[6] defended the idea of a state based on the rule of law;[7] maintained a basic distinction between the public and the private;[8] envisaged a sovereign who respected personal freedom by permitting his subjects the liberty of commerce and contract, as well as the choice of profession, where to live, and how to raise their children;[9] held that a primary task of a good government was to secure a rudimentary welfare for all citizens;[10] affirmed that civil laws govern actions, not inner faith or conscience;[11] insisted on the utility of toleration;[12] and advanced a form of representative government based on the idea that the source of subjects' obligation to obey the law stems from the fact that each subject, in obeying the sovereign's law, is obeying a power that the subject himself could be seen as having consented to and authorized.[13]

No less striking than the similarities, however, are the differences that separate Hobbes's political theory from classic liberalism. In Hobbes's political theory the sovereign is above the civil law and his power is absolute, indivisible, and irrevocable; individual rights are narrow and weak; the equality and welfare that the sovereign is obligated to secure is minimal; censorship is one of the sovereign's key responsibilities; and supervising the church and regulating what is taught at the universities are the job of the state. Although the end Hobbes assigns to government—the attainment of peace and order—is limited in a manner that is consistent with modern liberalism, the means or powers Hobbes gives to the sovereign to achieve those limited ends are not.[14]

Perhaps no aspect of Hobbes's thought is less appreciated yet more instructive for what it can illuminate about liberalism's needs and limitations than the conclusions Hobbes draws about the fundamental importance of virtue—or a certain catalog of moral virtues—to politics.[15] One reason for this neglect is the assumption that a politics with so uninspiring an aim as securing peace and order has no need for—indeed, must be hostile to—the claims of virtue. Another is that Hobbes proceeds from a theory of nature and a moral psychology that impose substantial constraints on the form or kinds of virtue to which appeal can be made. Indeed, Hobbes's philosophy of nature and man could seem to leave no room at all for the very idea of virtue. His materialist metaphysics subverts the idea of a greatest good and undermines the idea of a specific human excellence. His mechanistic psychology appears to rule out the kind of choice, deliberation, and practical reasoning about what is right and proper in particular situations that are crucial to the conventional idea of good character. And his reduction of the passions to desire for power seems to preclude the possibility of acting contrary to passion on the basis of higher desires or reason, as virtue seems to require. Thus premises and notions crucial to Hobbes's philosophy create an environment in his thought that appears implacably hostile to virtue.

Or, rather, one should say implacably hostile to virtue understood in terms of human perfection. But, as I argued in the introduction, perfection of the soul, from Aristotle's point of view the best part of virtue, should not be regarded as the whole of virtue. Within an Aristotelian framework, virtue encompasses qualities relative to or supportive of a wide variety of ends, culminating in but not limited to the highest end. Accordingly, it does not follow from the opinion that human beings lack a specific perfection—affirmed by Hobbes in no uncertain terms—that subjects and sovereigns do not need specific virtues, or particular qualities of mind and character, to perform their tasks effectively. In fact, the discovery or hypothesis that human beings lack a greatest good or supreme perfection is bound to have a bearing on the specific virtues that subjects and sovereigns must possess so that they can play their parts in maintaining peace and order. And it is this line of thought, I shall argue, that Hobbes pursues in his political theory.

Despite his famous rejection of the idea of an ultimate end or greatest good[16] and notwithstanding his scathing attack on the Christian Aristotelianism of the Schoolmen, which he ridiculed as "Aristotelity,"[17] virtue of a kind is at the center of Hobbes's grand effort to clarify the human condition and to prescribe remedies for the inconveniences that attach to it. To be sure, this honor is usually accorded to Hobbes's doctrine of the laws of nature. But in chapter 15 of *Leviathan*, at the end of his enumeration of nineteen laws of nature, Hobbes acknowledges that, properly speaking, the laws of nature are not really laws at all: "These dictates of reason men use to call by the names of laws, but improperly; for they are but conclusions or theorems concerning what conduceth to the conservation and defence of themselves, whereas law, properly, is the word of him that by right hath command over others."[18]

If the laws of nature are not really laws, what, then, are they? They are, as Hobbes says, principles of right reason about the actions that conduce to peace. But they are also more than that. For they proclaim the dependence of politics on certain qualities of mind and character that enable individuals to overcome restless and unruly passion so as to perform the actions that, as principles of right reason, they dictate. Indeed, the laws of nature in Hobbes's view are most satisfactorily thought of as moral virtues. So states Hobbes without apology or embarrassment:

> all men agree on this, that peace is good; and therefore also the way or means of peace (which, as I have shewed before, are *justice, gratitude, modesty, equity, mercy*, and the rest of the laws of nature) are good (that is to say, *moral virtues*), and their contrary *vices*, evil.
>
> Now the science of virtue and vice is moral philosophy; and therefore the true doctrine of the laws of nature is the true moral philosophy.[19]

Far from erecting a theory of the state that dispenses with virtue, Hobbes's Leviathan is firmly grounded in reflections on the virtues that conduce to peace.

Hobbes's recognition of the dependence of his political theory on the virtues of peace does not at all reflect a failure on his part to understand the implications of his own ideas or to grasp the essential logic of political action. To the contrary. When the laws of nature are understood as Hobbes explicitly and repeatedly said they ought to be—as moral virtues—the question of how the moral virtues arise and what can be done to foster them comes into focus as more critical to his thought than the questions that have recently preoccupied so many scholars concerning political obligation or how the laws of nature can be binding. To use a mechanical metaphor, virtue lubricates the joints and moving parts of Hobbes's complex political machine. The indispensable role of virtue is part of Hobbes's design, although I shall conclude that Hobbes's political theory requires more virtue than Hobbes manages to provide for or recognize. But my main emphasis shall be on the considerable justice that Hobbes manages to do to virtue within the confines of his own framework.

While he wrote his works on political philosophy during a period of high political drama and declares that his study of government was "occasioned by the disorders" of his own time, Hobbes understood his specific contribution to reestablishing order to be the clarification, through an elaboration of the one and only science of politics, of the fundamental principles of politics.[20] Thus while he believed the "science of natural justice" that he had worked out in his *Leviathan* clarified the great political controversies of his own day and had immediate practical implications, Hobbes held that his political theory contained a utility that transcended the turmoil of his times.[21] One element of that enduring utility is Hobbes's account of the moral and intellectual virtues crucial to the attainment of peace, the limited and, by Hobbes's principles, the only legitimate goal of politics. Inasmuch as this goal is also a liberal goal, liberalism has a stake in understanding Hobbes's particular catalog of virtues, the reasons for restricting virtue to those qualities serving the end of peace, the role that Hobbes assigns to the sovereign in fostering his subjects' virtue, and the virtue the sovereign requires to meet the demands of his role.

The Critique of Virtue

In the "Epistle Dedicatory" to *Leviathan*, addressing his "Honor'd Friend Mr. Francis Godolphin," Hobbes warmly records his debt to Francis's brother Sidney, whose good opinion of his work Hobbes cherished because of Sidney's excellence of character:

> For there is not any virtue that disposeth a man, either to the service of God, or to the service of his country, to civil society, or private friendship, that did not manifestly appear in his conversation, not as acquired by necessity, or affected upon occasion, but inherent, and shining in a generous constitution of his nature.[22]

Unfortunately, as Hobbes goes on to indicate, most men are not so generously constituted. And owing to the poorer material out of which most men are made, Hobbes anticipates that his book is bound to be generally misunderstood: those in power will decry the work on the grounds that his political theory unduly diminishes authority; and private men will decry it on the suspicion that it inordinately diminishes liberty.[23] What distinguishes those— such as Sidney and Francis Godolphin—who are capable of appreciating his book from the many who will be offended by it is a certain kind of virtue, the capacity to control immediate passion and look beyond interest narrowly conceived, so as to accurately assess the implications of rational argument and act on them.

But is this introductory invocation of virtue not just a fine rhetorical flourish? After all, Hobbes makes it difficult for his readers to take seriously his insistence on their need for virtue. In chapter 4 of *Leviathan*, he introduces virtue as a prime example of "insignificant sounds"; and he uses the names conventionally given to virtues and vices as a chief illustration of "inconstant signification," that is, names that reflect the speaker's interests and appetites, but which the speaker seeks to pass off as eternal and immutable principles.[24] In chapter 6, Hobbes appears to eviscerate the specifically moral content of a wide range of traditional or Aristotelian virtues—including courage, magnanimity, and liberality— by reducing them to passions and then reducing the passions to appetites and aversions.[25] And Hobbes continues the work of explaining morality in nonmoral terms by systematically redefining manners, "those qualities of mankind that concern their living together in peace and unity," in terms of desire, in particular, the desire to exercise greater power.[26] Before too long in his account of human nature in the first part of *Leviathan*, Hobbes appears to have so drastically reinterpreted virtue that it can seem preferable to devise a new term for the quality he discusses in the "Epistle Dedicatory" under the traditional name.

Hobbes thus gives conflicting indications concerning the status of virtue. On the one hand, he summons the language of virtue to express his gratitude toward a cherished friend and to describe a moral quality necessary to one who would understand his philosophy and put it into effect. On the other hand, he condemns the inherited language of virtue as an offense against clear thinking and presents virtue as a puffed-up name for passions and appetites. These conflicting indications, however, need not involve Hobbes in a contradiction. It is conceivable that virtue is a notion easily abused but which can nevertheless be employed profitably by one who has understood its proper uses and characteristic abuses, and, indeed, must be employed with precision by one who wishes to understand the nature of men and to lay bare the fundamental principles of politics.

Yet there remains a major obstacle preventing our appreciating the pride of place that Hobbes gives to virtue: the harsh and uncompromising attack Hobbes himself directs against Aristotle's understanding of virtue, or more precisely the understanding of virtue found in the tradition of Christian Aristotelianism that Hobbes believed had corrupted the universities of his day.[27] Hobbes's harshness has had its costs. Throwing nuance and qualification to the wind, Hobbes blurs the important distinction between Aristotle, or the views Aristotle actually develops in his writings, and Scholastic Aristotelianism, or the centuries-old tradition of Christian interpretation of Aristotle's works that prevailed at the time.[28] By going beyond what Hobbes says about Aristotle's views on virtue to what Aristotle actually said, and by moving from Hobbes's highly charged rhetoric to his constructive practice, one can gain much-needed perspective on Hobbes's appreciation of the political importance of virtue. Hobbes's un-Aristotelian denial of a greatest good and his un-Aristotelian effort to explain human conduct exclusively in terms of the desire for power and fear of death do not imply a break in every important way with the Aristotelian tradition. Indeed, as one reads Hobbes, it is precisely by keeping in mind the Aristotelian distinction between virtues relative to a greatest good, or the qualities that conduce to human perfection, and the virtues relative to certain lesser ends—the qualities, for instance, that conduce to peace—that one can see that notwithstanding their important differences, Hobbes and Aristotle are in agreement that specific qualities of mind and character are an indispensable means to the preservation of political society.

One way in which Hobbes makes the important connection between his own political theory and that of Aristotle rather difficult to see is by portraying Aristotle's philosophy and political science as thoroughly disreputable scholarly nonsense: "And I believe that scarce anything can be more absurdly said in natural philosophy than that which now is called *Aristotle's Metaphysics*; nor more repugnant to Government, than much of that he hath said in his *Politics*, nor more ignorantly than a great part of his *Ethics.*"[29] While he does not undertake anything like a point-by-point refutation of Aristotle's alleged absurdities, repugnant doctrines, and ignorant opinions, Hobbes does identify two fundamental errors that he believes pervade Aristotle's writings and make them a source for fundamental instability in political life. One error informs Aristotle's natural philosophy and is rooted in bad metaphysics; the other error underwrites Aristotle's moral philosophy and stems from a misunderstanding of the relation between the passions and the good.

The natural philosophy of the Greeks, according to Hobbes, "was rather a dream than science."[30] Greek philosophy failed to understand that nature consisted of matter in motion and nothing more; nor did it grasp that the means to understanding such a materialist universe was the method exemplified by the science of geometry. The language that Christian Aristotelians developed to speak about virtue was one of Hobbes's favorite examples of the "senseless and insignificant language" that arose in the absence of right method and sound premises about the basic elements of the world. The doctrine of the virtues taught at the universities pre-supposed the "doctrine of *separated essences*," a doctrine, Hobbes asserted, that was "built on the vain philosophy of Aristotle."[31] Sep-arated or abstract essences are essences that are separated or ab-stracted from matter; but since in Hobbes's view there is nothing in the universe but matter or body, such essences must be "the names of *nothing*."[32] It is these fanciful names of nothing, these essences that are supposedly intelligible and incorporeal, which, Hobbes holds, lie at the foundation of the doctrine of virtue that he mockingly calls "Aristotelity."

Aristotelity is both absurd and dangerous. Its absurdities in-clude such metaphysical nonsense as the belief that "faith, and wisdom, and other virtues are sometimes *poured* into a man, some-times *blown* into him from Heaven—as if the virtuous, and their virtues could be asunder."[33] Although his rhetoric obscures the point, what troubles Hobbes is not the introduction of virtue into politics but, rather, the introduction into politics of pernicious misunderstandings about virtue. The doctrine of virtue Hobbes calls Aristotelity is pernicious because it "serve[s] to lessen the dependence of subjects on the sovereign power of their Coun-try."[34] Conceiving of virtue in terms of separated or abstract es-sences causes political mischief by providing subjects make-believe standards that, as they imagine, entitle them to disobey the civil law when a conflict arises between what the standards dictate and what the civil law commands. Hobbes thus does not scorn the virtues as expounded by Christian Aristotelianism be-cause he rejects the very idea of virtue. He scorns the virtues prom-ulgated by Christian Aristotelianism because he regards them as fictitious entities, belief in which produces civil strife by promot-ing disrespect for, and grounds for disobeying, the laws of the commonwealth.

Similarly, in identifying the fundamental defect in Aristotelian moral philosophy, Hobbes does not condemn the very idea of a moral philosophy based on the virtues but, rather, objects to the particular virtues licensed by what he presents as Aristotle's approach. Indeed, the trouble with Aristotle's approach, according to Hobbes, is that it licenses any and all moral virtues. In Aristotle's kind of moral philosophy, as Hobbes understood it, what is called good and virtuous is nothing other than what particular moral philosophers happen to desire and hence "but a description of their own passions."[35] Moreover, Aristotelian moral philosophy obscures the actual end that true virtue serves—the attainment and preservation of peace—while encouraging individuals to engage in groundless speculation about a nonexistent supreme perfection, a vain activity that serves only to sow discontent and division and thus places in peril virtue's true end. In effect, Aristotelity teaches each individual to do whatever he believes to be good or right, and such practice, Hobbes thinks, cannot but lead to chaos in the commonwealth. Curiously enough, then, Hobbes criticizes Aristotelian moral philosophy as a kind of emotivism that encourages individuals to treat their passions and private judgments as authoritative conclusions about right and wrong. And more curious still, in opposition to what he regards as Aristotle's relativizing misunderstanding of virtue, Hobbes seeks to advance a rational, objective, and universal account of the moral virtues, which he contends is the basis of "the true moral philosophy."[36]

Hobbes can provide a rational, objective, and universal account of moral virtue because he believes that he, in contrast to Aristotle, has identified the real and only end that moral virtue serves. Whereas Aristotle sought to define virtue in terms of some inherently elusive, controversial, and ultimately nonexistent human perfection, Hobbes seeks to explain virtue exclusively in relation to a worldly good that all individuals can understand and embrace. And this is not an implausible way to think about virtue. The nonexistence of a heavenly good or supreme perfection does not preclude a worldly good that can be known through reason, a good that does not pertain to perfection but can be enjoyed by all and in principle serves as the precondition for the enjoyment of all practicable desires.[37]

Indeed, in Hobbes's view, peace was the good in question. Peace is the social and political condition that best enables individuals to satisfy their fundamental desire, the desire for self-preservation. And, according to Hobbes, whatever other goods individuals may happen to desire, they will be more likely to satisfy them where peace prevails. The moral virtues are those qualities of mind and character that conduce to self-preservation—and hence the satisfaction of desire—by making peaceful existence possible.[38] To understand the full importance of moral virtue, however, one must acquire intellectual virtue. And one may achieve this, on Hobbes's view, by making a science out of the study of politics.

VIRTUE AND THE SCIENCE OF POLITICS

On Hobbes's view, political science can contribute to the preservation of political society by bringing to light the rational principles of political life and the moral virtues that enable subjects and sovereigns to honor them. However, virtue for Hobbes is not simply part of the subject matter of the science of politics. It is also a prerequisite of such a science, because success in the science of politics depends on the virtue of those who practice it.

Hobbes is famous, along with Bacon and Descartes, for having helped lay the foundation for modern philosophy by not only introducing a new method for but also making the issue of right method central to the study of morality and politics. All true forms of inquiry, Hobbes argued, are forms of science, and all science proceeds on the basis of right method, including the scientific or true study of politics.

Partly because of his own emphatic insistence on the scientific character of his studies of morality and politics,[39] and partly because of a confusion about what he means by the term "science," one can easily overlook the fundamental differences between the method of Hobbes's science of politics and the method of the natural sciences. Unlike the fundamental axioms of physics, which are rooted in the evidence of the senses and phenomena in principle readily observable by all, the premises from which the principles of politics are deduced, according to Hobbes, come from a form of self-knowledge that is rare and difficult to achieve. Consequently, the practice of political science requires a greater degree of moral and intellectual virtue than any other science.

According to what Tom Sorell has called the "standard interpretation," Hobbes's science of politics is either modeled on the natural sciences or can be deduced from his physics and physiology.[40] Yet, as Sorell and several before him point out, there is strong evidence that Hobbes developed his arguments about morality and politics on the basis of hard-won observations gleaned independently of the distinctive methods of natural sciences.[41]

Indeed, in each of his three major works on politics, Hobbes stresses the foundations of the science of politics in prescientific experience. In the *Elements of Law* (1640), Hobbes argues that reliable experience of fact is the beginning of scientific knowledge.[42] In *De Cive* (1642), where Hobbes declares himself the inventor of civil philosophy, he explains that his civil philosophy is "grounded on its own principles sufficiently known by experience," and is therefore not dependent on knowledge gained through physics or derived from the principles of a mechanistic psychology.[43] In *Leviathan* (1651), Hobbes holds that his speculations about political science are grounded in a prescientific knowledge of the passions.[44] In addition, in *De Corpore* (1655), a work that treats of matter and its general properties, Hobbes emphasizes that the subject matter of natural philosophy is "very different" from that of civil philosophy; and he presents the inquiry into the "dispositions, affections, and manners of men" as separate from the investigation of the properties and movements of natural bodies.[45] Although Hobbes, I shall argue, does not, in fact, derive the principles of politics from the principles of matter in motion or from the principle that the universe consists of matter in motion and nothing else, his mechanistic psychology and materialist metaphysics, as I have already indicated, do shape his diagnosis of the human condition and circumscribe the kinds of remedies he can prescribe to enable human beings to overcome the defects of their natural condition.

The science of politics, like all sciences, produces knowledge of consequences or draws out implications of axiomatic premises in the manner of the exemplary science, geometry.[46] Political science produces knowledge about the nature of the commonwealth by drawing out the consequences of propositions, culled from experience, about the basic structure of what Hobbes calls human nature. As Hobbes understands and practices it, political science is concerned with neither identifying the historical origins of particular political orders nor formulating lawlike causal generalizations about political conduct. Rather, it deals with the logic of political life—that is, what, given the nature of man, are man's reasonable ends, and what form must political life take for man to achieve them? But ascertaining the nature of man is not itself a matter of logic; it is, as the introduction to *Leviathan* explains, a matter of experience, or experience rightly interpreted, and the right interpretation of the relevant experience, as Hobbes himself also indicates in the introduction, requires actions that express virtue.

In the introduction to *Leviathan*, Hobbes forthrightly argues that the science of politics, as well as effective governance of commonwealths, rests on one and the same attainment. This moral and intellectual excellence—which Hobbes explicitly claims for himself and which, he asserts, others must acquire if they wish either to understand or to practice politics—is self-knowledge, the means, according to Hobbes, by which human beings can imitate God's virtue.

"Nature," Hobbes declares in the opening sentence of the introduction, "(the art whereby God hath made and governs the world) is by the *art* of man, as in many other things, so in this also imitated, that it can make an artificial animal."[47] The excellence of man, this "rational and most excellent work of nature," the created thing in which God manifests most clearly his own virtue, is the power to reason, a power that sets man apart from all other created things. Although man is not, on Hobbes's view, by nature

47

a social and political animal, man can imitate God's virtue by creating an artificial animal of the most excellent sort, that is, an artificial man or a commonwealth. A commonwealth is excellent insofar as it is created in accordance with the principles of reason and as a creature of reason the commonwealth represents the supreme social and political animal.

Because it conforms to the strictures of reason, the leviathan, or the well-made commonwealth, has a soul or nature that can be known. But only a man of particular nature and attainments can attain knowledge of the leviathan's nature. The first thing a man who wishes to understand the well-made commonwealth must understand is the nature of the commonwealth's maker, the nature of man. Such understanding, however, is not acquired easily or by any old means. Indeed, it is not ultimately acquired by empirical observation, the reading of books, the study of history, or the positing of parsimonious assumptions. Rather, Hobbes explains, one gains knowledge of man through introspection, through looking within and grasping the shape and structure of one's own passions. Hobbes places a Socratic maxim, "Read thyself," at the foundation of political science and indicates that on the grounds of a knowledge of human passion secured through self-knowledge a true science of politics can be erected that will overcome the errors of all previous efforts to understand moral and political life.[48]

Introspection is an appropriate method for the acquisition of general knowledge about human beings because human beings share a nature: "the similitude of *passions* . . . are the same in all men."[49] While the objects of human passion vary from one individual to another, the form of desire is the same in all, and this form, in Hobbes's view, is capable of being known by the human mind. But the human mind is prone to distraction and easily deflected by passion from the path of accurate observation and right reason. Thus it is more precise to say that the forms of passion can be known by a human mind that has overcome the obstacles to self-knowledge that the passions present.

Although such introspection does not require elaborate instruments or exacting calculations or uncommon erudition, Hobbes claims that to read in oneself the character of mankind is "harder than to learn any language or science."[50] This hard undertaking, which is not political science proper but, rather, furnishes the constitutive elements investigated by political science, must be engaged in by both political scientists and rulers. Political scientists must undertake introspection because it furnishes the point of departure or axioms from which the nature of political life and the structure of the commonwealth are deduced. The ruler must undertake introspection in order to assure himself that the conclusions reached by the political scientist about the laws of nature, the sovereign's authority, and the things that preserve and dissolve commonwealths stem from correct premises. Accordingly, both the political scientist and the ruler must overcome their passions in order to read in their own natures the universal structure of human passion and must, then, keep their passions in place as they infer the nature of politics from its "constitutive cause," the nature of man. This discipline of passion in the service of reason is a crucial part of what Hobbes means by virtue.

Hobbes claims that his new science of politics avoids the absurdities involved in the traditional accounts of virtue. What Hobbes does not emphasize, but which is of the first importance to the understanding of the structure of his thought, is that if he had rejected the idea of virtue altogether, he would not have avoided absurdities of his own and could not have hoped to form a more adequate understanding of politics. His debt to his predecessors is in part reflected in, and in part obscured by, his claim to have surpassed them by exercising more perfectly than did they the traditional virtue of self-knowledge.

Virtue and the Natural Condition
of Mankind

In analyzing Hobbes's state-of-nature teaching, commentators typically challenge his depiction of human nature, or raise theoretical questions about the grounds of the laws of nature, or explore whether Hobbes has accurately described the rules of cooperation in the absence, and for the establishment and preservation, of a common coercive power. These are important concerns, but the interest they have attracted has crowded out other significant issues. What I wish to draw attention to is a central and neglected issue concerning virtue. Namely, the logic of Hobbes's account of the natural condition of mankind indicates that no escape from the misery of their natural condition is possible for human beings unless they exercise certain demanding moral virtues.[51]

Hobbes derives his account of the natural condition of mankind, which marks the transition point between his theory of human nature and his theory of the state, from the knowledge of the passions that he wins through introspection. But to grasp the political implications of the passions, one must do more than look accurately within. Since passion in political society is held in check by law, to understand the full power of the passions, what they are capable of causing men to do and what they make it difficult or impossible for men to achieve, one must view the passions in action outside of the commonwealth, freed of artificial constraint. One can accomplish this, in Hobbes's view, in one of two ways: either by observing the consequences of civil war, which dissolves actual commonwealths, or by undertaking a thought experiment whereby one imaginatively places human beings in a condition without a settled common authority and infers their conduct from the logic of the passions.

Although his depiction of the natural condition of mankind is obviously in part motivated by, and sharpened through, his observations of the English civil war,[52] Hobbes states explicitly, consistent with the introduction to *Leviathan*, that his depiction of the natural condition of mankind is based on an "inference made from the passions."[53] This natural condition of mankind represents the absence of political life, the form relations among men must take in the absence of an agreed-upon common power.

In the absence of a common lawmaking power, each individual has a right to all things.[54] This right is nothing to be particularly proud of since it reflects the nonexistence of inherent limitations on conduct that an individual judges will serve his self-preservation. Moreover, this natural or absolute liberty proves unprofitable because it produces a savage and vulnerable condition in which each can take what he pleases but no one can be pleased for too long with what he takes for fear that it will be taken away, with perfect right, by someone else.[55] Thus as Hobbes famously held, the natural condition of mankind is thoroughly miserable, a war of all against all in which the life of each is "solitary, poor, nasty, brutish, and short."[56]

The condition of war, which is a war of every man against every man, is not defined by actual violence and fighting but, rather, by the prevalence of a certain inclination in the minds of men, a disposition to settle disputes not by law but by subterfuge and violence.[57] It is only by agreeing with others to renounce, in accordance with the laws of nature, one's natural right to all things and transfer it to a common power that one can escape the terrors of the condition of mere nature and enjoy the security and comfort that peace or civil society brings.

The necessity for virtue springs from the fact that the fundamental human passions drive men to act in irrational ways. Far from having a rational actor model of politics, Hobbes may be said to have an irrational actor model.[58] The most fundamental passions or desires are the desire for preeminence and the even more fundamental fear of, or desire to avoid, violent death. The desire for preeminence or glory and honor—by definition scarce goods that are diminished by being shared—produces a dangerous competition not merely for wealth and honor but for more wealth and honor than others have. This competition for preeminence is dangerous because it results in proud winners and envious losers.[59] Since pride and envy prompt individuals to reckless acts that imperil life and limb, the desire for preeminence turns out to be in permanent tension with the fundamental human passion for the preservation of one's life.

The dangers generated by the competition for preeminence are not the only inference that Hobbes makes from the logic of the passions. Reflection on the natural condition of mankind also reveals that human beings are fundamentally equal. Human beings are not only equal in the sense that they are moved by the

51

same inherently destabilizing passions and in the state of nature have an equal right to all things. Once the artificial constraints of civil society are stripped away, they can also be seen to be equal in the sense that they are equally vulnerable to injury and violent death. Some are weaker and some are stronger, but, particularly in the absence of government, "the weakest has strength enough to kill the strongest."[60] This fundamental equality prevails inside as well as outside the commonwealth, although both strong and weak are decidedly more vulnerable outside the commonwealth than inside.

The fundamental passions that constitute human nature combined with the fundamental equality of human beings make political life unstable. But reason shows, Hobbes argues, that the instabilities in political life are vastly more desirable than the one and only alternative: war, or the natural condition of mankind. Individuals, however, do not always see what reason shows. They frequently do not understand, for example, that political society of any sort is preferable to the breakdown of political society; they often fail to see clearly which actions preserve and which destroy political society; and they sometimes, having understood exactly what reason prescribes, fail to act reasonably.

Nevertheless, if political society is to be maintained, or if the condition of war is to be brought to an end and political society established or reestablished, passion must be constrained. The most reliable constraint on passion is the passion of fear,[61] provided that it is fear wisely directed. Unfortunately, people often fear the wrong things, "the power of spirits invisible,"[62] the fear of which serves not to contain but to inflame the passions. So fear, "the passion to be reckoned upon," must be disciplined and educated. Among other things, individuals must learn to fear the vulnerability to sudden and violent death in the state of nature more than the loss of natural liberty incurred in the obedience to common laws. And they must learn to fear the consequences of violating the civil law more than the threat of punishment in a world to come, a threat with which designing clergy induce them to disobedience of the sovereign's command. Hobbes's political solution therefore requires enlightenment.

The purpose of such enlightenment is to make fear the cornerstone of the moral virtues. Fear is the foundation of moral virtue in the sense that all the moral virtues are justified by reference to the fearful condition—the war of all against all—that their exercise keeps at bay. The moral virtues can be understood as those qualities of mind and character that secure peace by suppressing pride and containing the competition for glory, but the motive that sustains them is fear rightly understood.

It still remains puzzling, however, just how, on Hobbes's account, the sort of excellence on which all the other moral virtues rest—the learning to fear the right things, in the right way, at the right time, for the right end—is to be developed and refined. In the condition of war, the constraint of passion by the passion of fear cannot by definition be the result of law. On the contrary, in the condition of war the creation of an institution for making law effective, that is, a commonwealth, is itself the result of the constraint of passion. Accordingly, in the absence of law and the institutions of political society, the constraint of passion must come from the exercise by individuals of moral virtue. But how can moral virtue be acquired and preserved in man's natural condition?

Hobbes recognizes two qualities that, in the condition of war, enable men to preserve their lives. While there is neither justice nor injustice in the condition of war—for justice is a creature of civil law—there are "two cardinal virtues," and they are force and fraud.[63] In the condition of war, these two cardinal virtues serve the good of self-preservation. In the absence of a common power, force and fraud help one achieve one's basic ends: the increase of power and the avoidance of death. Outside of political society and without the aid of force and fraud, one's basic desires are doomed to frustration. Yet as with the virtuous fear that fits men for social and political life, so too with the cardinal virtues that enable one to prevail in the condition of war: Hobbes gives little clue as to how they might arise or be cultivated and maintained in the state of nature.

Although he does not say very much about how it is possible and gives reasons for believing that it will be very difficult, Hobbes nevertheless reasonably holds that if the ugliness and anxiety of the condition of war are to be brought to an end, it is necessary for the passions to submit to the dictates of reason. Reason provides "articles of peace," or "laws of nature": general rules of peaceful living in society that, taken together, constitute a basic framework of principles and practices for establishing and maintaining a commonwealth.[64] Nevertheless, the possibility of escape from the condition of war depends upon more than knowledge of the right rules and practices. It requires as well the capacity to make the dictates of reason effective. And this capacity involves the discipline of the passions. The trouble, as I have noted, is that "the passions of men, are commonly more potent than their reason."[65]

Men are so constituted that they can in principle understand and, when things go well, bring into existence the peace that reason declares is in their long-term or genuine interest. But they are also constituted so that they do not easily grasp or stay focused on their genuine interest, and thus they cannot achieve peace without overcoming severe obstacles arising from their basic nature. Since, on Hobbes's account, the capacity for the requisite qualities of mind and character for securing and preserving peace is by nature in man but such qualities do not, to put it mildly, arise naturally, it is essential to the logic of Hobbes's argument that such qualities be acquired and maintained in the condition of "meer nature." Although it is not an inference that Hobbes himself explicitly makes, the necessity for the cultivation of moral virtue in the condition of nature is, in accordance with Hobbes's procedure, an inference that can be drawn from the passions as Hobbes understands them. That such cultivation of the virtues and, once they are acquired, the maintenance of them in the natural condition of mankind will be a formidable challenge is an equally valid inference.

Thus while Hobbes famously insisted that the "notions of right and wrong, justice and injustice" have no place outside of political society, the same cannot be said, and Hobbes does not say so, about moral virtue as a whole. Indeed, it is the logic of his own argument that clarifies why, in addition to force and fraud—the cardinal virtues in war—virtues relative to the good of peace must already be present in men in the condition of "meer nature"; otherwise they could not cooperate in such a way as to extricate themselves from the inconveniences of the war of every man against every man.[66]

VIRTUE AND THE LAWS OF NATURE

Given the importance for philosophy that he attaches to precise definition, it is a striking peculiarity of Hobbes's exposition of the laws of nature in chapters 14 and 15 of *Leviathan,* a peculiarity to which Hobbes himself calls attention, that what he refers to as laws of nature can at best be understood as laws only in a loose or equivocal sense.[67] Hobbes's point is not that the laws of nature cannot be understood as laws in, say, the Stoic or Catholic sense of natural law. It is, rather, that the laws of nature cannot be understood as laws in view of Hobbes's own carefully conceived formal definition.

On the one hand, Hobbes defines a law of nature as "a precept or general rule, found out by reason, by which a man is forbidden to do that which is destructive of his life or taketh away the means of preserving the same, and to omit that by which he thinketh it may be best preserved."[68] On the other hand, Hobbes defines law as "not counsel, but command; nor a command of any man to any man; but only of him whose command is addressed to one formerly obliged to obey him."[69] Reason, which is the source of the laws of nature, is not a person but a faculty or power; its commands, in the last analysis, are recommendations. In Kantian terms, the imperatives of the natural law are hypothetical and not categorical. Indeed, as I pointed out earlier, in chapter 15 of *Leviathan,* at the end of his enumeration of nineteen laws of nature, Hobbes himself goes so far as to acknowledge that, properly speaking, the laws of nature are not laws at all: "These dictates of reason men use to call by the names of laws, but improperly; for they are but conclusions, or theorems concerning what conduceth to the conservation and defence of themselves, whereas law, properly, is the word of him, that by right hath command over others."[70] If it is improper to do so, why does Hobbes refer to the laws of nature as laws?

In part, no doubt, to "pay homage" to the tradition of natural law, so long as this is understood to mean not only showing respect but also cloaking innovations through the use of venerable terminology.[71] Hobbes himself provides a justification for his acknowledged impropriety when he suggests in the very last sentence of chapter 15 that the theorems of peace he chooses to refer to as laws of nature can be "properly called laws" if they are considered "as delivered in the word of God, that by right commandeth all things."[72] But in light of what Hobbes rather consistently says about God, there are serious obstacles to the consideration of the laws of nature as so delivered. The main problem is that, strictly speaking, Hobbes's God cannot be conceived of as a commander or lawmaker. Nor indeed, on Hobbes's account, can God be understood as any other kind of acting or intervening presence in history. This is because reason, on Hobbes's view, cannot move beyond conceiving of God as a first mover or eternal cause about whom nothing else can be said, and who must therefore remain essentially incomprehensible to human beings.[73]

There is, however, another route by which the laws of nature may be understood as commanded by God. The conclusions of natural reason about how men can secure peace could be understood by the Christian world that Hobbes was addressing as laws insofar as these conclusions or theorems could be shown to be the command of God as revealed in Scripture. Indeed, part 3 of *Leviathan* (as well as the third part of *De Cive*) is in significant measure devoted to just such a demonstration. Yet even if Hobbes had shown that Christians have an obligation, grounded in the authority of Scripture, to observe the laws of nature as commanded by God, he would leave open the question of the status of the laws of nature for non-Christians, or what their moral status was as derivations from natural reason.

If the laws of nature, then, are, as Hobbes acknowledges, properly speaking not laws, what sort of thing, speaking properly, are they? As I have emphasized, the answer comes at the end of chapter 15 where Hobbes offers an alternative and more satisfactory name for the subject matter he introduces under the rubric of laws of nature: "all men agree on this, that peace is good; and therefore also the way or means of peace (which, as I have shewed before, are *justice, gratitude, modesty, equity, mercy,* and the rest of the laws of nature) are good (that is to say, *moral virtues*), and their contrary *vices,* evil. Now the science of virtue and vice is moral philosophy; and therefore the true doctrine of the laws of nature is the true moral philosophy."[74]

Perhaps the most obvious objection to Hobbes's characterization of the laws of nature as moral virtues is his own thesis that good and evil are names for appetites and aversions and hence conventional or artifacts of human will.[75] But, in fact, this thesis, rightly understood, is one of the grounds of his view that the laws of nature understood as essentially moral virtues are "immutable and eternal."[76] What Hobbes means when he declares that good and evil are merely apparent is not that reason is altogether silent about morality or right and wrong, but that reason reveals that there is no *greatest* good or *ultimate* end for human beings.[77] And by this Hobbes means some conception of the most choice-worthy life, some view of human perfection.

The absence of a standard of human excellence is, for Hobbes, a fundamental fact about the moral life. It is precisely the persistent and often violent disagreement among human beings about the greatest or ultimate good—a disagreement for which nature, in Hobbes's view, furnishes no standards of adjudication—that suggests to reason the goodness of peace everywhere and under all circumstances, as well as the way or the means, in particular the qualities of mind and character, that conduce to it. In the absence of a greatest good, the best that human beings can hope for is felicity, or "*continual success* in obtaining those things which a man from time to time desireth."[78] But felicity is not equally available under all conditions. Reason reveals that the wretchedness of the natural condition of mankind makes felicity unattainable in it. Reason also reveals that peace is the essential social and political precondition for the satisfaction of one's desires, whatever they may be. Although it is not a greatest good in the sense of human perfection or salvation, peace for Hobbes is a kind of primary good, because without it, in the state of nature, all conceivable satisfactions must be fleeting, and fear must hang over every undertaking.[79]

The qualities that conduce to the establishment and preservation of the primary good of peace are virtues; the defects that prevent or subvert peaceful relations among men are vices. Although what is counted just in one state may be held unjust in another, justice, understood as obedience to the civil law, is everywhere the same.[80] The whole of moral virtue is peaceableness or sociability.[81] Sociability comprises both a set of rules for the maintenance of a social life and a cluster of dispositions to act on the appropriate rules. The rules can be summed up in a single familiar formulation: *"Do not that to another, which thou wouldest not have done to thyself."*[82]

The familiarity of the formulation, however, should not be allowed to obscure Hobbes's crucial point: complying with the demands of sociability is reasonable but difficult. For a rule is one thing; the ability to translate it into action is quite another. People often break rules, even rules they think reasonable and in their long-term interest, because they are too weak to resist the prospect of satisfaction of immediate desire. Others, out of laziness or self-indulgence, fail to think through the likely consequences of casual transgressions. Some neglect to consider long-term interest at all. And what is generally true about the failure to make long-term interest the principle of one's conduct is especially so for Hobbesian people, who are essentially creatures of pride and passion.

To avoid doing to another what one would not have done to oneself requires more than the ability to recognize the wisdom or prudence or efficiency of such conduct. In addition to discernment, such forbearance also requires the qualities of mind and character that enable one to perform the reasonable acts that embody one's best interest. In general the qualities in question must include the ability to reason about consequences; the imaginative capacity to put oneself in the place of another; and the discipline to constrain passion, especially pride and envy, so as to comply with reason's prescriptions. One implication of Hobbes's analysis of the natural condition of mankind is that human beings are not endowed by nature with the discipline or dispositions to comply with the rules for the preservation of life that Hobbes calls natural because of their reasonableness. Or as Aristotle remarked (in his critique of the hyperrationalist Hippodamus), good laws are worthless without habits of obedience.[83]

The nineteen laws of nature Hobbes enumerates in *Leviathan* may be divided into four categories: the first two laws specify the fundamental political end and framework; the third through the eleventh govern social relations; the twelfth through the fourteenth identify principles for the fair distribution of property; and the fifteenth through the nineteenth concern rules for the fair adjudication of controversies.[84] While Hobbes does not mean his list of laws to be exhaustive, he does argue that the laws of nature he enumerates are necessary and universal in the sense that "peaceable, sociable, and comfortable living"[85] cannot be achieved without their exercise.

The connection between the laws of nature understood as precepts for self-preservation and understood as qualities of mind and character can be seen with greatest clarity in Hobbes's account of the laws of nature governing social relations, but the connection is already apparent in the first and fundamental law of nature. "Seek peace, and follow it" is the first and fundamental law of nature because it contains or determines all the rest.[86] It is reasonable because peace is always a better means to self-preservation than war. Like all of the laws of nature, it binds always "*in foro interno*" (in conscience) but not always "*in foro externo*" (in external conduct), which means that one should always seek peace and, once it is established, do all in one's power to preserve it, but in a condition of war one need not expose oneself by renouncing one's natural right to all things before such time as others are prepared to do the same.[87] Peace is never automatic, partly because circumstances are not always propitious, and partly because people are not always capable of taking advantage of propitious circumstances. But peace is always good or to be preferred; it should always be sought, and after it is established, the rules for preserving it should always be followed.

There are, however, no clear-cut rules that aid one in following the rules that reason prescribes. This is another reason that the rules of reason are not automatically or easily observed. "Following" like "seeking" is a complex activity that involves desiring the right object at the right time in the right way. Seeking peace and following it, once it is acquired, depend on a settled disposition to act in ways that conduce to peace even when peace is absent, or when peace is in place but nobody seems to be watching too carefully; an ability to discern the opportunities that arise for the attainment of peace and to distinguish them from vain hopes and wishful thinking in dangerous situations where the first performance of promises will lead to injury or worse; and the capacity in civil society to make one's long-term interest in peace the principle of one's habitual conduct.

The second law of nature—establish peace by contracting with other men to lay down one's right to all things—especially depends upon the third law of nature, justice, the essence of which is performing valid covenants or keeping promises.[88] Although "successful wickedness hath obtained the name of virtue,"[89] Hobbes holds that it can never be reasonable or just to violate promises, because one who breaks his covenants shows himself untrustworthy and thereby proclaims his unfitness to be accepted into any society. Hobbes, of course, does not deny that men, while secretly breaking their promises, can establish an appearance of trustworthiness. What he does deny is that it is reasonable for any man to count on getting away with such deceit for very long. The reasonable view Hobbes argues is the long-term view, and with a view to the long term what counts are the conditions necessary for preserving society. One's long-term interest in preserving society consists not only in appearing to keep covenants but in actually keeping them. This is because one can never be sure when one's fraud will be found out; and to be found to be a breaker of covenants—an activity that endangers the commonwealth by calling into question its fundamental framework—is to declare oneself unfit for society. This cost Hobbes contends outweighs any conceivable benefit that comes from breaking but appearing to honor them.

One could, of course, quarrel with this judgment. Indeed, one should notice that at this crucial juncture Hobbes introduces the dubious empirical claim that the cost of violating a promise or law, however small and seemingly insignificant, and whatever the apparent odds of getting away with it, always exceeds the benefits. But if we are to understand the logic of Hobbes's argument, the point that needs to be stressed is that justice, or keeping covenants, is a law of nature not because it promises heavenly rewards or escape from punishment after death, and not because it makes the soul of the man who practices it better, but because in the here and now justice is the practice best suited to promote self-preservation.[90] Justice, like all the laws of nature, is self-interest rightly understood.

And self-interest rightly acted upon. While justice for Hobbes is the best policy, the success of the policy that reason declares the best depends upon the practice of justice understood as a moral virtue. Justice so understood is the settled disposition to keep promises. Promises can be kept for good and bad reasons, and Hobbes even recognizes an elevated reason for promise keeping: "That which gives to human actions the relish of justice is a certain nobleness or gallantness of courage, (rarely found) by which a man scorns to be beholden for the contentment of his life to fraud or breach of promise. This justice of the manners is that which is meant where justice is called a virtue, and injustice a vice."[91] But what is necessary for peace is a middle ground between a settled disposition to do what is just for the sake of integrity and independence, and the lack of any settled disposition to perform just acts at all. In the pursuit of the middle ground, the passion to be counted on, as it is ultimately for all the moral virtues, is the pervasive and reliable one of fear.[92] Accordingly, peaceful relations, Hobbes believes, depend on a settled disposition among men to perform just acts out of self-interest enlightened by calculation or fear of the immediate or worldly consequences of nonperformance.[93]

This settled disposition is not self-sustaining. It presupposes an effective civil power or sovereign capable of enforcing covenants through the fear of punishment. And it is not self-generating. It requires a cultivated capacity for self-restraint whereby individuals take the measure of the sovereign's credible threat of force and learn to regard it as the most fearful thing, more fearful, say, than the prospect of otherworldly punishments that could give grounds for violating the civil law in the here and now. In other words, politics depends upon fear rightly understood. And fear rightly acted upon.

Hobbes's leviathan, it could be said, is a commonwealth of cowards, but not ordinary cowards. Since it is essential to the success of Hobbesian politics that subjects learn to fear the right things in the right way for the right ends, the rational pursuit of peace requires that Hobbesian subjects become virtuosi of cowardice. Accordingly, and in sharp contrast to Aristotle, for whom courage was the paradigm of the moral virtues, Hobbes reduces courage to a passion—the hope of avoiding hurt through resistance—and does not even count it among the moral virtues.[94]

The reinterpretation of virtue in terms of rational fear does not eliminate practical judgment from the exercise of moral virtue. And this creates problems for Hobbes's political theory that he does not pursue. Hobbes distinguishes a number of qualities—including good judgment, discretion, and prudence—under the rubric of intellectual virtue.[95] The problem is that while the logic of his presentation implies what Aristotle expressly asserted[96]—the dependence of moral virtue on intellectual virtue—Hobbes does not grapple with the challenges this dependence poses to his account of politics.

For example, the practice of gratitude, the fourth law of nature, is a necessary and universal requirement of peaceful relations among men because benevolence, trust, and mutual help, qualities whose exercise is crucial to the functioning of society, will never develop if individuals cannot count on receiving benefit from those on whom they confer benefit.[97] Gratitude is an endeavoring or disposition to cause no regret to a benefactor. It is not based on a sense of nobility or gallantry but on a fear of consequences, in particular the fear that society would be destroyed should the practice of gratitude cease. Yet even if the disposition to gratitude were firmly established in the individual, the problem of exercising the virtue would remain. First, I must be able to recognize my benefactors and distinguish them from my nemeses, a difficult task for Hobbesian human beings who are prone to confusion about their long-term interest. Then, once my benefactor is correctly identified, I must determine what sorts of acts are appropriate to the benefit he has conferred: a suitable sum of money, faithful companionship, a knowing nod and friendly smile. And this determination cannot but depend on precise judgments about changing circumstances and individual needs. While the need to return benefits may be based on calculations, the returning of benefits is not a calculation but an art from which the exercise of the practical wisdom is ineliminable.

Likewise, the tenth law of nature, which prohibits arrogance, requires that individuals not demand for themselves any rights they are unwilling to accord others.[98] As a virtue, the prohibition of arrogance or the requirement of modesty is the fixed disposition, rooted in fear of the consequences for the maintenance of society, not to make for oneself special demands. But what counts as a special demand? As Hobbes himself allows in this context, men in political society must retain certain inalienable rights, including the "right to govern their own bodies, [the right to] enjoy air, water, motion, ways to go from place to place; and all things else, without which a man cannot live, or not live well."[99] This formulation leaves many difficult issues unsettled, issues that can be resolved only by considered judgments resting in part on contingent circumstances. Is the demand that the state provide a minimum level of subsistence for all citizens so that each can have a chance at living well a demand of modesty? Or is it a violation of what modesty demands? What determines the minimum? And aren't even the minimal rights that modesty requires be protected bound to collide unless individuals exercise these minimal rights judiciously? And what counts as judicious exercise of one's individual rights?

As with justice, gratitude, and modesty, so too with equity, mercy, and the other moral virtues Hobbes presents under the rubric of laws of nature: they denote the rational precepts that conduce to peaceful relations as well as the fixed disposition, rooted in fear of society's dissolution, to act in accordance with them. And the practice of each of the moral virtues is inseparable from the exercise of such intellectual virtues as good judgment, discretion, and prudence. Indeed, the further one inquires, the more it seems that Hobbes's political theory is vulnerable not because it places too little weight on virtue but because it places far more than it recognizes and can gracefully acknowledge. And this forces one to inquire about the source of the virtues on which maintenance of Hobbes's well-made commonwealth rests. The short answer is an energetic, vigilant, and indeed, in Hobbes's sense of the term, virtuous sovereign.

The Sovereign's Virtue

The logic of politics, as Hobbes infers it from the passions, reveals that moral and intellectual virtue are necessary for the attainment of peace but hard to come by in a state of war. Matters stand somewhat differently, however, in connection with his account of the supports for, or source of, virtue in civil society. Safeguarding the virtue in his subjects is, in fact, among the leading tasks of Hobbes's sovereign. The chief means available to the sovereign for supporting virtue, according to Hobbes, are the regulation of church doctrine and the supervision of ideas taught at the universities. Yet to execute these and his other tasks well, Hobbes's sovereign himself must possess moral virtues, or qualities of mind and character that conduce toward peace. The sovereign's virtues, however, cannot be the result of his regulation and supervision because they are presupposed by the regulation and supervision he undertakes in behalf of his subjects and with an eye to the preservation of peace. Hobbes, however, does not leave the sovereign's virtue entirely unaccounted for. In fact, he argues that in the most reasonable case, when the sovereign is a monarch, the sovereign's virtues have their primary source in the influence exerted by the interests attached to his office. I shall suggest, however, that this is a very unsatisfactory argument.

Sovereign authority is indivisible and the powers of the sovereign are inseparable.[100] This absolute sovereignty may be embodied in one person, in a few, or in many. Rejecting such designations as tyranny, oligarchy, and anarchy or mob rule—corrupt or defective regimes, according to the classical scheme—as merely terms of disapproval applied by disgruntled subjects to monarchy, aristocracy, and democracy, Hobbes could appear to banish morality from politics.[101] And by repudiating the classical scheme according to which good regimes are those in which the ruler rules for the common or public advantage, and bad regimes are defined as those in which rulers seek their private advantage, Hobbes could seem to sever the connection between ruling and virtue. In fact, Hobbes's main purpose in rejecting the classical scheme is to eliminate appeals by subjects to their own private judgment about what measures conduce to the peace and defense of the commonwealth. What Hobbes cannot eliminate from his system—and does not think he has eliminated by repudiating the classical scheme—is the need for moral virtue in sovereigns.

Although he downplays the difference between ruling for private advantage and ruling for the common good, Hobbes does, in fact, surreptitiously reinstate the distinction in order to show the superiority of monarchy to both aristocracy and democracy in achieving the aim of good government: the preservation of peace and security. Hobbes's principal argument for preferring monarchy to aristocracy and democracy is that monarchy provides a harmony of interests between ruler and ruled:

> . . . for the passions of men are commonly more potent than their reason. From whence it follows that where the public and private interest [of the ruler] are most closely united, there is the public most advanced. Now in monarchy, the private interest is the same with the public. The riches, power, and honour of a monarch arise only from the riches, strength and reputation of his subjects. For no king can be rich, nor glorious, nor secure; whose subjects are either poor, or contemptible, or too weak (through want or dissension) to maintain a war against their enemies, whereas in a democracy, or aristocracy, the public prosperity confers not so much to the private

fortune of one that is corrupt, or ambitious, as doth many times a perfidious advice, a treacherous actions, or a civil war.[102]

The problem, however, with Hobbes's assurance that the interests attaching to the monarch's office—the very human interests in wealth, glory, and security—will impel the monarch to maintain the material well-being of his subjects and preserve the commonwealth is suggested by Hobbes himself. For Hobbes's account of human beings as creatures of pride and passion gives us good reason to doubt that the monarch, notwithstanding the incentives created by his office, will choose, or be able, to perform the deeds that satisfy his interests rightly understood.[103]

The conflict between the private interest of the sovereign and the public interest is intrinsically more severe in a democracy or aristocracy, Hobbes believes, because in these regimes public prosperity does not directly translate into the private advantage of the ruler. Perhaps.[104] But if, as Hobbes has argued in his account of human nature, passion requires the discipline of virtue to bring it in line with the prescriptions of reason, then the mere fact that reason prescribes to the monarch that he rule for the sake of his subjects to satisfy his own interests in riches, power, and honor provides no guarantee that the monarch will comply with reason's prescriptions. Indeed, it is reasonable, even likely, given Hobbes's own understanding that "the passions of men are commonly more potent than their reason,"[105] that the monarch will overlook the actual convergence between his private advantage and the public interest and recklessly pursue wealth or honor or sensual pleasure at the expense of both the public interest and his private interest rightly understood. Indeed, Hobbes's own view that "the *understanding* is by the flame of the passions, never enlightened, but dazzled"[106] suggests that a monarch possessing absolute power but bereft of moral virtue is likely to do what actual monarchs have always routinely done: loot the treasury, despoil the countryside, impoverish the masses, allow the military to grow weak and bloated, while living a life of extravagant luxury.[107]

Hobbes's argument that in monarchy there is a convergence of interest between ruler and ruled in fact glosses over in regard to

the monarch one of the key implications of Hobbes's own examination of the logic of politics in regard to all other individuals:
to act on what reason indicates to be one's rational interest (or
in accordance with those dictates of reason Hobbes calls laws of
nature) requires the moral virtues (to which he also gives the
name laws of nature), and the moral virtues cannot be presumed
but must be acquired. In explaining the reasons for a preference
of monarchy over democracy and aristocracy, Hobbes simply
equates monarchy with its perfect form, casually assuming that
monarchs will rule in accordance with the laws of nature because
their office gives them incentives to comply with reason's dictates.
But granting that a rational monarch would have a powerful interest in pursuing the public interest, the force of Hobbes's own central argument about the proclivity in man for irrational conduct
shows that a rational interest is not enough; it must be accompanied by moral virtue. In short, Hobbes's arguments in favor of
monarchy over aristocracy and democracy surreptitiously presuppose virtuous monarchs and covertly assume craven aristocrats
and democrats. And Hobbes's failure to account for the virtue
that will enable a monarch to advance the public interest by tend-
ing rationally to his private interest reflects another way in which
his political theory depends on a reservoir of virtue for which it
supplies inadequate explanation.[108]

The sovereign's virtue and its sources are important issues because peace and order require that the sovereign effectively support the virtue of his subjects. The main route through which
Hobbes's sovereign supports virtue is by forming opinions that
counteract the destabilizing doctrines that stimulate subjects to
disregard their duty to obey the law. In general, it is the sovereign's duty to appoint public ministers to instruct the people
"in the knowledge of what is just and unjust, thereby to render
them more apt to live in godliness and in peace amongst themselves."[109] Censorship, or control of what opinions are taught—
but not interrogation to determine fundamental beliefs or test
conscience[110]—is crucial because "the actions of men proceed
from their opinions; and in the well-governing of opinions consisteth the well-governing of men's actions, in order to their peace

and concord."[111] Hobbes singles out two institutions in particular over which the sovereign must exert firm control in order to guard against the promulgation of false and harmful beliefs that weaken the disposition in subjects to comply with the laws of nature: the church and the university.

The sovereign is the final arbiter of what Scripture means and the highest authority for how religion should be practiced because sovereign power is indivisible and supreme. It is necessary for the sovereign to exercise this responsibility energetically and wisely because of the power of false religious ideas to corrupt conduct.[112] Religion as commonly understood consists of false and fear-inspiring beliefs in "powers invisible" that arise out of men's perpetual anxiety about their future welfare. These false and fear-inspiring beliefs are sustained by men's general ignorance of natural causes.[113] To say that most religion springs from ignorance of causes is to declare that most religion is a result of a defect or deficit of intellectual virtue.[114] Lack of intellectual virtue leaves "simple people" open to the machinations of "crafty ambitious persons" who promulgate superstitions that encourage disobedience of the civil law.[115]

While the causes of religion lie in human nature and are universal, the ceremonies through which religion is institutionalized take an infinite variety of shapes.[116] The sovereign must authorize those forms of worship that support correct opinions about God and forbid those forms that breed habits of disobedience to the established laws. When it is properly cultivated, rather than exploited or allowed to run wild, religion serves the function of making men "more apt to obedience, laws, peace, charity, and civil society."[117] In other words, when skillfully supervised by the sovereign, religion is a valuable resource for fostering the moral virtues; when it is employed by corrupt clergy, there is hardly a more pernicious force for the destruction of the moral virtues on which civil society depends.

The second great institution where beliefs that underlie moral virtue are formed is, on Hobbes's account, the university. Hobbes deplores how in his own day the universities of England promulgated absurd doctrines and promoted the use of unintelligible language.[118] In particular, Hobbes condemns the university for teaching the false and destructive principle, derived from religious opinion, that individuals should use their private judgment or conscience to determine what is lawful and what is not.[119] Instead, the universities, "the fountains of civil and moral doctrine," should be used to teach the true doctrine about the roots of civil authority and the absolute power of the sovereign.[120] The true civil and moral doctrine is, of course, in Hobbes's view, the one he sets out in the pages of *Leviathan*.[121] And this doctrine openly states that political life depends on moral virtues which must be maintained by the sovereign power.

Hobbes is famous for indulging the dubious aspiration to construct a geometry of politics. And Hobbes himself is partly to blame for having left so many readers with this impression. But readers must be alert and discerning. The intention to reduce politics to geometry could seem to be implied in the distinction he draws in *Leviathan* between political science and tennis: "The skill of making and maintaining commonwealths consisteth in certain rules, as doth arithmetic and geometry; not (as Tennis-play) on practice only; which rules, neither poor men have the leisure, nor men that have had the leisure have hitherto had the curiosity or the method to find out."[122] Yet what Hobbes's overall argument in each of his three major statements on politics actually implies is that whereas excellence in tennis depends on practice *only*, success in politics depends on the exercise of right reason to discern the laws of nature *as well as* on the acquisition of appropriate virtues—the qualities of mind and character that conduce to peace. Indeed, so much is implied in Hobbes's consistent claim that the laws of nature are also, and more properly speaking, moral virtues.

CONCLUSION

In his *Lectures on the History of Philosophy* Hegel refers to *De Cive* and *Leviathan* as "much decried" works.[123] Hobbes has, indeed, always offended traditional pieties. In his own time he was known as the "beast of Malmesbury"; he was forced to flee both England and France owing to his political views; his *Leviathan* was denounced as "a farrago of Christian atheism"; and late in his life a bill concerned in part with doctrines set out in *Leviathan* and directed against atheism and heresy was introduced into the House of Commons.[124] Yet, as Richard Ashcraft has pointed out, Hobbes's writings would not have provoked attacks from "more than 50 volumes and countless sermons [that] appeared in print" if his opinions had not reflected common concerns of seventeenth-century Englishmen, and if his ideas had not had roots in dominant religious and philosophical conceptions.[125]

The fact that Hobbes offends traditional pieties certainly does not entail that he rejected all things associated with tradition and piety. This is particularly so in the case of virtue. Far from simply decrying virtue or urging its elimination from serious reflection on politics, Hobbes gives a certain interpretation of moral virtue a place of honor in his new political science. Virtue, according to Hobbes, is an indispensable support to right method in the true science of politics. Without the virtue, which Hobbes emphasizes is rare and difficult, that enables one to control one's private passions so as to discern in them the universal form of human passion, political science cannot be placed on secure ground, nor can the logic of politics be accurately elaborated. Moreover, a firmly grounded and accurately elaborated political science will reveal, according to Hobbes, that virtue rightly understood is indispensable to political life. As Hobbes unfolds its logic, political life can be seen to require citizens who exercise the moral virtues that Hobbes identifies with the laws of nature; a sovereign who exercises virtues produced by the interests that attach to his office; and active supervision of religion and education by a virtuous sovereign who forms in subjects or citizens the opinions that support moral virtue.

To be sure, Hobbes's catalog of virtues differs dramatically from that of Aristotle or Aquinas. So too does his account of why the moral virtues are good. Hobbes has little use for the manly or brilliant virtues such as courage and magnanimity. More fundamentally, he rejects the idea of a heavenly good or supreme perfection. But, as I have argued, Hobbes's political theory vividly demonstrates that rejection of the idea of a greatest good or ultimate end does not require the abandonment of every form of virtue. Even for Aristotle and Aquinas, who understood human beings in terms of a supreme perfection or ultimate end, virtue implies qualities of mind and character that relate not only to perfection but also to more modest tasks, such as upholding the beliefs, practices, and institutions that make possible living together in a political community.

Instead of understanding virtue also in the light of a human being's greatest good or supreme perfection, Hobbes understands virtue exclusively in terms of an earthly and immediate goal—peace. Peace has a special status among ends, according to Hobbes, because it is the indispensable means to all other actually attainable ends. And instead of understanding virtue as relative to a specific regime, Hobbes again understands virtue in terms of peace, the goal common to all regimes. Peace, for Hobbes, is a rational and universal goal to which all men can in principle agree and to which most can be brought to give actual assent.[126]

The moral virtues, those qualities of mind and character that conduce to the rational and universal good of peace, are good everywhere and always. Even in the condition of war, where it would be foolish to exercise the moral virtues in their fullness, it is reasonable to endeavor to create a condition—that is, a commonwealth—where the moral virtues can become effective. While Hobbes flatly rejects the notion that the aim of politics is to make citizens good in the sense of a highest perfection, he emphatically teaches that politics cannot achieve its one legitimate goal—the self-preservation of individuals in civil society—unless both citizens and ruler exercise the virtues that conduce to the universal good of peace. Hobbes is no less convinced than Aristotle that certain virtues are necessary for the maintenance of political life, and is in agreement with Aristotle that it is the task of government to promote such virtues. Thus the area of agreement between Aristotle and Hobbes about the political importance of virtue is

71

considerable, despite the fact that Hobbes's excellences of character are, from Aristotle's point of view, at best excellences of a lesser order.

At the same time, because he understands the virtues in relation to the goal of peace, a condition that enables men to exercise more effectively their natural and inalienable rights, in particular the right to self-preservation, Hobbes's account of virtue is pertinent to liberalism. Liberalism, too, recognizes such a right and holds it to be fundamental. But on Hobbes's understanding of the logic of politics, the logic of liberalism must appear fatally flawed. It is not just that from Hobbes's perspective liberalism gives too much scope to the public exercise of private judgment, but that liberalism circumscribes too narrowly government's role in promoting virtue.

For Hobbes, the sovereign has a basic obligation to promote virtue in his subjects through political education. In particular, the sovereign must supervise churches and universities, because that is where opinions are formed, and false opinions, according to Hobbes, are the basis of destructive action. It turns out that those parts of Hobbes's political theory most obnoxious to liberal sensibilities—absolute sovereignty, and censorship or supervision of the church and universities by the state—concern the sovereign's freedom and need to take measures to insure virtue in citizens. However, these aggressive and, to the liberal spirit, intolerably intrusive measures are aimed at producing what may be seen, even from the liberal perspective, as only a modest kind of virtue, the virtue necessary to the maintenance of the institutions that underwrite peace and cooperation for mutual advantage.

The nonliberal aspects of Hobbes's political theory allow government to provide more generously than do liberal political theories for virtues that seem to be as necessary for liberal citizens as they are for Hobbesian subjects. Because it shares much with liberalism without really being liberal, Hobbes's political theory can help throw into sharper relief the nature of liberalism's need for virtue. It is not that liberalism is less in need of the moral virtues that Hobbes identifies as indispensable to his leviathan, but, rather, that liberal regimes are less free than Hobbes's sovereign to promote the virtues which are indispensable to them both.

It has been remarked, from a variety of vantage points, that Hobbes lowers the aims of politics. Whether or to what extent he was justified must remain controversial. But within the framework he helped establish, Hobbes shows that a politics which no longer aims at perfecting souls or leading human beings to salvation is not for that reason a politics that can do without virtue. To the contrary. The logic of politics, as Hobbes expounds it, reveals that a state freed from what Hobbes views as the false and pernicious idea that it is the task of government to perfect citizens or save souls—for example, a liberal state—is still very much in need of "equity, justice, gratitude, and other moral virtues."[127]

Locke: Private Virtue and
the Public Good

Hobbes is one of the founders of liberalism because he gave early, systematic, and influential expression to constitutive elements of the liberal tradition. Not all founders, however, are founding fathers. Founding fathers are those who not only originate, or play a fundamental role in the establishment of, a tradition, but ones who also get recognized and revered as founders by those in the tradition who come later. Because he is routinely disowned or disparaged by liberals, Hobbes cannot be regarded as more than one of liberalism's founders. In contrast, John Locke—who perhaps is a founder of the practice within the liberal tradition of establishing distance from Hobbes's *Leviathan* by glossing over his agreements with it—is one of liberalism's founding fathers because of the respect accorded to him by liberals themselves. Although they may criticize or even abandon particular Lockean doctrines, liberals have no trouble recognizing in Locke's thought a powerful expression of their own premises, principles, and spirit, and they are not embarrassed to acknowledge Locke's tremendous influence or their far-reaching debt.

There has been, of course, lively disagreement about the ideas that lie at the center of Locke's thought. Political theorists have put forward powerful portraits of Locke as an early and seminal apologist for capitalism;[1] as a Hobbist who disguised his Hobbism by mitigating in his political theory the more severe aspects of Hobbes's leviathan;[2] as a libertarian champion of the natural right to private property;[3] and as a seminal contributor to the theory of liberal constitutionalism.[4] While each of these interpretations captures important elements in Locke's thinking, each passes by and leaves unexplained prominent features of his thought.

Thanks, however, to a variety of recent writings, it has become increasingly clear that Locke's opinions on morality and politics form a complex and many-sided whole. John Dunn, for example, has argued that a "deeply Puritan pattern of sentiment" holds together such apparently conflicting ideas as Locke's skeptical view about the severe limits of human knowledge and his strong defense of the goodness of toleration.[5] Nathan Tarcov has brought out the "non-Lockean elements in Locke" by clarifying the political significance of Locke's seminal contribution to educational theory, *Some Thoughts Concerning Education*.[6] And Charles Taylor has made a powerful case that Locke's moral psychology represents a peculiar and complex form of hedonism, one that is a constitutive element in a larger, theologically grounded vision of freedom, reason, and natural law.[7]

Though incompatible in important ways, the distinctive interpretations of Dunn, Tarcov, and Taylor converge in the view that Locke's moral and political thought is best understood as an integrated, if tension-riven, whole, and that the source of the unity of this whole is bound up with Locke's opinions about human nature and man's place in the universe. In what follows I shall not attempt to reconcile the particular interpretations put forward by Dunn, Tarcov, and Taylor nor adjudicate the fundamental issues that divide them. But in the effort to clarify Locke's opinions about virtue and politics, I shall try to respect the methodological lesson common to all three. While Locke nowhere systematically pursues the question of virtue, the subject arises in a variety of ways and places in his thought. And when the various strands of his treatment of virtue are brought together, his writings can be seen to yield a compelling account of the dependence of legitimate government on the character of citizens and officeholders.

As in Hobbes's case, the importance of virtue to Locke's moral and political thought has been generally neglected. A major reason for this neglect, as it was with Hobbes, is that Locke's critique of inherited ideas about virtue has been mistaken for a wholesale repudiation of virtue. Another reason, which also helps account for many misunderstandings of the status of virtue in Hobbes's political theory, is that scholars take Locke's rejection of the classical view that the *purpose* of politics is to promote virtue to imply that politics for Locke in no way *depends* on virtue. This inference, however, does not follow logically from the theories of Locke or Hobbes. Nor is it a position either holds.

Just as Aristotelian terms provide a means for clearing up the confusion with Hobbes, so too an appeal to Aristotle's distinction between the virtues that conduce to human perfection and the virtues that serve other ends can clarify Locke's understanding of the relation between virtue and politics. In Aristotelian terms, Locke's political theory as a whole shifts attention from the virtues of the human soul to the virtues of a good citizen of a regime based on natural freedom and equality, and to the social virtues that are necessary for the maintenance of any sort of human association. This shift of attention, however, does not involve for Locke—as it did for Hobbes—a repudiation of the very idea of a greatest good or ultimate end. Indeed, in his writings on morality and politics, Locke suggests that the virtues of a good citizen coincide to a considerable extent with human excellence, so that many of the very same qualities which enable an individual to conform to the moral rules that make all society possible and enable him to prosper in a free and commercial society also involve the perfection of the understanding, the "most elevated faculty of the soul."[8]

A good point of departure for an appreciation of Locke's views on virtue is provided by a famous passage from *The Reasonableness of Christianity*, in which Locke advances an important criticism of an older understanding of virtue:

> The philosophers, indeed, shewed the beauty of virtue: they set her off so as drew men's eyes and approbation to her; but leaving her unendowed, very few were willing to espouse her.[9]

On Locke's account, however, virtue was not fated to remain as she was left by the ancient philosophers, a luxurious ornament too costly to maintain. For Christianity made virtue the most profitable of investments:

> But now there being put into the scales, on her side, "an exceeding and immortal weight of glory," interest is come about to her; and

virtue now is visibly the most enriching purchase, and by much the best bargain. That she is the perfection and excellency of our nature; that she is herself a reward, and will recommend our names to future ages, is not all that can now be said for her. 'Tis not strange that the learned heathens satisfied not many with such airy commendations. It has another relish and efficacy to persuade men, that if they live well here, they shall be happy hereafter. Open their eyes to the endless unspeakable joys of another life; and their hearts will find something solid and powerful to move them. The view of heaven and hell will cast a slight upon the short pleasures and pains of this present state, and give attractions and encouragements to virtue, which reason and interest, and the care of ourselves, cannot but allow and prefer. Upon this foundation, and upon this only, morality stands firm, and may defy all competition. This makes it more than a name, a substantial good, worth all our aims and endeavours; and thus the gospel of Jesus Christ has delivered it to us.[10]

But ultimate profitability is not the only kind of profitability. In his writings on knowledge, politics, and education, Locke may be said to offer another and independent, if less exalted, ground for virtue's profitability: the preservation of a political order based on the consent of the governed—the only form of government, in Locke's view, consistent with the fundamental premise of his political theory, which is also liberalism's fundamental premise, the natural freedom and equality of all human beings.

With resigned melancholy John Dunn has declared that Locke has almost nothing to offer in the way of insight into contemporary political thought because of "the intimate dependence of an extremely high proportion of Locke's arguments for their very intelligibility, let alone plausibility, on a series of theological commitments."[11] Whatever the proportion of Lockean arguments supposedly rendered unfit for contemporary use by theological entanglements, such anxieties are out of place in connection with Locke's arguments about the dependence of representative self-government upon virtue. Doubts about human perfection could impair the beauty of virtue, and disbelief in Christianity could diminish virtue's ultimate profitability. Such doubts and disbelief, however, would have, from Locke's point of view, little effect on the importance of virtue to the establishment and maintenance of regimes based on the natural freedom and equality of all human beings, the consent of the governed, and the principle and practice of toleration. This is because the necessity for such virtue in Locke's scheme rests neither on premises about human perfection nor on beliefs about God's order but, rather, on the logic and requirements of liberal constitutional government.

VIRTUE AND HUMAN UNDERSTANDING

Sometimes Locke's indifference or downright hostility to virtue is inferred from his famous critique of innate ideas. But in his seminal contribution to modern philosophy, *An Essay Concerning Human Understanding* (1689), Locke's purpose is essentially moral, and the moral intention that animates his critique of the belief in innate principles is the defense of virtue through the clarification of its true grounds.

To understand the true grounds of virtue one must understand the understanding, the "most elevated faculty of the soul"[12] yet among the most difficult to observe and evaluate.[13] Although to understand human understanding, the inquirer must employ "Art and Pains" so as to place the understanding "at a distance, and make it its own Object,"[14] the attainment of such understanding is both pleasant and advantageous.[15] It is pleasant because it involves the exercise of man's most noble faculty. And it is advantageous because the understanding, if left to its own devices, is exceedingly liable to lead conduct astray by mistaking for knowledge certain fanciful conceptions that tempt individuals to ruinous adventures. By exercising the qualities of mind and character that enable one to establish the limits beyond which the understanding is not equipped to venture, Locke hopes to teach the mind to mind its own business. And virtue is a crucial part of that business.

It is a fundamental premise of Locke's thought that the intellectual equipment with which human beings are endowed, though limited, is adequate to the practical and spiritual tasks we face: "Men have Reason to be well satisfied with what God hath thought fit for them, since he has given them (As St. *Peter* says,) . . . Whatsoever is necessary for the Conveniences of Life, and Information of Virtue; and has put within the reach of their Discovery the comfortable Provision for this Life and the Way that leads to a better."[16] An inquiry into human understanding, so far from undermining virtue, is necessary, in Locke's view, to clear the mind of the clutter that causes it to lose sight of the knowledge of virtue which is readily at hand. While there is much that the mind cannot know, "[t]he Candle, that is set up in us, shines bright enough for all our Purposes."[17] And Locke understands our primary purpose to be the fulfillment of our duties for the right governance of our conduct.

Locke's prime example of a fanciful and widespread opinion that creates obstacles to right conduct and interferes with the discharge of our duties is the notion, taken by many to be a precondition of the moral life, that there are innate principles "stamped upon the Mind of Man."[18] The leading argument in favor of the view that innate principles inhere in the souls of men is that of "Universal Consent" or general agreement.[19] However, such agreement, Locke points out, may arise from a variety of causes, prominent among them the power of convention and the human predilection to credulity. In fact, simple observation reveals not universal agreement about moral principles but more nearly the reverse: vast numbers know nothing about basic theoretical ideas, while among nations wide and intractable disagreement prevails about the structure of a proper and well-lived life.

Locke doubts the possibility of adducing an example of even a single "moral Rule" which could be understood as an innate speculative principle that commands universal assent.[20] The most plausible—"Justice, and keeping of Contracts"—actually belongs to those "Rules of convenience," the common ties of all human association, that must be honored not only in decent and civilized societies but even among "Outlaws and Robbers" if they are to succeed in their criminal exploits.[21] What this suggests to Locke is not the threat of moral relativism but, rather, that the denial of innate practical principles is no obstacle to a recognition of universal, necessary, and objective rules for the maintenance of political life.

Nor is the denial of innate practical principles in the mind an obstacle to a recognition that persons are, by nature, governed by "a desire of Happiness, and an aversion to Misery," as well as by certain "natural tendencies" to pursue some objects and avoid others.[22] What Locke insists upon is the nonexistence of "Principles of Knowledge, regulating our Practice," that somehow inhere in the soul or the mind's structure.[23] So, according to Locke's hedonistic moral psychology, while moral rules are not part of the basic equipment of human nature, the ability to determine the rules governing the moral life is a distinguishing or constitutive element of the human mind.[24]

The mind, for example, is capable of identifying "that most unshaken Rule of Morality, and Foundation of all social Virtue."[25] A version of what Hobbes calls "that Law of the Gospel" and the sum of the laws of nature is for Locke a universal, objective, and necessary moral rule: "That one should do as he would be done unto."[26] This rule is not innate or self-evident, but it is reasonable because, as a part of morality, it is capable of demonstration.[27] Nor is the rule self-enforcing. In fact, it is more often than not transgressed, for complying with it is not some low-level, easily learned task but a strenuous and hard-won achievement.

The fundamental obstacle to doing as we would be done to is not that human beings are moved by a desire for happiness and aversion to misery, but that human beings have a propensity to confuse "imaginary for real happiness,"[28] to mistake immediate pleasure for "true felicity" and "real Bliss,"[29] and to make "wrong Judgments" about what is "really good," by which Locke means what brings the greatest pleasure over the long term.[30] Like Hobbes, Locke believed that human beings are endowed with reason but very often are driven by passions to disregard reason's dictates.[31] Indeed, in *Some Thoughts Concerning Education*, which contains his most thorough treatment of the subject, Locke defines virtue in terms of overcoming the wrong judgments to which our immediate appetites incline us, and seeking to satisfy those desires of which reason approves.[32] To achieve happiness or the satisfaction of desire, one must cultivate particular qualities of mind and character in order to place the passions under reason's guidance. On the basis of such a view Locke could be labeled, with equal plausibility, a rationalist, a hedonist, or a virtue theorist. This does not show that Locke was confused; it reveals, rather, the inadequacy of the labels.

Although no moral principles are innate, the reasonableness of some basic ones can be discerned from a variety of vantage points, and such rules can come to be respected by men on the basis of very different fundamental moral perspectives. While Christians, Hobbists, and heathen philosophers may have different reasons, grounded in conflicting accounts of nature, man, and God, they can in principle all agree, without violating their ultimate beliefs, on the importance of honoring promises.[33] Locke takes the possibility of such agreement about the rules of morality notwithstanding disagreement about morality's foundation as a proof that in the absence of innate practical principles human reason can discern basic "Moral Rules" about how to act in society, and that men can reach agreement about them "without either knowing, or admitting the true ground of Morality."[34]

This is not to say that the true foundations of morality are not of ultimate importance. Locke himself affirms that the ultimate ground of morality "can only be the Will and Law of a God, who sees Men in the dark, has in his Hand Rewards and Punishments, and Power enough to call to account the Proudest Offender."[35] What Locke's analysis does suggest, however, is that the lack of agreement about the true foundations or ultimate ground of morality is consistent with the need for and existence of social virtue, or the virtues that conduce to the observance of the rules that make social life possible.[36]

Just as universal agreement cannot establish the true grounds of morality, pervasive disagreement does not refute them or weaken the evidence of political society's need for virtue. Indeed, thanks to a happy arrangement that Locke attributes to God, but whose logic he discerns on his own, the virtues necessary for the preservation of society are also virtues which God rewards:

"For God, having, by an inseparable connexion, joined *Virtue* and public Happiness together; and made the Practice thereof, necessary to the preservation of Society, and visibly *beneficial* to all, with whom the Virtuous Man has to do; it is no wonder, that every one should, not only allow, but recommend and magnify those Rules to others, from whose observance of them, he is sure to reap Advantage to himself."[37] The convergence of the practice of virtue with the achievement of public happiness is another reason that one does not have to discern or affirm the ultimate ground of what one might call true virtue to discern or affirm the necessity of particular qualities of mind and character for politics. In fact, Locke holds that careful reflection on the logic and presuppositions of public happiness leads to the affirmation of many of the same virtues as does knowledge and embrace of the will and law of God. Although careful reflection is rarely accomplished, and for political purposes Locke believes that it should not be counted upon, it does follow that knowing and embracing the law of God provides a powerful additional incentive to virtuous conduct that advances the public good.

Locke knows that many will hypocritically sing the praises of moral rules that they do not find venerable or binding. Others will lazily affirm moral rules because of habit or custom, rather than as a result of the exercise of their own understanding or because of true belief about God. And Locke is acutely aware of virtue's elusiveness: "the name, or sound *Virtue*, is so hard to be understood; liable to so much uncertainty in its signification; and the thing it stands for, so much contended about, and difficult to be known."[38] In fact, there are almost as many conceptions of virtue as peoples, because all societies tend to use the term "virtue" to signify "what is in its own nature right and good,"[39] while disagreeing with each other on what is in its own nature right and good. Or perhaps one should say that there are as many conceptions of human perfection and the greatest good as there are peoples. For by distinguishing, as people and societies (and many scholars) tend not to, between virtues relative to human perfection and those that conduce to the preservation of political society, one can simultaneously affirm that disagreement about human perfection and the virtues supporting it is pervasive and likely to endure, and hold that reason is competent to discern—and human beings, from a variety of viewpoints, can, at least in principle, achieve agreement upon—the virtues necessary for the preservation of political society.

In sum, Locke's attack on the doctrine of innate ideas in the *Essay*, far from showing that virtue is meaningless or unnecessary, argues that the moral and political necessity for virtue cannot be derived from or clarified by what traditional authorities say about it. The doctrine of innate practical principles is especially pernicious, in Locke's eyes, because it makes people fearful of questioning custom and received opinion. Without such questioning, though, the weight of custom and the tyranny of tradition, Locke believes, will obscure the conduct God truly commands and the virtues actually required for the preservation of society. By rooting out the false ideas that fetter or infantilize the human spirit, Locke's polemic against the doctrine of innate ideas is meant to pave the way to a better understanding of the fundamental moral rules of society and the virtues that sustain them.

Virtue and the Origin, Extent, and End of Civil Government

Sometimes Locke's indifference or hostility to virtue is inferred from how little he has to say about it in his most famous contribution to modern political theory, the *Second Treatise* (1689). But to draw such an inference is to look for virtue in the wrong way and in the wrong place. In the *Second Treatise*, Locke explicitly focuses on a circumscribed part of politics: the part, his title page explains, "concerning the True Original, Extent, and End of Civil Government." While there is little reason to expect that a treatise concentrating on the *form* of legitimate government will delve into questions of virtue, there are also no grounds for inferring that the absence of an exploration of virtue in such a work implies the irrelevance of virtue to politics or the author's general neglect of, or indifference to, the subject.[40]

Indeed, although his primary concern in the *Second Treatise* is the form of, or principles that constitute, legitimate government, Locke makes the presence of virtue felt at crucial junctures in his analysis, and the very logic of his argument calls attention in a variety of ways to the inescapableness for politics of questions about virtue. Locke's account of the *origins* of civil government indicates that a minimum of virtue is necessary in the beginning, if men are ever to leave the state of nature and bring political society into being. Moreover, Locke's analysis of the *extent* of civil government shows that mankind needs virtue both to maintain the fundamental political institutions of legitimate government and to achieve the purposes for which they were established. And, finally, his examination of the *end* of civil government reveals that virtue is necessary for citizens if they are to discharge their most fundamental political duty and to exercise their most basic political right.

Nor is that all. In the *Second Treatise*, Locke even goes so far as to identify the family as the institution crucially responsible for fostering the virtues supporting a political society that respects the natural freedom and equality of all human beings.[41] What he does not pursue in the *Second Treatise*—the catalog of such virtues and the structure and content of the education for virtue—does not, however, go unpursued in his thought. Indeed, so important to Locke is the subject of virtue that he devoted an entire pamphlet, the *Letter Concerning Toleration* (1689), to the defense of a single virtue and wrote an entire book, *Some Thoughts Concerning Education* (1693), to enumerate a catalog of virtues that support a life of liberty, and to spell out the most appropriate manner to instill them. By considering Locke's treatise on the principles of legitimate government together with his considered reflections on the virtues, one can achieve a better understanding of how Locke's political theory is not only open to but presupposes an account of the virtues, and how his account of the virtues shapes, and is shaped by, his account of the "True Original, Extent, and End of Civil Government."

Virtue and the Origin of Civil Government

In his clarification of how the commonwealth originates out of the state of nature, virtue is neither Locke's first thought nor what he stresses. But the need for virtue is implied by the things Locke regards as of first importance about the state of nature, and by the issues he deems worthy of being stressed: natural freedom and equality; the fundamental instability that inevitably transforms life without government into a dangerous state of war; the pre-political right to property; and consent as the founding act of political society.

The fundamental premise of Locke's political theory, the natural freedom and equality of all, means that no man is by nature subject or subordinate to the will of any other man.[42] It does not mean that individuals enjoy, or are built to attain, freedom from the constraints of physical nature, or material want, or civil law. Nor does it mean license, in the sense of doing exactly as one pleases. This is because the law of nature, which Locke holds is accessible through the exercise of human reason even in the state of nature, dictates that "no one ought to harm another in his Life, Health, Liberty, or Possessions."[43] As has often been pointed out by Locke's defenders, Locke himself explicitly distinguishes between freedom's right use and its abuse, or liberty and license. But there is an additional implication that Locke's defenders have tended to show less alacrity in emphasizing: to avoid the descent into license and achieve freedom through the observance of law requires the exercise of virtue.[44]

Owing, however, to the natural scarcity of virtue, individuals in the state of nature—that is, a condition without government—frequently disregard the obligations imposed by the law of nature, especially the obligations to respect the person and property of other individuals.[45] Locke finds that those in the state of nature have an equal right to execute the law of nature by judging and punishing transgressors; but he also finds that this right is of little use in ensuring the intention of the law of nature, which is "the peace and *Preservation of all Mankind*."[46] The fragility of peace in the state of nature is a result of human imperfection. But it is not just that individuals lack the wherewithal in the state of nature to enforce their right against occasional bullies and transgressors. They also lack the ability to act reasonably and judge wisely and so themselves often fail to avoid bullying and transgressing. Because he perceives that in the state of nature men will be prone to "passionate heats" and "boundless extravagancy," Locke emphasizes that punishments for transgressions against the law of nature may extend only as far as "calm reason and conscience dictates."[47] Not every judgment that issues forth from an individual is valid; the right to punish transgressions against the state of nature extends only so far as the individual "soberly judges the Case to require."[48] But given the human proclivity to wrong judgments, especially in matters pertaining to one's own interest and happiness, sober judgment is not a quality that may be counted on.

The unruliness of the passions, which under the best of circumstances makes obedience to the dictates of reason difficult, is greatly exacerbated by the "perfect freedom" of the state of nature. In the face of the weakness of reason, the power of the passions, and the absence of a common judge with authority, men in the state of nature constantly succumb to the temptation to use force without right. The result in Locke's political theory is that life in the state of nature is for most practical purposes what Hobbes says it is in its essence, harsh and miserable—or, in Locke's words, "a State of enmity and destruction."[49] A crucial implication of Locke's acknowledgment of the qualities that peace in the state of nature presupposes, and of the passions that overwhelm them, is that the state of nature must always tend toward, and sooner or later become, a state of war.[50]

As in Hobbes's analysis, Locke's account requires in individuals a substantial supply of virtue if they are to escape from the state of war. On the one hand, Locke argues that the victory of passion over reason which transforms the state of nature into a state of war is inevitable, because in his natural condition man lacks the qualities of mind and character to control his passions and use his reason well. On the other hand, if men in the state of war were completely bereft of the ability to exercise reason and restrain passion, they would be unable to adopt the prescribed remedy to the inconveniences of war: the institution of political society through the establishment of rational agreements to live under a common judge. Like Hobbes, Locke implies that life outside of political society is made intolerable by the scarcity of moral virtue, while putting forward an account of how political society comes into being that presupposes a minimum of moral virtue already present in man's intolerable prepolitical condition.

For example, moral virtue, or a part of moral virtue, is a presupposition of Locke's account of the natural or prepolitical right to property. This prepolitical right to property is grounded in and limited by the exercise of virtue. In the beginning, and outside of political society, each human being has a right to everything because God has given the Earth and all that is on it "to Mankind in common."[51] One acquires a right to property in land or material, a right that allows one to exclude others from the use of what God has given to men in common, by mixing one's labor with it.[52] This title to property is legitimate provided that the purpose of acquisition is to preserve life or make it more comfortable and does not result in spoiling or destruction.[53] Moreover, to benefit from the right to property, individuals must exercise concentration and perseverance or industriousness, and intelligence or rationality.[54] For those who are capricious, covetous, quarrelsome, and contentious, the right to cultivate land and acquire and improve the resources in which the earth abounds will prove of little worth.[55]

Exercising the right to property to the detriment of others was a negligible danger so long as human beings lacked the means and the motive to acquire more property than they could use to defend and ease their lives.[56] The invention of money provides both means and motive. Money enhances the value of the right to property but also creates new opportunities for its abuse, and so heightens the need for virtue. By providing a nonperishable good that can be exchanged for perishable items, money encourages human beings to produce and acquire more than they themselves immediately need. Moreover, by breaking the connection between immediate need and the right to property, money exacerbates the tendency to acquire useless or harmful goods.[57] At the same time, money raises human productivity and leads to an increase in "the common stock of mankind."[58] By giving the industrious and rational greater incentive to apply themselves to work and production, money amplifies differences in virtue and makes it more profitable.[59] So money is a source of both vice and virtue.

To yield its full benefits, especially once money has been invented, the natural right to property requires virtue and such virtue requires the support of law. The cultivation of virtues relative to labor, which *"makes the far greatest part of the value* of things, we enjoy in this world"*[60] depends upon the exercise of both industriousness and rationality in the organization and protection of the system of labor:

> numbers of men are to be preferd to largenesse of dominions, and
> . . . the increase of lands and the right imploying of them is the
> great art of government. And that Prince who shall be so wise and
> godlike as by established laws of liberty to secure protection and
> incouragement to the honest industry of Mankind against the op-
> pression of power and narrownesse of Party will quickly be too hard
> for his neighbours.[61]

In other words, Locke envisages, if not the legislation of virtue, the making of laws of liberty that have as one of their purposes promoting and protecting the virtues exercised in the acquisition of property and the development of production and commerce.

The need for virtue can also be seen in the consideration of consent.[62] Consent is part of the moral foundation of political society and the act by which political society comes into being. It is because men are by nature free and equal that only consent, or choice based on private judgment, can rightfully subject an individual to any man-made law. The consent that forms political society involves the individual's deliberately divesting himself of his natural liberty to judge and execute his judgment, and uniting with other men so that the making and executing of laws is carried out by a common authority. The reason one abandons all the liberty to which one is entitled by nature for a lesser liberty in political society is that political society provides more effective preservation of one's liberty, as well as one's life and estate, than one could attain outside of political society with one's natural liberty intact. But this voluntary and calculated renunciation could not occur without virtue, or the discipline of desire that enables reason to determine what is necessary, and the discipline of passion involved in obeying reason's commands.

The practice of consent presupposes a common language and basic acquaintance with, and trust of, one's fellow consenters. And, in the context of common beliefs and practices, consent requires a range of qualities including the ability to calculate long-term interest and resist the lure of more immediate pleasures, proficiency in negotiation and cooperation, facility in recognizing fair compromises, and the art of keeping promises and respecting the claims of others. In contemporary terms, the very practice of consent presupposes not only "social capital" but also the "cooperative virtues"[63] and "democratic dispositions."[64]

Virtue and the Extent of Civil Government

The need for virtue in Locke's political theory by no means abates once the practice of consent has established political society. Like his account of the origins of civil government, Locke's analysis of the extent of government, or the overall boundaries of government power and the relations among specific powers, demonstrates the importance of virtue to the legitimate exercise of political power.

Locke's delineation of the legislative power, the supreme power in the commonwealth, presupposes virtue in legislators. But it also assumes that such virtue will never be in abundance. Supreme over the other powers, the legislative power is neither absolute nor arbitrary, but is limited in principle by the good for which government is constituted and all political power is exercised: the preservation of life, liberty, and estate, or the public good.[65] Thus the making of legislation requires the discipline of the passions that in political society, as in the state of nature, incline one to disregard one's duties in favor of one's private advantage, narrowly understood. And the restraint of passion and the exercise of judgment are the province of virtue.

If virtue were abundant, there would be no need for the separation of governmental powers. But in view of the scarcity of virtue,[66] if those who made the law also had the power to enforce it, then, Locke argues, the universal human tendency to seek one's own advantage narrowly understood would impel them to craft laws to their own immediate benefit and to devise ways to exempt themselves from laws that should be applicable to all. To mitigate this temptation, Locke separates the legislative power from the executive power. While his aim in separating those who make the law from those who execute it is to economize on virtue, in the process of separating the powers Locke throws into sharper relief the inescapableness of virtue in a representative government based on consent.

Locke separates what he calls the federative power from both the executive power and the legislative power,[67] partly on the basis of reflections about virtue. Usually held by the same person or persons who hold the executive power, the federative power deals with security and foreign affairs. Like the executive power, the federative power is not involved in the making of laws. But whereas the executive power is guided by, and supervises, the implementation of standing law, the federative power operates in a domain into which law can neither reach very far nor operate all that effectively. In areas like security and foreign affairs, areas where settled law and standing rules provide little guidance because actions are so involved, designs so complex, and interests so entangled, "Prudence and Wisdom," which are inseparable from virtue, must govern.[68]

Virtue is no less essential for characteristically executive actions. Executive power is above all characterized by prerogative, the "Power to act according to discretion, for the publick good, without the prescription of the Law, and sometimes even against it."[69] The necessity of prerogative stems from the inherent limitations of law. Since law is formal and abstract, while the actions and situations that it governs are particular and concrete, laws must always be overinclusive or underinclusive, embracing instances that do not correspond to their purposes and excluding cases that do. Frequently, laws will be overinclusive and underinclusive at the same time. Moreover, because of the uncertainty and variableness of human affairs, even the most carefully crafted laws will in some cases give directions that lead to injustice, and on other occasions will give no clear direction at all. It is for such unavoidable occurrences that prerogative must be exercised. Where the law is silent, or likely to defeat the purposes for which it was enacted, the executive not only may but is obliged to use his prerogative to exercise discretion to defend the public good. That is, he must act on the basis of a reasoned judgment, one that is not determined by the law but is governed by the same good that governs the making of laws—the public good, or the preservation of the life, liberty, and estate of the members of society.

The account of federative power and the doctrine of executive prerogative show that Locke's liberalism is incompatible with any facile distinction between the rule of law and the rule of men, and hence with any hope that government can function independent of the qualities of mind and character of the individuals entrusted with its operation. Recognizing that in many instances duly enacted laws will be silent or will speak incorrectly, and that wise and prudent human beings must be on hand to complete the intention of the law—effecting the public good—Locke fortifies the institutions of free government by building into them a flexibility that allows officeholders to exercise practical judgment. To exercise such judgment soberly, effectively, and with a view to the public good is to exercise virtue.[70]

By making explicit what Locke left latent, one can come full circle and see the need for virtue not only in the federative and executive powers but also in the legislative power. For just as there can be no rule that fully determines the conduct of security and foreign affairs, and no algorithm that prescribes the precise steps for executing legislation, so too there is no law or procedure that completely regulates the making of new laws which fit the community's changing circumstances. On reflection, it turns out that what Locke said of foreign affairs and executive action is ultimately true as well for legislation: actions are involved, designs complex, and interests entangled. Once one sees that actions, designs, and interests in domestic affairs resemble in relevant ways actions, designs, and interests in foreign affairs, one must conclude that "Prudence and Wisdom" are crucial—though perhaps in less conspicuous ways—to that part of government devoted to making settled laws and standing procedures. In other words, individual virtue is indispensable even to the legislative power, the part of government that in Locke's account least relies on it.

Virtue and the End of Civil Government

Once political society is established, the political need for virtue is still not exhausted by the demands involved in the effective carrying out of the various governmental powers. Attention to the end of civil government reveals one very important reason why legitimate government can never do without a minimum of virtue in the people. While the very institution of government is, on Locke's view, a response to a lack of virtue in the state of nature, the virtue of the people is the last barrier in political society to despotism, or a state of war introduced by government. When government abuses the people's trust by failing to govern in accordance with the public good, the people are formally released, Locke holds, from their obligation to obey the ruler or magistrate.[71] But who is to say at what point government has betrayed its trust? While government is the umpire that settles all other disputes in political society, it is the people, on Locke's view, and not the government who are the umpire when it comes to controversies concerning whether government has honored the public trust.

One implication is that political society can never be purged of every last vestige of the state of nature. The state of nature is defined as the condition in which there is no settled standing power to decide disputes; political society is defined as the condition in which there is such a power. Since the people as a whole, and, indeed, ultimately each individual alone, must perennially be prepared to judge whether government has violated its trust in the making and execution of standing laws designed for the public good, judgments not governed by a settled standing power are an ineliminable feature of legitimate politics. So the necessity for private judgment that is the defining feature of the state of nature is present as well in political society.

In agreement with Hobbes, Locke holds that political society properly aims to exclude "all private judgment of every particular Member";[72] but Locke, like Hobbes, reaches the conclusion that this aim cannot—indeed, must not—ever be fully accomplished. However, whereas Hobbes reinstituted the right to private judgment only on the brink of one's physical destruction,[73] Locke defends a right of resistance which provides that every particular member ultimately retains his private judgment concerning the fundamental question of whether the established government is honoring its trust. So Locke, in principle, accords substantially greater room to the exercise of private judgment in political life, and therefore his political theory requires a greater degree of prudence and wisdom in citizens.

Anticipating the objection that his insistence on a right to resistance in the people opens the door to permanent instability and constant revolution, Locke contends that the people are not easily moved to action; that it would take dramatic and prolonged betrayal of the public trust to rouse the people against the established authority; and that when the people are moved to action, it is more likely that the true rebels will be the rulers who have betrayed their trust by disregarding the public good.[74] Locke, of course, wished to diminish the threat to stability created by the permanent role he reserves to the exercise of private judgment in politics. But he cannot remove the threat altogether. The exercise of the right of resistance will always require a judgment by citizens about the public good and the means to securing it, a judgment that is not subject to but, rather, stands judge over the standing law, and is not determined by but, rather, ascertains the fairness of settled procedures. And this means that politics, as Locke understands it, is dependent on the people's virtue.

Accordingly, not only can discretion, in a broad sense, not be the monopoly of the executive among the powers of government; discretion cannot be the monopoly of government as a whole. In

the last analysis, the people, because they cannot altogether renounce private judgment, must be constantly prepared to exercise discretion. For the people are obligated, in Locke's political
theory, to maintain vigilance and determine when the federative
power has become reckless, when the executive power has over-
stepped its prerogative, and when the legislative power has failed
to make laws consistent with the preservation of life, liberty, and
possessions. In sum, in Locke's account, the people must be per-
petually prepared to exercise "Prudence and Wisdom" in judging
whether their representatives in the legislative, executive, and federative powers have exercised "Prudence and Wisdom" in pursuit
of the public good. Although Locke does not stress the fact, the
very logic of politics as he expounds it reveals the impossibility of
eliminating moral and intellectual virtue from the practice of limited constitutional government. Thus, though it is not his theme
there, in the *Second Treatise* he sets forth a system of government
that depends on virtue in its beginnings, in its organization, and
in achieving its end.[75]

Virtue and Toleration

It is pertinent in this context to consider Locke's famous "doctrine of toleration"[76] because it too is in large measure concerned
with the extent and proper end of civil government and at the
same time displays political society's dependence on virtue. In his
Letter Concerning Toleration (1689), Locke sharply distinguishes the
role of religion from that of civil government. Religion is responsible for the care and salvation of men's souls. In contrast, "all the
power of civil government relates only to men's civil interests, is
confined to the care of the things of this world, and hath nothing
to do with the world to come."[77] But toleration is not merely a
"doctrine" that declares man's duty to honor the boundary between religion and politics.[78] Toleration, for Locke, also names a
virtue that involves the control of powerful human passions.

Toleration is always necessary and usually urgent because peace
and order are perennially threatened from opposite directions.
The civil government is constantly tempted to overreach and il-

legitimately interfere with religion. For their part, the religious authorities frequently succumb to ambition for temporal power and persistently seek to meddle in affairs of the state. The duty of toleration requires, on both sides of the division between church and state, the restraint of desire and the exercise of judgment. The magistrate must restrain the passion for dominion from extending beyond its proper domain and seeking to instruct the soul. The clergy must control their zeal to do God's work on earth by carrying forward the deity's will, as they understand it, into every last corner of other people's lives. Through such restraint and control, magistrates and clergy both can succeed in tolerating beliefs about religion that differ from their own, and can manage to keep to their proper spheres. As with Hobbes's laws of nature, which are also and essentially moral virtues, toleration is not only a principle of reason but also a quality of character. Indeed, "toleration" should be understood as naming the virtue that enables one habitually to execute the duty to tolerate.

Toleration is a virtue that is well grounded in, or "agreeable to," both "the Gospel of Jesus Christ," which has as its end the care and salvation of men's souls, and "the genuine reason of mankind," which allows for differences of opinion about what leads to ultimate salvation.[79] Despite the efforts of corrupt religious leaders to impose articles of faith or forms of worship through the coercive force of government, true Christianity supports the virtue of toleration because the truly Christian life involves disciplining desire, especially the ambition for worldly gain. At the same time, toleration, as a virtue that conduces to peace and political stability, falls within the sphere of civil government.

The duty to tolerate religious beliefs and practices different from one's own is not boundless. Civil government need not tolerate—and, indeed, has an obligation to prohibit—"opinions contrary to human society, or to those moral rules which are necessary to the preservation of civil society."[80] Locke himself believed that such opinions will seldom be found in any church (with the rather large exception of the Catholic Church). The end of legislation is the "the worldly welfare of the commonwealth";[81] however, since certain extreme opinions "manifestly undermine the foundations

95

of society"[82] by so inflaming the passions as to make the observance of the fundamental rules of social life impossible, legislation that aims at the public good must sometimes touch beliefs in order to safeguard social virtue.

Virtue and Paternal Power

Locke is not guilty of developing an account of politics that depends upon virtue but ignores its sources. Nor does his political theory suggest that the necessary virtues can be fostered through legislation alone or, as some contemporary liberals suggest, somehow arise automatically from the experience of living under free institutions. Nor again must one look beyond the pages of the *Second Treatise* to discover the institution that Locke believes is crucially responsible for fostering the necessary virtues. In chapter 6, "Of Paternal Power," Locke indicates that parents have both the authority and the obligation to form the minds and mold the actions of their children, or educate them in the moral virtues.

Parents' power over children—shared equally, according to Locke, by father and mother—does not violate the principle of natural freedom and equality because children "are not born in this full state of *Equality*, though they are born to it."[83] Lacking the physical strength to provide for their own material well-being, and wanting the intellectual and moral proficiency to govern their actions by reason, children are dependent on their parents for preservation, nourishment, and education.[84] But the governance of children by their parents has a fixed purpose. Just as political power is defined in terms of, and rendered legitimate by, its end—the public good—so too paternal power is determined and limited by its goal—enabling children to become self-governing adults. Self-governance means living in accordance with the law of reason, or acting on the basis of an understanding of the rights and duties entailed by man's natural freedom and equality. While human beings are born for freedom in the sense that they are endowed with the capacity for rationality, the ability to exercise their freedom rationally comes only with age, proper rearing, and education.[85]

The education that makes the essential human capacities for freedom and reason effective is, on Locke's account, principally the duty of parents. Rather optimistically, especially in light of his own observations on the power of passion and the tendency for individuals to misunderstand what truly lies in their long-term self-interest, Locke argues that human nature, as formed by God, is such that parents will almost inevitably exercise their authority over children in tender and affectionate ways, and nurture and educate their children with a view to the children's good.[86] Understandably, given the limited means available to government in his day, Locke does not consider the role of government in cases in which parents discharge their duty to their children poorly. But he seems to acknowledge a role for the state in providing for education by arguing that if a father dies without having appointed a deputy or tutor to educate his child, the law must step in and provide for the child's governance and education.[87]

What, however, is the shape, the structure, and the content of a good education? Though he does not stress it in the *Second Treatise*, Locke was acutely aware that an education for liberty is an arduous, time-consuming, and involved activity, and that even in the best case, parents cannot be counted on to do all and exactly what needs to be done. For it is precisely to provide such guidance, to educate educators about the components of an education designed to foster virtues fitting a life of liberty, that Locke published *Some Thoughts Concerning Education.*

Virtue, Education, and the Family

Locke began writing what became *Some Thoughts Concerning Education* as private correspondence with Edward Clarke, a friend and landed country gentleman, who had sought advice on the education of his son. We must recognize that the *Education* was designed for members of a class that comprised only about 4 to 5 percent of the English population, but we must not conclude that therefore it retains little relevance today. We must also appreciate that it was the members of this class who, in the seventeenth century, governed England and managed her commercial affairs. Thus Locke's prescriptions for education address in one sense a very narrow audience but in another sense a general or universal readership. While his *Education* is a guide to the education of what in effect was an elite in his age, it is at the same time a basic education for all those who exercise the rights and responsibilities of full citizenship in a state based on the consent of the governed.[88] And a striking feature of Locke's view is that the primary aim of such education is not the transmission of particular knowledge, be it classical learning or natural philosophy, nor the acquisition of skills or a trade; Locke advocates, rather, that kind of moral education which seeks to form character by providing a training in "the principles and practice of virtue."[89]

Locke's "Epistle Dedicatory" brings out the dependence of the public good on private education and the dependence of private education on voluntary acts done by parents with a view to the public good. Worried that his book still bore the imprint of its origin in private correspondence with Clarke and thus in many places looked more like "the private conversation of two friends than a discourse designed for public view," Locke explains that he was persuaded to make public his thoughts on education by those whose judgment he trusted, and who had convinced him that by doing so he could advance the public good and fulfill his obligation to his country.[90]

Indeed, in putting his obligation to his country before his personal concerns about publishing an unworthy book, Locke hopes he can benefit the state by helping parents fulfill their duties:

> The well educating of their children is so much the duty and concern of parents, and the welfare and prosperity of the nation so much depends on it, that I would have every one lay it seriously to heart and, after having well examined and distinguished what fancy, custom or reason advises in the case, set his helping hand to promote everywhere that way of training up youth with regard to their several conditions which is the easiest, shortest, and likeliest to produce virtuous, useful, and able men in their distinct callings: though that most to be taken care of is the gentleman's calling.[91]

Each must do his share to promote right education: parents must fulfill their duties toward their children, and they are in part enabled to do so by individuals such as Locke who put aside their personal preference to perfect their thoughts in private in order to benefit the public by indicating to parents how their duties might best be discharged.

The importance of education derives from the fact that "of all the men we meet with, nine parts of ten are what they are, good or evil, useful or not, by their education."[92] In its prescriptions for rearing children to become useful and good adults, Locke's *Education* covers a remarkable range of subjects. It includes detailed recommendations for the strengthening of the physical constitution of young children, offering advice on clothes, diet, personal hygiene, toilet training, and sleep habits. It contains long discussions of the curriculum of reading for a young gentleman and the place of classical learning and knowledge of natural philosophy in the life of a man of affairs. It examines the contribution that music, dance, recreation, art, gardening, and travel make to a well-educated man. But the main subject of Locke's *Education* is virtue, or, more specifically, the formation of the qualities of mind and character that support the life of a gentleman.[93]

The virtue toward which Lockean education is directed is not relative to the highest perfection or to eternal salvation. In fact, in the *Education* Locke rarely mentions Christianity, and although he reaffirms that the correct idea of God is the true ground of virtue, he indicates that probing such matters does not belong to the business at hand.[94] This is not to say that the virtue with which he is primarily concerned, the virtue relative to an English country gentleman, is not connected to the highest perfection as Locke understands it. For virtue of all sorts involves the governance of desire by reason. And "the right improvement and exercise of our reason . . . [is] the highest perfection that a man can attain to in this life."[95] For a detailed account of the means by which the mind is to be improved, one must turn to *Of the Conduct of the Understanding*, where Locke argues that, like the body, the understanding must be exercised, habituated, and disciplined to achieve the excellence of which it is capable.[96] Locke's *Education*, however, aims not at *perfecting* this highest power but, more modestly, at teaching men of affairs to use their reason reasonably well: "since it cannot be hoped, he [the pupil] should have time and strength to learn all things, most pains should be taken about that which is most necessary; and that principally looked after which will be of most and frequentest use to him in the world."[97] What is most necessary and useful in this world, according to the *Education*, are the qualities of mind and character that enable a gentleman to maintain his possessions, prosper in commercial affairs, and govern well.

To form a gentleman, one must begin young and habituate a child to right conduct.[98] Reasonable habits must be "woven into the very principles of his nature."[99] This is accomplished not through the mastery of reasoning or rules of instruction, but through repetition and the observation of examples of good and bad qualities.[100] Whereas rules can be difficult to understand and easy to forget,[101] "nothing sink[s] so gently and so deep into men's minds, as *example*."[102] Locke's aim is to make the rational habitual. His reasoning is that the acquisition of habits which accord with reason is more reliable in practice than reasoned calculation of one's interest as each new situation arises, because reason, "when we have most need of it[,] is seldom fairly consulted, and more rarely obeyed."[103]

So that the young child can acquire rational habits and observe examples of moral excellence, Locke recommends a tutor.[104] Locke's standards, however, are high, and the task he has in mind for the tutor is demanding and far-reaching. The most important prerequisite is that the tutor come to his job generously endowed with a range of moral virtues:

> In all the whole business of education, there is nothing like to be less hearkened to or harder to be well observed than what I am now going to say: and that is, that I would from their first beginning to talk have some some *discreet, sober,* nay, *wise* person about children, whose care it should be to fashion them aright, and keep them from all ill, especially the infection of bad Company. I think this province requires great *sobriety, temperance, tenderness, diligence,* and *discretion,* qualities hardly to be found united in persons that are to be had for

ordinary salaries nor easily to be found anywhere. As to the charge of it, I think it will be the money best laid out that can be about our children, and therefore though it may be expensive more than is ordinary yet it cannot be thought dear. He that at any rate procures his child a good mind, well principled, tempered to virtue and usefulness, and adorned with civility and good breeding, makes a better purchase for him than if he laid out the money for an addition of more earth to his former acres.[105]

While no better investment is to be had than a father's investment in his child's virtue, even a gentlemen of means, Locke anticipated, was likely to pause before the financial outlay for education that he was advising.[106] In other words, even in Locke's time the steps one had to take to provide children with the virtues befitting a free man were dauntingly complex, arduous, and expensive.

Education in virtue is primarily a matter of learning to take pleasure from the right kinds of things.[107] And the right kinds of things are defined by reason: "the great principle and foundation of all virtue and worth is placed in this, that a man is able to *deny himself* his own desires, cross his own inclinations, and purely follow what reason directs as best, though the appetite lean the other way."[108] The work of education consists in making desire "subject to the rules and restraints of reason"[109] so that the right sorts of things are desired. The aim is not to extirpate the appetites but to cultivate reasonable desires and resist the unreasonable ones.[110] Accordingly, "the true secret of education" consists in the teacher's maintaining the pupil's liveliness of spirit while teaching the spirit to submit to reason.[111]

In reconciling the need for discipline with the importance of liveliness, Locke recommends "those softer ways of shame and commendation"[112] and "the *milder methods* of government."[113] These "softer ways" and "milder methods" involve the application of rewards and punishments rightly understood. Locke opposed the beatings and other corporal punishment prevalent in his day. He did not oppose them, though, on the grounds that discipline was antithetical to freedom, but because discipline based on beatings forms a slavish character. The correct form of discipline consists in teaching children to take pleasure in the approbation that comes from acting rightly or in accordance with reason, and teaching them to suffer the pain of shame when they act badly or contrary to reason. In other words, Locke seeks to replace physical pleasure and physical pain as motives for conduct with the pleasure that comes from esteem or good reputation, and the pain that comes from shame or disgrace.[114] "*Esteem* and *disgrace* are, of all others, the most powerful incentives to the mind, when once it is brought to relish them"; and love of esteem and apprehension of shame form the "true principle" that inclines children to "the right."[115] However, for all their utility, desire for esteem and aversion to disgrace are not, according to Locke, the true principle of right and virtue.

Love of reputation is not the principle of virtue pure and simple but the closest practical approximation to it:

> though it [reputation] be not the true principle and measure of virtue (for that is the knowledge of a man's duty and the satisfaction it is to obey his Maker in following the dictates of that light God has given him with the hopes of acceptation and reward), yet it is that which comes nearest to it; and being the testimony and applause that other people's reason, as it were by common consent, gives to virtuous and well-ordered actions, it is the proper guide and encouragement of children, till they grow able to judge for themselves and to find what is right by their own reason.[116]

Although love of reputation is not the ultimate justification of, or the greatest reward for, virtue, it is the cornerstone of the education of a gentleman. Accordingly, it is not inconsistent for Locke to credit Christianity with making virtue "the most enriching purchase,"[117] and to hold that "[s]hame of doing amiss and deserving chastisement is the only true restraint belonging to virtue."[118] Locke's reasonable argument is that the true foundation of virtue and the best reason for exercising it cannot generally be counted on in education or in politics. It must, however, also be acknowledged that in relying so heavily on reputation or the good opinion of others, Locke exposes his education in virtue to the danger of becoming a training in conformity to the prejudices of the day.

Nevertheless, the considerations that impel Locke to assign a critical role in education to concern for reputation do not stem from his own reliance on public opinions or common consent but, rather, grow out of his reflections on human nature. Locke designs his education to discipline dominant desires that he believes are typical of all human beings. Typically, one of the desires most in need of discipline is the child's natural desire for what Locke calls dominion.[119] Dominion looks like the love of liberty, but in contrast to the love of liberty, which focuses on freedom from the arbitrary rule of other men or their laws, dominion seeks power over others. Children show their love of dominion in the wish to have their way, to possess objects and do with them as they please.[120] It is this love of dominion, Locke argues, that is the root of injustice and strife in society. And it is this tyrannical desire to have one's way that early education must most combat, so that children learn to be pleased with what is right and proper.

Dominion is tempered by the virtue of liberality, which consists in easily sharing one's things with one's friends.[121] It is, however, justice and not liberality that Locke calls "this great social virtue."[122] Since justice involves an understanding of what property is and how it is acquired, an understanding children cannot be expected to possess, the foundations of justice must be laid in liberality, or learning to part easily with one's belongings. Injustice and dishonesty must be emphatically associated with the feeling of shame.

Courage or fortitude is "the guard and support of the other virtues," because it enables one to discharge one's duty and respect the dictates of reason despite the presence of danger and the expectation of evils.[123] Whereas for Aristotle a man expressed courage in the primary sense of the term when he faced death nobly on the battlefield,[124] Locke, in keeping with his tendency to understand virtue in terms of the gentleman's life (and in the process contributing to the democratization of virtue), stresses how courage is exercised off the battlefield and wherever human beings combat "pain, disgrace and poverty."[125] And whereas Hobbes downgraded courage from a virtue to a passion and then downgraded courage further by grounding the moral virtues in the passion of fear, Locke sees that the exercise of even the more modest moral virtues can call for courage.

Civility, the ability to put another at ease in conversation and dealings without flattery or servility, is in a sense the first of the social virtues.[126] It "is that general good will and regard for all people which makes anyone have a care not to show in his carriage any contempt, disrespect, or neglect of them, but to express, according to the fashion and way of that country, a respect and value for them, according to their rank and condition."[127] Civility combines respect for the dignity of individuals with knowledge of convention and circumstance. It requires finely calibrated practical judgment about the varying ways in which respect is showed another. It is a difficult-to-master art and crucial to men's ability to live together in a political society based on natural freedom and equality.

As with liberality, justice, courage, and civility, so too with industry, thrift, truthfulness and the other moral virtues that Locke expounds: all are affirmed by Locke because they place reasonable restraint on desire and contribute to happiness by enabling men to live together in peace and prosperity.

Conclusion

Few doubt that Locke wrote the *Second Treatise* (as well as the *First*) with a view to the political upheavals of his time. Yet Locke's response to the crisis over the throne in England is of more than antiquarian interest, because it consisted, according to his own self-understanding, in the articulation of universal principles of political right and legitimate government.

Legitimate government, according to Locke, is based on the consent of the governed. It has as its aim the public good, which Locke consistently defines as the protection of life, liberty, and possessions. While it is not government's job to promote human excellence or save souls, government cannot protect life, liberty, and possessions unless citizens practice virtue in private life and bring specific social and moral virtues to political life. The specific virtues on which the public good depends are, in Locke's view, learned in private life, but a private life that imposes formidable demands on parents as well as children.

Locke maintains that such virtues as self-denial, liberality, justice, courage, civility, industry, and truthfulness are necessary to public life and acquired by a moral education that takes place in the family. The success of moral education as Locke conceives it depends crucially upon parents who understand what kinds of actions deserve praise and what kinds deserve blame; who through their own conduct provide vivid examples of the virtues in action; and who have the good luck to find, and the financial resources to employ, a virtuous tutor to direct their children's education. In other words, Locke's scheme for moral education—and, more generally, his solution to the problem of the source of virtue in regimes dedicated to the protection of liberty—presupposes stable and prosperous families, parents with a generous endowment of moral virtue, and an immense concentration of parents' time and resources on the moral education of their children. However, if parents should cease to praise and blame as Locke recommends, or if the two-parent family dissolved as a basic unit for the rearing of children, or if it became infeasible for families to devote to each child the intensive care and attention that Locke believed was necessary to form adults capable of self-government, it does not quite follow that Lockean liberalism would cease to be viable. Such developments, however, would mean that a substitute source would have to be found to foster the virtues for which, on Locke's account, there is no substitute.[128]

Kant: Virtue within
the Limits of Reason Alone

Two great strands of thought have dominated contemporary liberalism. One strand locates the ground of freedom and the source of human equality in the humble side of human nature. It is typified by the utilitarianism of Jeremy Bentham, but it has deep roots in the political theory of the protoliberal Thomas Hobbes. Hobbes grounded freedom in the natural right of each individual to secure his self-preservation and found the source of human equality in common weakness and vulnerability to sudden and violent death. The other great strand of liberal political theory locates the ground of freedom and the source of human equality in what is lofty in human beings. Its greatest representative is Immanuel Kant. Kant grounded freedom in, and found the source of human equality to consist in the common dignity that derives from, the capacity of rational beings to act out of respect for the moral law.

According to a thriving tradition dating back to Hegel and sustained today in large measure by critics of liberalism, Kant's philosophy distorts the moral life by removing virtue from ethics. His moral philosophy, the critics charge, is marred by a *rigorism* that narrowly defines morality as a set of universal and necessary rules indifferent to circumstances and a *formalism* that deprives morality of substantive content.[1] However, a wave of revisionist scholarship in recent years has constructively challenged this venerable view, arguing that there is greater subtlety and flexibility in Kant's moral philosophy than his Hegel-inspired critics have acknowledged, and rich, untapped resources for his proponents to develop.[2] I shall suggest that the question of virtue is one on which Kant's philosophy proves more fertile and flexible than has been commonly supposed, but perhaps not quite so fertile and flexible as the revisionists would have us believe.

A good point of departure is to recall the status of virtue in Rawls's political theory, very likely the best developed form of Kantianism in contemporary moral and political philosophy. As is well known, Rawlsian liberalism views the right as prior to the good; focuses on freedom and procedure rather than the uses of freedom and the outcomes of procedure; articulates the principles of justice for the basic constitutional framework of a well-ordered society rather than the concrete institutional arrangements for the governing of an actual liberal society; and emphasizes the capacity in human beings for choosing and revising ends rather than the skills and capacities necessary for individuals to choose ends wisely and make wise choices effective.[3] Opinions about virtue are not what first springs to mind in connection with Rawls's political theory.

Nevertheless, what is not central or emphasized in a political theory is not therefore absent from the theory or unimportant to its coherence and viability. Indeed, as I suggested in the introduction, Rawls's account of the development of the virtues in a well-ordered society in part 3 of *A Theory of Justice* suggests that Kantianism in moral and political theory does not preclude, and actually requires, reflection on the moral virtues that support a stable and just liberal regime.[4] At the same time, the marginal role that these reflections play in Rawls's theory, and the lack of interest in them over the years displayed by sympathetic commentators, also suggest that Kantianism in moral and political theory encourages a neglect of the virtues necessary to preserve liberal societies and the variety of means for cultivating them.

Judith Shklar was of a different opinion. In *Ordinary Vices*, an attempt to sketch the moral psychology or character of good liberals, Shklar showed little patience for the view that Kant's moral philosophy had a share of responsibility for diminishing the concern within liberal theory for character or the moral virtues. To the contrary, Shklar blames Kant's interpreters for having "superficially" opposed Aristotle's "ethic of character building" to Kant's ethics of duty.[5] Shklar insists that for liberals Kant is an exemplary teacher about the structure of good character, and his examination of the ethics of character in the *Doctrine of Virtue*, the second part of *The Metaphysics of Morals* (1797) is, she declares, "particularly significant for liberalism, for it reveals the degree to which it [liberalism] may encompass a theory of character."[6]

On Shklar's interpretation, Kant, no less than Aristotle, put forward an ethic of right dispositions. Where they differed was in the interpretation of the content of good character, a difference that in her judgment redounded much to Kant's advantage. Whereas Aristotle's good man, according to Shklar, is aristocratic, dependent on wealth and honor, aloof, and devoted to his own self-perfection, Kant's moral individual is democratic, egalitarian, and benevolent; requires no special intellectual endowment, material wealth, or social standing; and simply seeks to respect humanity in his own person and in that of others.[7] Kant, Shklar also notes, differed with Aristotle over the relation between politics and the formation of character. Whereas Aristotle believed that the cultivation of virtuous citizens was the aim of politics, Kant held that the state had no business caring for citizens' virtue.

In "The Liberalism of Fear" Shklar again invoked Kant's *Doctrine of Virtue* as providing the exemplary account of good liberal character.[8] There, however, Shklar delicately acknowledged, without really pressing the point, a certain inadequacy in Kant's moral and political theory. On the one hand, she asserts that the dispositions, as Kant describes them, of a person who respects humanity in his own person and in that of others are dispositions that support personal freedom. On the other hand, she holds, as I observed in the introduction, that while the experience of living in a liberal regime which administers fair procedures and upholds the rule of law fosters dispositions that support personal freedom, it cannot be part of the purpose of a liberal regime to take steps to promote the character necessary for the maintenance of liberal institutions. When it comes to caring for virtues, even those it recognizes as critical to its survival, Kantian liberalism, according to Shklar, must tie its hands.

Shklar's restatement of Kant's account of good character and her contention that living under political institutions that protect personal freedom is the key condition for cultivating liberal virtues provide a timely reminder of a neglected dimension in Kant's practical philosophy and therewith in the liberal tradition as well. But Shklar avoids directly confronting the ambiguities and weaknesses in Kant's ethics of virtue. In particular, she does not investigate whether it is correct that life under liberal institutions fosters the virtues that support them; she does not even clarify what the relevant issues would be in such an investigation. Nor does she ask whether nongovernmental institutions such as commerce, the family, voluntary associations, and religion must play a supporting role. Or whether virtues other than those fostered by liberal institutions are necessary to the support of a life of liberty. Or whether specific features of Kant's thought have encouraged the widespread perception that his philosophy disparages the moral worth of the virtues and depreciates the political significance of good character. Or why it is that so many scholars have misread Kant as an enemy of virtue.

Striking features of Kant's own thought suggest that concerns about virtue and its sources are, in fact, unimportant for liberal morality and politics. The distinction fundamental to Kant's *Critique of Pure Reason* (1st ed. 1781, 2d ed. 1787) between a phenomenal or empirical world strictly governed by the laws of nature and a noumenal or intelligible world governed by the laws of freedom seems to deprive of moral worth the everyday world of sense, experience, and circumstance in which virtue operates.[9] The contrast basic to Kant's *Groundwork of the Metaphysic of Morals* (1785) between nonmoral inclination (including wants, needs, and desires) and moral motivation (obeying the moral law out of respect for the moral law) appears to rob our particular attachments, passions, and tasks of moral worth and dignity.[10] And the famous assertion in *Perpetual Peace* (1795), central to Kant's thinking on politics, that the problem of the state can be solved even for a nation of intelligent devils apparently implies that citizens do not need to possess even a minimal level of virtue to make a liberal republic work.[11] It can easily seem that if Kant is to give virtue any place at all in his practical philosophy, then it must be a narrowly defined place occupied by a desiccated notion of virtue.

This appearance is neither altogether misleading nor entirely adequate. In fact, Kant may be said to exalt the meaning of virtue by equating it with purity of moral intention. At the same time, by altogether depriving them of the title "virtue" he may be thought to have left open to neglect a wide range of other qualities that are, even from his own point of view, indispensable to the moral life and to politics.

Indeed, one key to a better understanding of the position of virtue in Kant's practical philosophy—as I have argued in connection with virtue's role in the political theories of Hobbes and Locke, and as I shall argue in the case of Mill as well—is the distinction between virtues relative to human perfection and qualities of mind and character that serve less exalted ends: virtues, in other words, of a lesser order. On the basis of the Aristotelian distinction between kinds of virtue one can see more clearly that within a Kantian framework specific qualities of mind and character are necessary to the actualization in life of the moral law; that Kant's particular catalog of moral virtues displays integrity and coherence; and that Kant's political theory, without doing violence to his practical philosophy, invites supplementation by a richer and more compelling account than Kant provides of the sources of the qualities of mind and character that enable individuals to cooperate for mutual advantage, respect the rights of others, and maintain the political institutions of liberal republics. In short, the decisive justification for introducing, contrary to Kant's usage, the distinction between virtues relative to human perfection and virtues of a lesser order into Kant's thought is that it brings into focus significant aspects of his moral and political philosophy which Kant's critics as well as Kant and the Kantians have generally neglected, and sheds light on important implications which for the most part they have failed to pursue.[12]

Virtue and the Moral Law

The moral law—the idea of a universal, necessary, and objective principle binding without exception on all rational beings—is the central idea in Kant's practical philosophy. But Kant's practical philosophy gives to virtue an important—if sometimes understated by Kant—role in sustaining this central idea. To bring out the connection between virtue and the moral law, I shall first connect a crucial feature of Kant's moral philosophy—the idea that freedom consists in giving or legislating for oneself the moral law—to a dominant idea about freedom in the liberal tradition. Then, I shall sketch Kant's understanding of the moral law, stressing Kant's own awareness of how the actualization of the moral law presupposes certain qualities of mind and character, qualities that, though not "genuine virtue" in Kant's sense, are nevertheless excellences of a lesser order and intelligible as virtues from the point of view of not only Aristotle but also Hobbes and Locke. Finally, I turn to Kant's *Doctrine of Virtue* to examine the catalog of virtues or internal dispositions of character that, on Kant's account, enable one to give to oneself and others "the respect owed to humanity as such." Attention to the supporting role that a variety of qualities of mind and character can and must play in Kant's practical philosophy reveals the extent to which autonomy for Kant, while in one respect a matter of right, is in another an achievement and mark of distinction.

From Individual Liberty to Autonomy

It has been observed, as I noted in the introduction, that in contrast to ancient and medieval political philosophy, where the promotion of virtue was generally understood to be the proper aim of politics, in modern political theory, particularly in the liberal tradition, the basic goal of politics came to be seen as the protection of personal freedom. This generalization, of course, must be qualified in a variety of ways. In the introduction I qualified it by stressing that modern thinkers in the Enlightenment and liberal tradition recognized that the achievement of freedom in political life, in fact, presupposes the exercise of virtue on the part of those who govern and those who are governed. Now I want to call attention to the peculiar way in which freedom is understood by a dominant current in the liberal tradition. Stated in abstract terms, freedom, as understood by key figures in the making of modern liberalism, was thought to consist in obedience to self-given law. Kant is in substantial agreement with Locke and in significant measure Hobbes as well that human beings are free, or making the most rational use of their natural freedom, when they live under laws they have legislated or prescribed. Where they differ is over the domain of freedom and the specific kind of laws that a self-legislating subject must make.[13]

In the social contract theory of the protoliberal Thomas Hobbes, the sovereign derives his powers from the authorization or consent of those over whom he rules. Individuals enter a commonwealth based on the calculation that they will be better off in political society under the civil law than outside of political society free from the constraints of civil law. Individuals form political society by renouncing the natural right to appeal to their own private judgment in determining what conduces to their self-preservation, in favor of a sovereign with the power to make and execute law and settle the controversies that arise under it. Yet in agreeing among themselves to obey the sovereign's laws, Hobbes emphasizes, subjects are really obeying only the dictates of their own most basic private judgment, the judgment that they are better off in society than outside it.[14]

Similarly, Locke holds that legitimate government is based on the consent of the governed. In forming civil society, men abandon the perfect freedom they naturally enjoy to exercise their private judgment, "within the bounds of the Law of Nature," as they see fit, and voluntarily incur an obligation to obey the laws and judgments of the commonwealth. In so doing, however, they express their freedom because the laws and judgments that they oblige themselves to obey are, in an important sense, their own—that is, made by them or made by their representatives within a constitutional framework to which they have consented.[15] Indeed, by limiting their natural right to judge in all matters as they think fit, individuals can be seen as enhancing the quality of their freedom by rendering their lives more secure.

Fundamental differences notwithstanding, both Hobbes and Locke agree that the natural freedom and equality of all human beings implies that the obligation to obey the law, where the law in question refers to the basic framework or the legitimating principles of the regime, is founded on the individual's ability to see the law as self-made or self-authorized. And, as I have argued, for both Hobbes and Locke a range of virtues must be present in subjects or citizens if they are to maintain a system where the laws reflect the most fundamental judgments of those who live under them about how to secure their lives and vindicate their rights.

The opposite of freedom for Hobbes and Locke was a specific kind of constraint, constraint on individual desire coming from another human being or group of human beings.[16] On the view they share, laws arising from a government that one has authorized or consented to is not really a constraint on desire but, rather, an expression of desire, or desire enlightened by reason. What this way of understanding freedom glides over is the further question concerning the origin, status, and worth of individual desires. For example, if my wants, needs, and desires have been imposed upon me by religion, society, family, peers, biology, or a dark and mysterious fate, they might well be seen to cease to be expressions of freedom and to be instead reflections of my dependence on external causes or my determination by alien forces. If my desires are not chosen but given or imposed from outside, then any law I formulate as an expression of them will simply inscribe in an external system of commands and prohibitions the very forces that hold me in thrall. Instead of being the author of my freedom, I become an accomplice in my enslavement.

This is the core of Kant's dissatisfaction with freedom understood as individual liberty. Embracing Newton's account of the physical universe, Kant argues that our wants, needs, and desires, or simply our inclinations, are indeed conditioned by alien or external causes, specifically the laws of natural necessity. As sentient beings living in a world governed by the laws of cause and effect, we are pushed and pulled this way and that by inclinations determined by antecedent physical events; and insofar as we are creatures of culture and convention, our supposedly higher pleasures are shaped by tastes and customs that are inherited or imposed from without. Human beings, in Kant's view, are thus essentially unfree in all activities in which desires can be understood as determined by causes external to the will.[17] To authorize or consent to a system of public laws on the basis of desire, or of fear, or of any calculation of costs and benefits, is to remain, in Kant's view, subject to external forces. From a Kantian perspective, one major problem with the social contract theories of Hobbes and Locke is that the liberty they rest content with securing bypasses the most fundamental question of freedom.

Kant in effect raises the standard for freedom.[18] Whereas Hobbes and Locke understand freedom in contrast to the submission to another human will, Kant understands freedom, in the main sense of the term, in contrast to a will determined by the natural necessity that governs the sensible or empirical world.[19] If one is to achieve freedom in the fullest sense, it is not sufficient, on Kant's view, to live under civil laws one has authorized or consented to. This is at best external freedom secured by public law in accordance with right. Inner or true freedom, according to Kant, is achieved when and only when one's actions can be seen as governed by a necessity beyond that of natural necessity. Freedom so understood is achievable, Kant believes, because human beings are not only sentient and conventional beings but also self-conscious beings endowed with a rational nature. On Kant's view, elaborated in the *Groundwork* and the *Critique of Practical Reason*, one transcends natural necessity and makes one's will effective by acting from a universal law that one recognizes and respects as prescribed by reason. In other words, freedom consists in giving to oneself the moral law. In the *Groundwork* and *Critique of Practical Reason*, Kant calls the simultaneous legislation of and obedience to the moral law autonomy. And in the *Doctrine of Virtue* he brings out in detail a crucial point only dealt with in passing in the *Groundwork* and the *Critique of Practical Reason*: such self-legislation depends upon certain qualities of mind and character in the legislator and the subject of the moral law, who, of course, are one and the same person.

The Necessity of Nongenuine Virtue

In the preface to the *Groundwork*, Kant explains that ethics consists of two parts. One part is concerned with what is contingent and empirical; Kant calls it practical anthropology (it includes moral psychology, comparative politics, and sociology), and it deals with the actual traits of flesh-and-blood human beings and the histori-cally diverse forms of social and political life. The other part of ethics is concerned with what is formal and rational; Kant calls it morals or moral philosophy, and it deals with a priori practical principles that can be known objectively, and that bind univer-sally. In Kant's understanding of ethics, moral philosophy is of substantially higher dignity than practical anthropology. Never-theless, it is not disdain or disinterest but a kind of philosophical modesty or appreciation of the limits of theoretical reason that compels Kant to largely refrain in his writings on moral philoso-phy from investigating issues of practical anthropology, even while his examination of theoretical reason itself shows that what belongs to practical anthropology is an ineliminable dimension of ethics.

Although Kant insists that the laws of morality must be formu-lated without reference to the facts of human nature or the cir-cumstances of particular men, he knows full well that it is only when assisted by the empirical part of ethics that these laws can be made effective in particular lives and actual circumstances:

> These laws [of morality] admittedly require in addition a power of judgement sharpened by experience, partly in order to distinguish the cases to which they apply, partly to procure for them admit-tance to the will of man and influence over practice; for man, af-fected as he is by so many inclinations, is capable of the Idea of a pure practical reason, but he has not so easily the power to realize the Idea *in concreto* in his conduct of life.[20]

Practical anthropology is crucial in two ways to the process by which the moral law is made effective. First, the application of universal moral principles to particular cases requires the exer-cise of practical judgment. This practical judgment, which is grounded in a variety of kinds of empirical knowledge—knowl-edge of human nature, of the proclivities and peculiarities of con-crete individuals, and of contingent circumstance—is indissolubly bound up with the empirical world, and so, along with the quali-ties that train and focus it, devoid of strictly moral worth. And

115

second, practical anthropology provides knowledge of the means for cultivating in human beings the dispositions that enable individuals to overcome impulse and inclination and embrace the moral law for its own sake. Thus while morals or moral philosophy, which comprehends the "ultimate norm for correct moral judgment," is, from Kant's point of view, the truly dignified part of ethics, practical anthropology, which he understands in terms of contingent experiences, critical reflection, prudent judgment, and self-discipline, is an ineliminable part of ethics because it prepares individuals to embrace that norm and enables them to apply it in their lives in relation to themselves and others.[21]

Kant reaffirms the connection between the higher and lower part of ethics in the famous opening of chapter 1 of the *Groundwork*:

> It is impossible to conceive anything at all in the world, or even out of it, which can be taken as good without qualification, except a *good will*. Intelligence, wit, judgment, and any other *talents* of the mind we may care to name, or courage, resolution, and constancy of purpose, as qualities of *temperament*, are without doubt good and desirable in many respects; but they can also be extremely bad and hurtful when the will is not good which has to make use of these gifts of nature, and which for this reason has the term '*character*' applied to its peculiar quality. It is exactly the same with *gifts of fortune*.[22]

Because empirical qualities of mind and character and the various external supports of happiness may be put to good as well as bad uses, Kant holds, quite reasonably, that they fall short of absolute goodness or inner unconditioned worth. They are therefore, on Kant's view, devoid of "genuine moral worth."[23] But while genuine moral worth is the only kind of *moral* worth Kant recognizes, to be devoid of "genuine moral worth" is not, even on Kant's strict view, to fall into utter worthlessness. This is because, once again quite reasonably, moral worth is not the only kind of worth Kant recognizes. Kant is committed to the view that while qualities of character and the external supports of happiness are entirely lacking in "genuine moral worth," they nevertheless play an indispensable role in supporting morality and giving moral worth to particular actions. Accordingly, although they are not good without qualification—and so cannot be said to possess genuine moral worth— such qualities as moderation or self-restraint, sober reflection, and the capacity to sympathetically enter into the outlook of another are good in a qualified way because, properly directed, they aid the individual in his efforts to act out of respect for the moral law.[24]

It is the rigid definition that Kant gives to the idea of morality which serves to deprive the qualities of character that support it of genuine moral worth. This rigid or philosophical definition, Kant maintains, merely makes implicit what is already a matter of "common knowledge" and "sound natural understanding," and is "generally in vogue."[25] What is already present in the common understanding of morality, Kant claims, is the idea that what is right is independent of whatever individuals may happen to need or want. To count as moral, a principle of right must hold for all human beings alike. Since morality takes the form of laws that are universal, necessary, and objective, dispositions—which not only can serve good ends as well as bad ones but are also particular, contingent, and shaped by forces beyond the individual's control—can never possess a genuine moral worth.

Only the good will possesses genuine moral worth. The good will, "the highest good and the condition of" all other goods,[26] is a will that wills in accordance with what is right or duty. Duty, "*the necessity to act out of respect for the* [moral] *law*,"[27] must be formal because it cannot refer to contingent ends. And to have moral worth, an act must not merely conform to what duty requires but must be done out of or for the sake of duty. The moral worth of an action is completely determined by the motive or intention that informs it—respect for the moral law—and is entirely independent of whatever consequences may flow from it. What makes an act moral, however, may be distinguished from what makes it possible, and therefore there is no contradiction in the assertion that certain qualities of mind and character, themselves lacking genuine moral worth, must be present for the successful completion of an act that is morally worthy.

Kant believed that most people most of the time know, without the aid of theoretical investigation, what duty commands. But theoretical investigation does yield a test for the determination of what duty requires, a kind of thought experiment in which one considers whether the maxim upon which one intends to act can be willed as a universal law.[28] Kant insists that the actual performance of this thought experiment—the putting of subjective maxims or plans of actions to the test of the categorical imperative—requires no special knowledge or skill, no peculiar capacities of judgment or philosophical acuity.[29] But he does not deny that the individual requires particular qualities of mind and character to honor the conclusions of the thought experiment which determines what duty commands, and to act in accordance with it. It is one thing to perform the intellectual act of excluding "sensuous motives" from one's determination of what duty commands; it is quite another to honor the conclusions of such a thought experiment, overcoming the blandishments of needs and wishes so as to do what is right because it is right.[30]

Indeed, such overcoming is so rare and difficult to discern that Kant is willing to acknowledge that it is "doubtful whether any genuine virtue [*wahre Tugend*] is actually to be encountered in the world."[31] The "true shape" (*wahren Gestalt*) of virtue is a mental disposition, untouched by any contingent empirical ground, to respect the moral law.[32] Virtue or "a morally good attitude of mind" is for Kant equivalent to dignity.[33] Genuine or true virtue is exercised in, and dignity so defined stems from, the activity of respecting the moral law by giving to oneself universal laws.[34] This is autonomy, and although Kant insists that evil actions are in a sense free,[35] it is only in acting out of respect for the moral law that one is free in the full sense. In all other actions one's will is determined by alien causes—appetites, passions, preferences, and opinions—all of which are themselves entangled in the web of cause-and-effect relations governed by natural necessity. By discerning the claims of reason on rational beings and acting out of respect for them, a human being escapes the causation of nature and becomes responsible for his or her deeds. The moral worth and the dignity of "genuine virtue" stem from the fact that through its exercise an individual achieves true freedom by "obeying only those laws which he gives himself."[36]

Among the duties that Kant specifies in the *Groundwork* as arising from the moral law is the duty to cultivate one's "natural aptitudes," "natural gifts," "talents," and "powers."[37] He argues for the duty to increase and improve such qualities on the grounds that they are always useful although, given the variety and changeability of circumstances, one cannot say in advance just how.[38] Despite their official lack of genuine moral worth in his system, Kant does not doubt the utility to morality of specific qualities of mind and character. Although he has little to say about the matter in the *Groundwork*, whatever dignity these useful qualities may be said to possess stems, he implies, from their role in facilitating the performance of duty for its own sake. In *The Metaphysics of Morals*, Kant elaborates the connection between morality and the qualities of mind and character that it both depends upon and expresses.

Kant's Catalog of Virtues

Kant provides a catalog of the virtues that conduce to moral perfection in the *Doctrine of Virtue*, the second part of the *Metaphysics of Morals*. While the first part, the *Doctrine of Right*, examines the basic principles of external freedom as they receive expression in private and public law, the *Doctrine of Virtue* explores the principles as well as the virtues that make possible internal freedom, or obedience to the moral law out of respect for it.

In the *Doctrine of Virtue* Kant understands by virtue only that which serves a moral end and perfects the highest or best part of us, our rational nature. Virtue is necessary because, as rational beings who are also finite and situated in the natural world, human beings are constantly tempted, even while recognizing its authority, to break the moral law.[39] Since executing the moral law because it is the moral law involves a perpetual struggle to resist and conquer powerful passions, virtue is "moral strength of the will."[40] Such strength is expressed through qualities of mind and character that enable one to subdue the inclinations deflecting one from taking the concept of duty as the incentive for carrying out the moral law. It is also expressed in qualities enabling one to perform actions that respect humanity in oneself and in others. As in the works of Hobbes and Locke, the virtues in Kant's thought can be understood as the qualities that enable human beings to act in accordance with the dictates of reason, but the dictates of reason for Kant are laws of morality and not prudence.

To clarify the difference between his own understanding of virtue and the traditional or Aristotelian understanding, Kant insists that virtue is not mere habit or aptitude but, rather, a set of inner dispositions rooted in firm, reflectively held, and purified principles.[41] In fact, this distinction does not set his conception apart from that of Aristotle quite as much as Kant implies. For Aristotle did not fail to accord to virtue a cognitive element and a connection to principle, inasmuch as he understood moral virtue as a habit in accordance with right reason.[42] Indeed, a certain family resemblance emerges as Kant explains that while human beings must be supposed to possess the capacity for virtue or "moral strength of the will," virtue itself (as Aristotle stressed) must be acquired and cultivated.[43] One crucial distinction, however, does bear emphasizing: Kant rejects Aristotle's inclusion, under the category of virtue, of excellences of character relative to intermediate and even mundane ends. Instead, Kant's pronounced tendency is to restrict virtue to the achievement of only one sort of excellence, moral excellence. Just as in the *Groundwork*, Kant's moralization of virtue in the *Metaphysics of Morals* seems to banish consideration of the qualities of mind and character that support cooperation for mutual advantage and competence in the routine activities of social and political life from the province of a purely philosophical inquiry of virtue. But, just as in the *Groundwork*, in the *Doctrine of Virtue*, the purely philosophical inquiry demands for its completion an inquiry into practical anthropology and, in particular, the qualities of mind and character that support the moral life.

In both works Kant obscures this by defining virtue wholly in terms of inner freedom or moral excellence. According to the *Doctrine of Virtue*, inner freedom or moral excellence involves two kinds of duties: the duty to oneself to promote one's own moral excellence, and the duty to others to promote their happiness. So virtue is singular in the sense that it is always essentially acting out of respect for the moral law, but virtue is also plural because individuals have various moral ends consistent with what reason prescribes, and various qualities are necessary to the attainment of these ends.[44]

The virtues one exercises in carrying out the duty to perfect oneself fall into two related classes: virtues that directly serve moral perfection,[45] and virtues that directly conduce to self-preservation.[46] To achieve moral perfection, one must cultivate the capacities that serve it, especially one's highest capacity, understanding, which is crucially involved in the process by which respect for the moral law becomes one's incentive for obeying it.[47] Fortitude, or "the capacity and considered resolve to withstand" strong but unjust natural impulses, and moderation, or control of physical desire, provide indispensable support to the disciplined exercise of the understanding.[48] In a related discussion in "What Is Enlightenment?" Kant argues that the failure to achieve enlightenment manifested by "a large proportion of men" has its sources in character. It is laziness, lack of resolution, and cowardice that keep so many in *"self-incurred immaturity."* The Latin phrase Kant designates as "the motto of enlightenment" expresses the dependence of intellectual virtue on moral virtue: *"Sapere Aude!* Have courage to use your *own* understanding!"[49]

But to be in a position to acquire enlightenment or respect the moral law by understanding its authority and honoring it in one's actions, one must be alive and well. One must abstain from vices such as lust, drunkenness, and gluttony that make one sluggish and inattentive to duty.[50] Other vices subvert duty more directly. Lying, avarice, and servility must be avoided at all costs because uttering falsehoods, lusting for possessions, and disavowing one's dignity as a creature endowed with a rational nature are all actions that of necessity reflect a maxim contradicting the idea that man is a moral being.[51] It follows that self-knowledge, or knowledge of what in man is worthy of respect, is a virtue. And so too is the disposition to heed the verdict of conscience, that is, "consciousness of an *internal court* in man."[52] In sum, the duty of virtue requires one to cultivate one's natural powers of spirit, mind, and body. But the justification is all-important. Virtue is not justified in terms of the increase that it may bring of wealth, power, or honor; rather, it is defended only on the principled consideration that since one can never know in advance what kind of actions will be required by duty, one must prepare oneself to honor what is right in whichever circumstances and in whatever manner one is called upon to act.

The virtues one exercises in fulfilling the duty to promote the happiness of others also fall into two classes: those that flow from what all human beings share, and those grounded in the practical conditions that distinguish one individual from another. Beneficence expresses a general respect for the humanity in other persons, gratitude a respect for benefactors, and sympathy a respect for the humanity in the poor and downtrodden.[53] One's duty toward others also involves the avoidance of the directly opposed vices, the "loathsome family" of envy, ingratitude, and malice, which cause one to neglect one's obligations to the humanity in the person of others.[54] The respect due the humanity in others requires moderation in one's demand for respect from other persons.[55] One must refrain from arrogance, defamation, and ridicule because they issue in acts that are contrary to the respect owed to humanity, whether in another or in oneself.[56] Friendship can be a virtue, but, though they may in practice fall short, only those friendships based on the principle of moral respect, and not those rooted in mutual advantage, express virtue.[57]

In an important observation at the end of the *Doctrine of Virtue*, Kant indicates that the virtues of social intercourse, "*affability, sociability, courtesy, hospitality*, and *gentleness* (in disagreeing without quarreling)," while only tokens of genuine virtue, nevertheless promote "the feeling for virtue itself."[58] What is striking in this assertion or concession is that it effectively admits back into morals and the account of virtue what Kant sought to expel in the beginning of the *Groundwork*, namely, the attribution of some qualified degree of moral worth to qualities of character whose exercise can be both good and bad. As Rousseau, whom Kant hailed as the leading inspiration for his moral philosophy, acutely observed, the virtues of social intercourse easily become the fashionable wrappings of a vile and decadent hypocrisy.[59] By nonetheless acknowledging that such qualities of mind and character play a substantial, if instrumental, role in fostering true or genuine virtue, Kant, at the end of the *Doctrine of Virtue*, opens the door to the kinds of inquiries he himself does not usually pursue, but which his theory implies are indispensable: inquiries of the sort, he indicates in the beginning of the *Groundwork*, that fall outside the scope of morals or moral philosophy but belong to practical anthropology and are a necessary component of ethics. Such inquiries must perhaps include not only investigation of the means for fostering the qualities of character that support genuine virtue; they must also involve study of the means that support the lesser virtues or qualities of mind and character which, one might say, form the conditions for the possibility of "peaceable, sociable, and comfortable living."

In his major works on morality, Kant affirms that respecting the demands of duty requires virtues of character, and he acknowledges that such virtues must be acquired and cultivated. But he barely begins to explore how this acquisition takes place and has little to say about who or what is responsible for insuring that the necessary and appropriate cultivation is carried out. In the *Doctrine of Virtue*, Kant acknowledges that the cultivation of virtue must rely on habit and example, but he discusses only the practice of moral reasoning as the means for virtue's cultivation.[60] At the same time Kant himself makes it difficult for the reader to believe that reason alone can generate "the force and herculean strength needed to subdue the vice-breeding inclinations."[61] Kant's approach does not prohibit or disable an inquiry into the variety of practices and institutions that promote the "moral strength of will" he calls virtue; but it does push the question of the acquisition and cultivation of the virtues into the background. In a time when traditional practices and institutions that foster the virtues are intact and functioning well, Kant's approach may encourage the illusion that such matters will always take care of themselves. In times of transition or upheaval, however, when such practices and institutions are undergoing substantial change and no longer performing their traditional functions, Kant's approach may foster the delusion that there is nothing useful or permissible to be done to promote the virtues. And by moralizing virtue, or assimilating virtue to genuine virtue or purity of will, Kant's moral philosophy obscures the very question of the virtues, or qualities of mind and character, that contribute to the maintenance of a political order that ensures freedom and equality.

Virtue and Liberal Republics

Kant's political writings are relatively short and, especially compared to his three great *Critiques*, accessible. On reflection this is not really surprising, for what one can say about politics independent of experience, as opposed, for example, to what one can say a priori about pure reason, is quite restricted. But not insignificant. Kant does not, as is sometimes said, reduce politics to legality. Nor does he reduce the science of politics to the science of law or jurisprudence. Rather, Kant limits the *philosophical investigation* of politics to what reason, independent of experience, can clarify about the principles according to which human beings ought to organize their collective lives.

Kant's philosophy certainly allows for the recognition that there is much more to politics than what philosophy can say about it. Just as he divides ethics into a formal component, which he regarded as philosophical, and a nonphilosophical empirical component, which he called practical anthropology, so too Kant distinguishes a formal or philosophical dimension of politics from an empirical or practical one. Kant's division of labor between the philosophical and empirical investigation in connection to politics—as I argued in connection to his twofold division of ethics—does not imply that the two dimensions are unrelated or that the nonphilosophical dimension is insignificant. But it must be acknowledged that Kant's strict exclusion of the empirical and practical from the philosophical investigation of politics encourages—as this exclusion did in connection to ethics—such a mistaken supposition.

To understand the relation between virtue and politics within a Kantian framework, one must grasp how the formal system of freedom, which in Kant's view it is the task of the philosophical investigation of politics to clarify, presupposes qualities of mind and character in the individuals who live under and maintain it. Kant presents a concise formulation of the external form freedom must take in politics in a discussion in the *Critique of Pure Reason* of the contribution that Plato's so-called doctrine of ideas makes to the understanding of virtue and politics. Kant contends that while Plato inaccurately understood the idea of the perfect state, it is entirely appropriate for philosophy to seek, like Plato, to articulate the idea of perfection in politics. On Kant's view, the necessary idea of perfection in politics consists of "A constitution allowing the *greatest possible human freedom* in accordance with laws by which *the freedom of each is made to be consistent with that of all the others.*"[62] Kant believes that this idea or formula, which rests on, and gives political expression to, the essential freedom and equality of human beings, must serve as the standard by which actual legislation and existing governments are judged, and the end with which they must be brought into harmony.

As in connection to morality so too in connection to politics: to articulate the idea of perfection, one must, on Kant's view, abstract from the vagaries of experience and the peculiarities of human nature. But, as in ethics, to even approach political perfection in practice, one must also, Kant holds, reckon with the vagaries of experience and the peculiarities of human nature. To choose the appropriate steps to bring actual political regimes closer to the ideal requires both formal and empirical knowledge. Thus the philosophical investigation of politics and the very idea of political perfection that it discloses imply the indispensability of the practicing politician and the need for practical anthropology. The practicing politician must be versed in practical anthropology to determine the qualities of mind and character that human beings must possess in order to actualize the political ideal. He also requires the knowledge gained from practical anthropology in order to provide, within the framework of political freedom, for the cultivation of such qualities.

Virtue, Liberalism, and Intelligent Devils

Despite the opening that Kantian political theory leaves for the empirical study of politics, Kant's most famous remark on politics may appear to suggest that as a purely theoretical matter a liberal republic based on the principles of public right does not depend on citizens endowed with virtue of any sort. On the one hand, Kant insists that a liberal republic is a formidable achievement, among political orders "the most difficult to establish, and even more so to preserve."[63] On the other hand, he asserts that a liberal republic can be founded and maintained by men who are entirely unangelic and wholly self-seeking:

> As hard as it may sound, the problem of setting up a state can be solved even by a nation of devils (so long as they possess understanding). It may be stated as follows: "In order to organize a group of rational beings who together require universal laws for their survival, but of whom each separate individual is secretly inclined to exempt himself from them, the constitution must be so designed that, although the citizens are opposed to one another in their private attitudes, these opposing views may inhibit one another in such a way that the public conduct of the citizens will be the same as if they did not have such evil attitudes." A problem of this kind must be soluble. For such a task does not involve the moral improvement of man, it only means finding out how the mechanism of nature can be applied to men in such a manner that the antagonisms of their hostile attitude will make them compel one another to submit to coercive laws, thereby producing a condition of peace with which the laws can be enforced.[64]

That establishing and preserving a liberal republic does not depend on virtue only follows from this analysis on the supposition that virtue is equivalent to genuine virtue or purity of motive in the performance of the moral law. Regardless of how one defines virtue, however, the capacity to submit to coercive laws that reason can show to be in one's best interest, and the ability to understand and respond appropriately to the right incentives, presuppose, as I argued in connection to Hobbes's political theory, a range of qualities of mind and character.[65] So Kant's claim that liberal republics can be preserved by unangelic, self-seeking men does not imply that such men need not possess particular qualities of mind and character, qualities that do not arise spontaneously but come from discipline and education. But one reason for the ease with which this may be overlooked is that Kant, wishing to deny a continuum, refuses to give such qualities the name "virtue."

Readers also misinterpret Kant because they overlook the important qualification he inconspicuously places inside parentheses—namely, that the self-serving devils for whom the problem of the state can be solved, though lacking virtue, must possess understanding.[66] Understanding, as Kant uses the term, includes more than the ability to determine what is in one's self-interest however understood. Kant's devils with understanding grasp long-term or enlightened self-interest; they possess the capacity to respond to institutional incentives and legal sanctions so as to perform the acts enlightened self-interest counsels. Therefore, just as it was necessary, on Kant's view, for individuals to acquire and cultivate qualities of mind and character relative to moral perfection so as to actualize the moral law in the concrete conditions of life, so too it will be necessary for a nation of intelligent devils, if they wish to establish and preserve a liberal republic, to acquire and cultivate the qualities of mind and character relative to the lesser end of respecting the coercive laws of state that secure external freedom. Whether one gives these qualities the name "virtue" is less important than appreciating that, on Kant's own account, liberal republics require them, and, though Kant does not delve deeply into the matter, that since they do not arise spontaneously, particular beliefs, practices, and associations must be instituted and sustained to foster them.[67]

Kant himself seems to acknowledge this in *Perpetual Peace* when he argues that before such time as perpetual peace is firmly established among the nations of the world—an achievement that does depend upon "the moral improvement of man" and is advanced by "good political constitution[s]"[68]—much knowledge of experience and human nature will be necessary for the determination of what policies will best secure the obedience and prosperity of the people. Although he consigns such questions to the realm of "political expediency," and while he disparagingly characterizes such undertakings as "mere *technical tasks*," Kant does allow government a role in insuring that citizens possess the qualities to maintain the conditions necessary for personal freedom.[69]

Virtue and History

In his *Idea for a Universal History with a Cosmopolitan Purpose*, Kant proposes history—or, rather, the laws of nature at work in history—as a source of the qualities of mind and character necessary for the preservation of civilized political society. Kant's view of history as governed by laws that advance the progress of mankind is perhaps the least plausible element of his political theory. But it is worth examining because it reflects Kant's awareness of the need to account for the development of the human qualities that support liberal republics. It also displays his awkwardness in doing so.

Although, according to Kant, we have no way of knowing whether nature indeed has a purpose that is carried out in history, we are entitled to posit that it does, and we have an interest in speculating on how the seemingly aimless conduct of mankind as a whole actually reflects a rational plan.[70] Nature's purpose in history, Kant suggests, is nothing other than to discipline men's passion and educate mankind for freedom. Nature does this by taking advantage of men's "unsocial sociability."[71] Man is social in the sense that he wishes to live in society, but unsocial in that he wants to be his own boss and do things his own way. The result is constant resistance and friction. Learning how to live together and manage the fundamental desire each has to govern himself is the art of civilization:

> Through the desire for honour, power, or property, it [resistance] drives him to seek status among his fellows, whom he cannot *bear*, yet cannot *bear to leave*. Then the first true steps are taken from barbarism to culture, which in fact consists in the social worthiness of man. All man's talents are now gradually developed, his taste cultivated, and by a continued process of enlightenment, a begin-

ning is made towards establishing a way of thinking which can with time transform the primitive natural capacity for moral discrimination into definite practical principles; and thus a *pathologically* enforced social union is transformed into a *moral* whole. Without these asocial qualities (far from admirable in themselves) which cause the resistance inevitably encountered by each individual as he furthers his self-seeking pretensions, man would live an Arcadian, pastoral existence of perfect concord, self-sufficiency and mutual love. . . . Nature should thus be thanked for fostering social incompatibility, enviously competitive vanity, and insatiable desires for possession or even power. Without these desires, all man's excellent natural capacities would never be roused to develop.[72]

Kant conceives of nature as a shrewd educator who uses the natural human propensities for competition, diffidence, and glory to develop in human beings qualities necessary for moral and political life.[73]

However unlikely it may be that nature works in the way Kant said it was reasonable to posit, one must understand Kant's underlying consideration: the need to provide some mechanism to foster the qualities of mind and character necessary to the preservation of just states. In Kant's account of the triumph of the liberal republic, the problem of political education is solved by the lawlike workings of nature which, taking advantage of man's "unsocial sociability," supply the qualities of mind and character that Kant suggests, consistent with the far more systematic argument of Hobbes, were necessary to the maintenance of political society.

In order to understand what is of lasting significance in his moral and political theory, one must establish what precisely is implausible in Kant's appeal to history to make up for the defect of better motives in citizens of liberal republics. That history is governed by rational laws is, in Kant's account, a hypothesis. But the dependence of liberal republics on particular qualities of mind and character is not hypothetical but an inference drawn from the logic of Kant's account of politics. The implausibility of Kant's hypothesis about purpose in nature and reason in history, coupled with the political need to develop men's natural capacities that his theoretical investigation implies, gives rise, from within the Kantian system, to the need to search for alternative, more reliable sources than those which Kant relies upon for the promotion of the qualities of mind and character necessary to the establishment and preservation of liberal republics. What his fanciful appeal to history actually testifies to is the price in plausibility that is paid when a theorist disregards, or glides lightly over, the questions of the sources that sustain the basic qualities of mind and character of liberal citizens.

In sum, when Kant suggests that the problem of the state can be solved without virtue, the virtue without which he believes the state can survive is "genuine virtue" or purity of motive in the performance of the moral law. Such a politics, however, is not politics freed from dependence on specific qualities of mind and character, certain natural capacities honed to a high degree. Kant's nation of intelligent devils will still have to acquire qualities of mind and character that enable them to cooperate for mutual advantage, respect promises, exhibit gratitude, refrain from pride, and so on. It is an implication of Kant's thinking that the dependence of liberal republics on such qualities cannot be abolished. These implications, along with the poverty of Kant's reflections on the sources of virtue, require a rethinking of what can be done, consistent with the imperative to protect external freedom, to provide for the presence of the necessary qualities of mind and character in the citizens of liberal republics. Indeed, Kant's reflections on the politics of intelligent devils invite the supplementation of Kant's reflections with something like Hobbes's account in chapters 14 and 15 of *Leviathan* of the virtues that self-interested individuals must possess in order to respect justice and keep the peace. And where the citizens of liberal republics fall somewhere between self-seeking intelligent devils and selfless angels, perhaps Locke's *Some Thoughts Concerning Education* would furnish guidance to the appropriate catalog of, and sources for, virtue. The more general point is that even in Kant's political philosophy, which has seemed to many to articulate a virtue-free liberalism, indications inscribed in the philosophy itself create space for, and show the necessity to morality and politics of, the cultivation of mind and character.[74]

CONCLUSION

Judith Shklar castigated as "superficial" the critics who alleged that Kant put forward a morality of rules which ignored, or was constitutionally unable to appreciate, the role of character in ethics.[75] To the contrary, Shklar replied, Kant's account of character was exemplary for liberals and liberal political theory. Shklar's view is a useful corrective to a common and long-standing complaint. But her opinion, too, is one-sided and also must be refined. It is a mistake to imagine, as Shklar rightly stresses, that Kant intended an account of morality that did away with virtue, and that he devised a theory of politics which made questions of character obsolete. It is, however, also a mistake to gloss over, as does Shklar, the awkwardness and rigidity of Kant's account of virtue and the inadequacies of his account of the sources whereby the virtues necessary to the preservation of liberal republics may be fostered.

Kant disconnects virtue from such ends as making men happy, prudent, or skillful in cooperating for mutual advantage. Virtue for Kant means "genuine virtue," and genuine virtue means purity of motive in the performance of the moral law. Understanding virtue exclusively in terms of the requirements of moral excellence, he refuses to give the name of virtue to the qualities of mind and character that serve the wide variety of other ends human beings pursue. But in his writings on politics, one can discern rising to the surface and struggling to make themselves felt claims about the dependence of liberal republics on certain basic qualities of mind and character. If only in connection with the ability to understand one's enlightened self-interest accurately and to conquer one's inclinations so as to act in accordance with interest rightly understood, Kant acknowledges the need for such qualities as self-restraint and prudent judgment. And Kant gives dramatic expression to the need to account for the acquisition and cultivation of such qualities by insisting that we must posit the dubious belief that nature works according to laws which both compel and enable human beings to maintain a system of private and public right.

Within the liberal tradition, Kant's view of morality and virtue stands at the opposite extreme from that of Hobbes. Whereas Kant equates virtue with purity or perfection in morality, Hobbes emphatically rejects the very idea of moral perfection and accorded the name of virtue only to those inner dispositions and forms of conduct that supported the political ends of peace and order. What I wish to suggest is that these two extreme approaches to the problem of virtue have cooperated to confuse the relation between politics and virtue in the liberal tradition. Kant puts forward an entirely nonprudential account of virtue: he moralizes virtue, making morality and virtue synonymous. Hobbes develops a purely prudential account of virtue: he drains much of the morality out of virtue, transforming it into enlightened self-interest. A third approach, one that is beholden neither to the restrictive metaphysical assumptions compelling Kant to equate virtue with morality nor to the restrictive metaphysical assumptions requiring Hobbes to reduce virtue to rational self-interest, could recognize virtues relative to human perfection as well as virtues relative to the preservation of political society. Such an approach would take its bearings from ordinary language and everyday experience and speculate in the space created by an open-minded and self-aware skepticism.

Liberalism derives a major advantage from this third approach. By maintaining a distinction between the noble virtues and the necessary virtues, liberalism can better understand its need to care for some virtues and its need to avoid using government to care for others that may nevertheless be crucial to its well-being. By avoiding the effort to promote virtues that are justified by appeal to human perfection or excellence, liberalism can respect the principle of restraining government from legislating morality. At the same time, liberalism can provide government a certain latitude for maneuvering to foster the qualities of mind and character citizens must possess for the more limited purpose of maintaining liberal institutions.

Kant was well aware that imperfect, finite, rational beings can make universal, objective, and necessary moral laws effective in practice only through the exercise of virtue. He displays a less satisfactory appreciation that if such beings, who constantly fall short of what the moral law requires, are to live together in peace and political freedom, they must cultivate a range of qualities of mind and character which, while lacking, according to his own scheme, genuine moral worth, nevertheless make possible the form of political life most appropriate to free and equal rational beings, a liberal republic. Liberals with a Kantian outlook on morality and political freedom, who have (with every good reason) abandoned Kant's faith in the beneficence of the laws of history, will have to look beyond the boundaries of Kant's philosophy and energetically investigate the sources for the cultivation of the qualities of mind and character—what one might, but need not, call the lesser virtues—that Kant's account of politics suggests must be present if liberal republics are to persevere.

Mill: Liberty, Virtue, and the
Discipline of Individuality

T HROUGH the eloquence, erudition, moral authority, and political engagement of his prolific writings, John Stuart Mill helped
to establish the character of English liberalism and in so doing established himself as England's greatest liberal. Until recently Mill
was routinely honored as a father of modern liberalism, and his
writings were habitually consulted as the indispensable point of
departure for the understanding of moral and political issues
surrounding the defense of individual liberty. But with the rise
in the 1970s of the Kantian-inspired deontological liberalism of
John Rawls, attention to Mill has declined as many liberals and a
good number of their critics have preoccupied themselves with a
host of relatively abstract issues—such as the constitution of the
self, the neutrality of law, and the legitimate forms of argument in
the public sphere—foreign to Mill's empirically oriented, histori-
cally grounded, and politically self-conscious liberalism.

One reason for the decline of serious study of Mill has been the
presumption shared by liberalism's critics and more than a few
liberals themselves that they need invest little time or energy in
studying Mill's thought because his ideas already constitute the
dominant moral and political orientation of the day and therefore
are ready at hand and easy to use, known to us without effort or
investigation. The presumption of familiarity, however, cannot
withstand the actual encounter with Mill's richly textured analyses
of such timely topics as the complementary roles of science and
poetry in the formation of an educated and complete human
being, the social and political preconditions for the effective exercise of individual liberty, and the competing claims of equality and
excellence in representative government.

Unfortunately, though, it is not the richly textured analyses but, rather, certain lifeless slogans about utility, liberty, diversity, and individuality that today tend to be associated with Mill's name. Thus Mill's thought has suffered the fate he himself asserted awaited ethical doctrines and religious creeds that become received opinion:

> not only the grounds of the opinion are forgotten in the absence of discussion, but too often the meaning of the opinion itself. The words which convey it, cease to suggest ideas, or suggest only a small portion of those they were originally employed to communicate. Instead of a vivid conception and a living belief, there remain only a few phrases retained by rote; or, if any part, the shell and husk only of the meaning is retained, the finer essence being lost. The great chapter in human history which this fact occupies and fills, cannot be too earnestly studied and meditated on.[1]

In the case of Mill's opinions, the loss of the finer essence is particularly unfortunate because at the heart of the remarkable body of work he has left, one encounters rare and instructive intellectual virtues: a supple dialectical intelligence, an exacting sense of the complementariness of opposites, and a discerning eye for both the element of truth in views he in many ways opposes and the partiality or falsehood inhering in the perspectives he more enthusiastically embraces.

Scholars, even some of those well-disposed toward what they take to be the core of Mill's thought, have not always appreciated Mill's penchant for finding truth in diverse sources. Some have suggested that Mill was caught in the grip of conflicting principles, some good and true, others bad and false. According to this way of thinking, Mill's deep admiration for the ideas of both the reformer of institutions Jeremy Bentham and the preserver of traditions Samuel Taylor Coleridge reflected the spirit of an indecisive man, one who on some days woke up in a liberal and rationalist mood and on other days got out of bed in a conservative and romantic frame of mind. Such possibilities would have to be taken more seriously had Mill not repeatedly remarked upon the importance of discovering the partial truth contained in conflicting opinions, sensibilities, and systems of ideas. But in light of his acute discussions of the dialectical character of serious thought, the interpretations of Mill as a contradictory thinker appear as flippant criticism by uninformed foes and, what is perhaps more damaging to Mill's reputation, the cavalier and patronizing apologetics of thoughtless friends.

Uninformed foes and thoughtless friends notwithstanding, Mill's defense of individual liberty has provoked at least three major criticisms. First, Mill has been accused of incoherently seeking to defend, on utilitarian grounds, an inviolable sphere of individual liberty. Second, he has been charged with indulging a romantic celebration of individual uniqueness that, in the domain of theory, lays the foundations for the postmodern celebration of untrammeled self-creation and, in practice, inevitably spirals out of control into narcissism and nihilism. Third, he has been condemned as a moral totalitarian who, under the banner of diversity, would impose a single conception of human flourishing, one that exalts individual choice and is aggressively hostile to revealed religion and tradition.

Much ink has been spilled in the expounding and rebutting of these criticisms, and coming to terms with them undoubtedly remains crucial to the determination of liberalism's future prospects. But much can be said about the structure of Mill's thought before a final judgment is reached about the ultimate coherence of his defense of individual liberty, the extent and implications of the romantic strand in his writings, and the depth of his devotion to promulgating a "Religion of Humanity."

My aim is limited. I shall argue that a crucial part of Mill's considered defense of the moral and political importance of individual liberty—even in *On Liberty,* his most single-minded defense of the principle of individual choice—is the articulation of a catalog of virtues that support it, and an account of the means by which such virtues might be fostered in a free and democratic society.

I shall focus on three major areas in which Mill connects virtue to morality and politics: his elaboration of the education of the free and complete mind; his account of the preconditions for, and benefits of, individual liberty; and his exposition of the aim and principles of representative democracy.[2] In fact, throughout his writings Mill saw that a political society based on freedom and equality could not sustain itself unless it had available effective means for the cultivation of certain necessary virtues. This is because a society that aspires to give the widest scope possible to individual choice and promote human development in its greatest diversity depends upon citizens who can seize the opportunities that liberty creates, and avert the peculiar dangers to individual freedom that modern democracy spawns. Indeed, a free society that not only tolerates but encourages experiments in living has perhaps a more acute need for virtue than do less open societies, because valuable experiments in living can be dangerous and volatile, and even relatively safe experiments may require for their successful execution refined qualities of mind and character.[3]

Like Aristotle, whom he regarded as the author of "many of the best observations of the ancients on human nature and life,"[4] Mill sees virtue as an irreducible feature of morality and politics. Mill, of course, differed with Aristotle over such matters as the status of specific virtues, the ends of a good life, and the goal of politics. But beneath the very real differences of opinion about virtue are important underlying continuities. Like Aristotle, Mill defends a particular conception of the good life for a human being. Like Aristotle, Mill believes that virtues are relative to a variety of ends and undertakings and not only to man's highest end. Like Aristotle, Mill explicitly calls attention to those lesser qualities of mind and character necessary to the maintenance of political society, qualities that Mill refers to as "social virtues." Finally, in agreement with Aristotle, Mill argues that the primary means for preserving a political regime is through education in the virtues.

As a champion of individual liberty understood as a way of life, and as a defender of representative democracy conceived of as the best practicable regime, Mill encounters difficulties in his treatment of virtue that are characteristic of liberal efforts to harmonize the political need for virtue with the political commitments to limited self-government, the protection of individual freedom, and the respect for human equality. On the one hand, Mill enthusiastically urges an expansion and protection of the realm of personal liberty; on the other hand, he recognizes the need to limit individual choice so as to preserve the institutions that form individuals capable of exercising choice skillfully, responsibly, and indeed boldly.[5] Perhaps the most fundamental difficulty is a variant on the well-known tension seemingly inscribed in the idea of liberal autonomy: namely, that the protection of autonomy means, in practice, that individuals will make bad choices which harm themselves and serve to restrict the autonomy of, or in other ways do injury to, others; yet every effort to direct by law, or set legal limits on, individual experiments in living threatens to subvert the principle of autonomy by legislating the meaning of right choice. In light of this tension, what, it might be asked, poses a more dire threat to the liberal ambition to protect individual choice than the invitation, implicit in the claim that virtue is relevant to politics and a fit subject for public policy, to legislate morals? Perhaps only the failure to appreciate that autonomy is an achievement, one that crucially involves the cultivation of particular qualities of mind and character. One of Mill's great lessons for liberals today, I shall argue, is that the achievement of autonomy, or what Mill sometimes called individuality, like spontaneity in athletic competition and improvisation in musical performance, requires the most exacting sort of discipline.

Virtue and the Free and Complete Mind

In the opening lines of his celebrated *Autobiography*, Mill announces that one reason he believes it useful to present to the public a sketch of his "unusual and remarkable" education is the great interest his age has in "education, and its improvement."[6] In harmony with the spirit of his age, Mill repeatedly argued that the public good was dependent on an improved education, one that was concerned with both intellectual and moral development. Indeed, in his account of the advantages and disadvantages of his own extraordinary private education—as well as in his lengthy tributes, published nearly two decades earlier, to Bentham and Coleridge, "the two great seminal minds of England in their age"[7]—Mill provides a consistent picture of the moral and intellectual virtues that form a free and complete mind.

The demanding curriculum ranging across the fields of human learning that James Mill fashioned for his son is well known, as is the cost that rigid focus on the cultivation of a critical rationality exacted from John Stuart. What has not been sufficiently considered is the debt that John Stuart Mill proclaims he owed, as a result of his education, to the ancients. From Greek and Latin authors he learned the art of rhetoric, general principles of legislation and government, and enduring ideas about education and culture.[8] And despite scholars' common tendency—common to students of liberalism and students of classical political philosophy—to stress what separates Mill's liberalism from the ancients, Mill himself stresses that the most enduring benefits he received from his formal education consisted in the lessons about, and training in, moral and intellectual virtue that he acquired through the study of Plato.

"There is no author," Mill wrote, "to whom my father thought himself more indebted for his own mental culture, than Plato, or whom he more frequently recommended to young students. I can bear similar testimony in regard to myself."[9] Plato's dramatic presentations of the way of Socrates exemplified "poetic culture of the most valuable kind," celebrated the most admirable of "the heroes of philosophy," and provided a model of "ideal excellence."[10] Above all, the Platonic dialogues offer a training in the Socratic method, a discipline in the practices that define an inquiring mind:

> The close, searching *elenchus* by which the man of vague generalities is constrained either to express his meaning to himself in definite terms, or to confess that he does not know what he is talking about; the perpetual testing of all general statements by particular instances; the siege in form which is laid to the meaning of large abstract terms, by fixing upon some still larger class-name which

includes that and more, and dividing down to the thing sought—
marking out its limits and definition by a series of accurately drawn
distinctions between it and each of the cognate objects which are
successively parted off from it—all this, as an education for precise
thinking, is inestimable, and all this, even at that age, took such
hold of me that it became part of my own mind. I have felt ever
since that the title of Platonist belongs by far better right to those
who have been nourished in, and have endeavoured to practise
Plato's mode of investigation, than to those who are distinguished
only by the adoption of certain dogmatical conclusions, drawn
mostly from the least intelligible of his works, and which the character of his mind and writings makes it uncertain whether he himself regarded as anything more than poetic fancies or philosophic
conjectures.[11]

What Mill found in Plato, and nowhere more adequately than in
Plato, was an image of, and a discipline that produced, freedom of
the mind. This freedom was not in the first place a right conferred
by nature or a liberty established by law but a quality of mind and
character, an intellectual and moral virtue. And this virtue was not
in the first place a social virtue necessary for the preservation of
society or a virtue of citizenship exercised in political participation and governing but, rather, a "heroic virtue" displayed in intellectual inquiry and exemplary of the highest type of human
excellence.

Human excellence, however, requires not only freedom of the
mind, but also elevation of the heart, and it was the job of education, in Mill's view, to provide both. Mill acquired a considerable
freedom of the mind from the notorious education he received
from his father. But it was in recovering from the severe one-sided-
ness of that education that he came to appreciate poetry's role in
educating the heart and making the mind complete. While cultivating the "analysing spirit" in his son to an unheard-of degree,
James Mill, his son eventually concluded, neglected the "natural
complements and correctives" that could nourish the feelings, en-
liven the passions, and sustain the virtues against the analyzing
spirit's "dissolving force."[12] The result, now the stuff of legend, was

that in the autumn of 1826, at the age of twenty-one, John Stuart sank into depression, having discovered that he lacked all desire to seek the goal—the good of mankind through the reform of existing institutions—for which he had been so rigorously trained by his father. In the process of his long recovery, Mill came to realize that a proper education required careful attention not only to the intellectual powers of analysis and speculation but also to "the internal culture of the individual."[13] Without poetry and art, without such educators of the heart as Wordsworth, Coleridge, and Goethe, a human being, Mill concluded, must remain stunted, a "reasoning machine" unable to feel sympathy with other human beings or nurture motives for pursuing worthy ends.

In its insistence that the formation of good character depends on a demanding education which disciplines the mind and elevates the heart, the *Autobiography* should not be thought to reflect a view about virtue and the liberal, or free and complete, mind peculiar to a single period in Mill's life. Present throughout his writings is the conviction that the acquisition of moral and intellectual virtue depends on a rigorous education incorporating the speculative truths won by philosophy with a knowledge of the heart that only poetry can reveal. For example, in 1867 in his "Inaugural Address Delivered to the University of St. Andrews" he reaffirms the importance of a "liberal education" in the making of "capable and cultivated human beings."[14] His firm conviction is perhaps nowhere more eloquently expressed than in companion portraits, written nearly twenty years before he began to draft the *Autobiography*, of two thinkers who, Mill indicates, decisively shaped his own mind: Jeremy Bentham and Samuel Taylor Coleridge.

In 1838 Mill wrote a long memorial essay for the *London and Westminster Review* (of which he was the editor) to honor the father of English utilitarianism and political progressive, Jeremy Bentham. Two years later in the same journal Mill published a thematically connected tribute to the romantic poet and conservative philosopher Samuel Taylor Coleridge. In both essays Mill begins by insisting on the kindredness of spirit of Bentham and Coleridge, an insistence that was bound to strike Mill's readers as quite absurd since the former was a rationalist reformer while the latter was a romantic preserver. Yet what made Bentham and Coleridge kindred spirits, in Mill's estimation, was that both were generously endowed with the philosophical spirit, and both employed that spirit—to be sure, with antagonistic styles and in opposite directions—for the benefit of the nation. Despite standing for opposing moral and political principles, each, according to Mill, deserved his country's gratitude as a "great questioner of things established."[15]

Because Bentham and Coleridge viewed "things established" from profoundly different perspectives, their questions brought to light quite different features of the the moral and political situation in England. But the truths each won separately were equally necessary to an understanding of the complexity of the situation. "[T]o Bentham," Mill wrote in his 1838 memorial, "it was given to discern more particularly those truths with which existing doctrines and institutions were at variance; to Coleridge, the neglected truths which lay *in* them."[16] And in his 1840 tribute to Coleridge, Mill reaffirmed this division of labor in the bringing to light of vital truths: "By Bentham, beyond all others, men have been led to ask themselves, in regard to any ancient or received opinion, Is it true? and by Coleridge, What is the meaning of it? The one took his stand *outside* the received opinion, and surveyed it as an entire stranger to it: the other looked at it from within, and endeavoured to see it with the eyes of a believer in it; to discover by what apparent facts it was at first suggested, and by what appearances it has ever since been rendered continually credible. . . ."[17]

The division of labor was not without its costs. The very abilities that enabled each to discover his portion of the truth blinded him to the truth discovered by the other so that "it was to be expected that Bentham should continually miss the truth which is in the traditional opinions, and Coleridge that which is out of them, and at variance with them."[18] The whole truth about morality and politics, Mill's two tributes suggest, involves a synthesis of Bentham's and Coleridge's profound half-truths. The two tributes suggest as well that such a synthesis depends upon "complete minds" which can combine and harmonize the distinct sets of intellectual virtues exhibited by such "systematic half-minds" as Bentham and Coleridge.

Bentham's intellectual virtues consisted in exact classification and rigorous examination of the empirical consequences of ideas and laws.[19] He sought to make moral and political thought precise, rational, and systematic by basing it on the principle of utility: in Bentham's eyes, the only practicable and coherent standard. Questioning the purposes and efficacy of existing institutions and laws, Bentham took nothing for granted and demanded that every particular practice prove itself by its clear and quantifiable contribution to human happiness. According to Mill, this single-minded insistence on utility as the standard in political reform and in the reform of philosophy helped eliminate much nonsense, backwardness, and grandiloquent rationalization of vested interest. But Bentham's virtues were also the source of his great deficiencies as a student of politics and philosophy. For, as Mill was to reiterate decades later in his *Autobiography*, the contribution to happiness of beliefs and practices cannot be easily weighed, measured, and translated into common units; and the demand for a precision appropriate to mathematics or bridge building in the study of human affairs blurs crucial aspects of moral and political life.

What moral and political philosophy requires above all, Mill argued, was precisely the knowledge that Bentham lacked, a knowledge of "the properties of man, and of man's position in the world."[20] Bentham's theory of human nature was radically incomplete. Convinced that human motivation was entirely intelligible in terms of the desire for pleasure and the aversion to pain, Bentham failed to see the limits of the usefulness of his guiding principle. It is not, Mill observed, that pleasure and pain do not have considerable jurisdiction in the determination of human affairs, but, rather, that they are considerably more complex and heterogeneous than Bentham imagined. Moreover, Bentham could not even recognize such motives for human actions as conscience or sense of right, the striving for perfection, the desire for honor and personal dignity, and the love of beauty.[21] This was in part because he contemptuously presumed that he had nothing to learn from other schools of philosophy.[22] But it was in large measure a result of the lack of a specific virtue. Bentham not only had no acquaintance with many experiences of the human heart, but owing to a deficiency of "Imagination"—a technical term that Mill uses to denote a faculty for entering into and representing to oneself the mind and circumstances of another—he was unable to make vivid for himself what he did not know firsthand.[23] So while Bentham's utilitarianism could illuminate the organization of, and suggest means for regulating, that rather large part of social arrangements governed by narrow self-interest, a different and no less indispensable teacher was needed for the other less conspicuous but not less essential domains of moral and political life.

That other indispensable teacher, according to Mill, was Coleridge. His dominant intellectual virtue was exactly that which Bentham lacked, a sympathetic imagination enabling him to discern the intricacies of the human heart and appreciate the moral and political imperative to accommodate the power and restlessness of human passion. In responding to this imperative, Coleridge showed that a discriminating knowledge of the past was indispensable. Within the venerable but corrupt institutions and practices of the past, Coleridge found important truths about the essential conditions for the preservation of political order. Mill emphasizes three such truths: the need for a moral education whose goal was a *"restraining discipline"* that would make an individual capable "of subordinating his personal impulses and aims, to what were considered the ends of society";[24] a certain underlying allegiance or loyalty, based upon the holding in common of sacred beliefs, fundamental principles, or shared values that enabled a society to negotiate the inevitable clash, in both domestic and foreign affairs, of conflicting interests;[25] and the existence of "a strong and active principle of cohesion among the members of the same community or state," by which, Mill emphasizes, he did not mean any kind of parochialism or xenophobia but, rather, a sense of solidarity, common ties, and a shared history and destiny.[26] These three "essential requisites of civil society"[27] must, of course, receive different institutional expression in different eras. Yet so far from making the mistake of many of today's communitarians and civic republicans that such notions represent stark alternatives to the spirit of liberalism, Mill insists that a restraining discipline, common principles, and a devotion to a shared history and common way of life are the irreducible preconditions of that progressive improvement which is inseparable from the defense of individual liberty.

Mill's companion accounts of Bentham and Coleridge together provide a vivid portrait of the liberal, or free and complete, mind. Such a mind, however, belonged neither to Bentham the rationalist reformer nor to Coleridge the romantic and reactionary poet but to the painter of their portraits, who, through the sharp rendering of his subjects, also exhibited the special virtues of his own mind, a mind that was strong and capacious enough to become home to what was best in two exceedingly different intellectual benefactors. That synthetic and synthesizing perspective—that capacity to allow "antagonistic modes of thought" to bring out what was best in one another, that "philosophical tolerance" and "liberality of opinion" which are essential to the apprehension of the complexities of moral and political life—is very much alive and on display in Mill's best-known work, *On Liberty*. In his seminal contribution to moral theory and political philosophy, Mill defends liberty in large measure for the virtues that it allows to prosper, and makes the defense of liberty depend to a significant extent on the capacity of a free society to promote the discipline of individuality.

VIRTUE AND LIBERTY

Mill's primary subject in *On Liberty* (1859) is "the nature and limits of the power which can be legitimately exercised by society over the individual."[28] The time was ripe, Mill believed, for a reconsideration of this subject because the "struggle between Liberty and Authority," a struggle as old as recorded political history, had taken a new shape in the advanced "stage of progress into which the more civilized portions of the species have now entered."[29]

In clarifying the limits of society's authority over the individual in the new democratic era, Mill does not offer a systematic examination of the relation between politics and virtue. Yet reflections on virtue and its political significance are woven into the very fabric of his famous defense of individual liberty. As I indicated earlier, I shall not rehearse, or defend Mill's doctrine against, the major criticisms that have been leveled at it. Much can be said on behalf of the familiar charges that his account of individual liberty is ultimately incoherent, that it suffers from a fatal romanticism, that it paradoxically sanctions a kind of moral totalitarianism. But there are also other things to say about Mill's political theory. My limited purpose is to show that Mill's exposition of the principles of individual liberty cannot justly be accused of failing to recognize or discuss perceptively the relation between politics and virtue under the conditions of modern democracy.

To begin with, Mill introduces liberty as a remedy to the tyranny of society, a subtle and insidious new danger posed to individual character in modern democracy. In ancient democracies the majority tyrannized the individual through the government; but in modern democracy, society, which tends to reflect the thinking of the majority, threatened to mold every individual in its own image.[30] By prescribing a single notion of good character through the powerful instrument of public opinion, society could, as effectively as any government action, fetter "human development in its richest diversity."[31] Individuals, however, were not the only losers. By depriving individuals of the opportunity to develop their talents and abilities, society deprived itself of energy and intellect.

To protect individual character—and thereby society—from the deadening effects of both the tyranny of society and that of government, Mill proposes the "one very simple principle"[32] for which *On Liberty* is famous: "the sole end for which mankind are warranted, individually or collectively, in interfering with the liberty of action of any of their number, is self-protection."[33] The inadequacies of Mill's famous principle have been much debated.[34] Indeed, in chapter 5 of *On Liberty* Mill himself suggests significant qualifications of his "one very simple principle," demonstrating an acute appreciation that the application of the principle to concrete instances often turns on difficult practical judgments about the quality and directness of harms to others which are caused by apparently self-regarding, but in reality substantially other-affecting, actions.[35] But perhaps the most important qualification to his "one very simple principle" is one Mill immediately introduces and that concerns society's legitimate interest in fostering certain qualities of mind and character and the appropriate means for doing so: "It is, perhaps, hardly necessary to say that this doctrine is meant to apply only to human beings in the maturity of their faculties. We are not speaking of children, or of young persons below the age which the law may fix as that of manhood or womanhood."[36] Education for liberty is, on Mill's view, not only perfectly compatible with the idea of the sovereignty of the individual or mature individual but, in Mill's judgment, necessary in the preparation of individuals to exercise, and coexist with others who similarly enjoy, sovereignty.[37]

A second place where virtue enters Mill's exploration of liberty is in the doctrine that utility is the proper standard for the judging of morality and politics. Of course, Mill did not use utility in what was then, or is still today, the ordinarily intended sense of the term. What he had in mind was "utility in the largest sense, grounded on the permanent interests of man as a progressive being."[38] Perhaps it was because he posited, among these permanent interests, a certain conception of flourishing or human excellence[39] that Mill could speak of Aristotle's "judicious utilitarianism."[40]

It is in *Utilitarianism* that Mill expounds the view that the foundation of morals is the principle of utility. The principle of utility, or "the Greatest Happiness Principle," holds that "actions are right in proportion as they tend to promote happiness, wrong as they tend to produce the reverse of happiness. By happiness is intended pleasure, and the absence of pain; by unhappiness, pain, and the privation of pleasure."[41] This is familiar. But in defending it against what he regards as the vulgar misunderstanding that looks on utilitarianism as a godless and soulless hedonism, Mill could seem to alter utilitarianism beyond recognition. He points out that much rides on how pleasure is defined; that is, whether happiness is identified with physical pleasure and regarded as essentially homogenous and quantifiable, or whether pleasure is considered as complex, heterogeneous, and, because bound up with both the passions and the intellect, very difficult to count, measure, or weigh.[42] As his essay on Bentham indicated, Mill took this latter path. His utilitarianism was grounded in a moral psychology, or understanding of human nature, that recognized a fundamental distinction between higher and lower pleasures;[43] that connected the development of "higher faculties" and "nobler feelings" to the overall increase of happiness;[44] that saw such development as hinging upon social arrangements, law, education, and culture;[45] and that understood virtue as a habit that lies "at the very head of the things which are good as a means to the ultimate end."[46]

Mill's considered view that virtue consists in those qualities of mind and character which conduce to human happiness does not involve him in any fatal inconsistency, either in connection with the principle of utility or in regard to his own overarching political theory. Human excellence, rightly understood, may be the highest pleasure and true source of happiness, and so choice-worthy on utilitarian grounds. Nevertheless, as Isaiah Berlin noted, Mill so enlarged and refined the meaning of happiness that "he left the true utilitarian spirit" far behind.[47] In other words, while Mill's appreciation of the complexities of character and the need for the development of the higher faculties does not contradict the logic of utilitarianism, it does frustrate a chief motive underlying the utilitarian approach: the aspiration to simplicity in moral and political judgment. More specifically, the supposition of complex, heterogeneous, and rank-ordered pleasures thwarts the ambition, characteristic of Bentham's utilitarianism, to measure happiness in simple units and to reduce moral and political questions to a calculus of pleasure and pain; at the same time it subverts the equally characteristic dream of an unambiguous decision rule for governance of moral and political life. Such a supposition, it should be noted, also makes virtue inseparable from the achievement of happiness by introducing the idea of conflicts between lower, ultimately less satisfying pleasures that are easy to gratify immediately, and higher and, in the end, more rewarding pleasures which require discipline and training for their achievement. It also connects Mill's thinking to Hobbes, Locke, and Kant on the crucial point that virtue is indispensable because human beings are inclined to make wrong judgments about what lies in their long-term or reasonably understood interest.

A third aspect of the moral and political importance Mill assigns to virtue comes to light in the best-known part of *On Liberty*, Mill's arguments in chapter 2 in behalf of liberty of thought and discussion. Consistent with his own "judicious utilitarianism," Mill does not defend liberty of thought and discussion as a matter of a fundamental right but in terms of the "permanent interests of man as a progressive being." Liberty, Mill argues, is an indispensable practice through which society and the state can develop the moral and intellectual nature of all men while creating an environment hospitable to, and in which political benefit can be derived from the presence of, exceptional human beings.

Freedom of thought and opinion would be of no value were it not for a particular "quality of the human mind."[48] Corrigibility, man's ability to correct his errors through the exercise of reasoned judgment, is "the source of everything respectable in man either as an intellectual or as a moral being."[49] In contrast to what Rousseau called "perfectibility," the capacity to undertake novel activities,[50] Mill's corrigibility denotes human beings' capacity to exercise right judgment in the activities they undertake. The ability to judge well, however, is acquired; and its acquisition depends upon learning, wide experience, and listening to "persons of every variety of opinion."[51]

But society impairs the capacity for reasoned judgment. It is disinclined to hear out all voices. Indeed, in the name of what is moral and pious, society is more likely to strike down the "best men and noblest doctrines."[52] Socrates was sentenced to death by his fellow citizens although he was justly renowned by the best men of his own age as the most virtuous among them and is rightly

regarded by modern men as the greatest teacher of virtue.[53] Jesus
was condemned to die as a "prodigy of impiety" although he was
exactly the opposite, the embodiment of "moral grandeur."[54] And
Emperor Marcus Aurelius, "the gentlest and most amiable of philosophers and rulers,"[55] was, in his persecution of Christianity,
brought low by the commonplace impulse to punish heterodox
beliefs and practices. Through the invocation of Socrates, Jesus,
and Marcus Aurelius, Mill brings out not only the enduring antagonism between human excellence and political society but also
the dependence of progress on society's capacity to restrain its
antipathy and make room for exemplars of intellectual, moral,
and political virtue.

Freedom of opinion is not only necessary for the protection of
outstanding individuals. More generally, it promotes diversity of
opinion, the social condition most favorable to the generation
and general dissemination of moral and political knowledge, and
to the promotion of moral and intellectual virtue. If received
opinion about morality and politics is false, diversity of opinion
preserves space for true opinions to openly confront false ones.[56]
If received opinion is true, but held, as it so often is, without conviction or understanding, the challenges to it made possible by
the presence within society of conflicting opinions can render
true opinions more vivid and secure.[57] And, in what is the most
common case, when received opinion is only partly true and opposing doctrines are partly true also, open expression of diverse
opinion allows alert individuals to weave the conflicting and partial truths about moral and political life together into a more subtle and comprehensive perspective.[58]

The utility of diversity of opinion is rooted in two factors: the
special character of moral and political knowledge and the general scarcity of virtue among individuals. In contrast to mathematics, "where there is nothing at all to be said on the wrong side of
the question," in moral and political matters there is always something to be said on the other side of the issue.[59] Some will infer
from this thought that Mill is denying the existence of right answers to moral and political questions. Others will seize upon
Mill's casually optimistic view that "as mankind improve, the num-

ber of doctrines which are no longer disputed or doubted will be constantly on the increase: and the well-being of mankind may almost be measured by the number and gravity of the truths which have reached the point of being uncontested."[60] They will conclude that Mill really believes that liberty of thought and discussion steadily builds up the supply of undoubted truths. Yet facile relativism and doctrinaire progressivism, tendencies all too well represented in Mill's thought, are neither the most weighty nor the most worthy part of it. Indeed, Mill is more concerned in discussing the liberty of thought and discussion to point out the dependence of the search for truth on moral and intellectual virtue, and to clarify what society must do given that such virtue tends to be in short supply:

> Truth, in the great practical concerns of life is so much a question of the reconciling and combining of opposites, that very few have minds sufficiently capacious and impartial to make the adjustment with an approach to correctness, and it has to be made by the rough process of a struggle between combatants fighting under hostile banners.[61]

It is because the virtue of sound judgment in moral and political matters is possible, necessary, and rare that freedom of thought and diversity of opinion must be actively encouraged.

The cultivation of sound judgment, the achievement of real understanding about "the great practical concerns of life," requires for its perfection a peculiar discipline. This peculiar discipline, which Mill found lacking in modern democracy, was best exemplified, according to Mill, in the Socratic conversations of Plato's dialogues and the school disputations of the Middle Ages.[62] Such dialectical exercises cultivate the quality of "many-sidedness," a virtue Mill associated with Goethe and Socrates, and which consisted in the capacity to appreciate what is true in diverse and rival perspectives.[63] But not everybody can receive a properly Socratic education, in part because Socratic educators are scarce, in part because the talents and abilities that enable students to receive a Socratic education are unevenly distributed among mankind. Freedom of thought and diversity of opinion on the level of society are imperfect contrivances for the cultivation of the mind but the best available substitutes for an exacting private Socratic education for each.

In order for the mind to be cultivated as the liberal spirit requires, on all important political questions both conservative and progressive opinions must be vigorously represented in public debate:

> Unless opinions favourable to democracy and to aristocracy, to property and to equality, to co-operation and to competition, to luxury and to abstinence, to sociality and individuality, to liberty and discipline, and all the other standing antagonisms of practical life, are expressed with equal freedom, and enforced and defended with equal talent and energy, there is no chance of both elements obtaining their due. . . .[64]

Indeed, contrary to the spirit of much contemporary liberalism—which seeks to articulate principles whose purpose is to circumscribe public debate, and whose effect in practice is to stigmatize as unreasonable, and ostracize from public life, a range of fundamental opinions held by law-abiding citizens—Mill goes so far as to argue that where fundamental moral and political truths achieve unchallenged sway, "teachers of mankind" should provide "some contrivance for making the difficulties of the question as present to the learner's consciousness, as if they were pressed upon him by a dissentient champion, eager for his conversion."[65]

Moreover, instead of relying on rules to regulate which opinions are admissible in the public sphere and which ought to be refused admittance, Mill argues that the "real morality of public discussion" deals with the virtues that make possible the free discussion of diverse opinion. In contrast to today's proponents of "the idea of public reason," "deliberative democracy," and the "discourse theory of ethics," it is not, Mill held, the business of "law and authority" to determine what kinds of opinions and arguments may be uttered and which ought to be heard in public debate. Rather, Mill calls on virtue to regulate the expression of opinion. Freedom depends on the capacity of individuals to distinguish virtue and vice in public debate, on citizens who can be counted on for

> condemning every one, on whichever side of the argument he places himself, in whose mode of advocacy either want of candour, or malignity, bigotry, or intolerance of feeling manifest themselves; but not inferring these vices from the side which a person takes, though it be the contrary side of the question to our own; and giving merited honour to every one, whatever opinion he may hold, who has calmness to see and honesty to state what his opponents and their opinions really are, exaggerating nothing to their discredit, keeping nothing back which tells, or can be supposed to tell, in their favour.[66]

In sum, it is not from radical skepticism about human understanding nor on the basis of a denial of a greatest good but, rather, out of appreciation of "the interests of truth"[67] and the moral and intellectual virtues bound up with its pursuit that Mill believes modern democracy must leave thought free and encourage diversity of opinion.

A fourth place where Mill connects virtue to liberty is in the argument he develops in chapter 3 that "individuality" is a discipline praiseworthy as a vital element of human well-being. Individuality does not mean doing whatever you please, or what Mill calls "miserable individuality."[68] Nor should it be confused with the pathology that Tocqueville diagnosed as "individualism," a condition in which "each man is forever thrown back on himself alone, and there is danger that he may be shut up in the solitude of his own heart."[69] Individuality, rightly understood, refers to the developed capacity to undertake experiments in living and form one's character in accordance with one's particular powers. Individuality does not develop in human beings naturally but is an achievement that requires a long and rigorous moral and intellectual education. Individuals must be "taught and trained in youth, as to know and benefit by the ascertained results of human experience."[70] The purpose of such education is to develop "the qualities which are the distinctive endowment of a human being."[71]

While no two individuals are exactly alike, every person who achieves individuality "must use observation to see, reasoning and judgment to foresee, activity to gather materials for decision, discrimination to decide, and when he has decided, firmness and self-control to hold to his deliberate decision."[72]

Mill denies that the development of the moral and intellectual virtues which express the discipline of individuality must be achieved at the expense of feeling and passion. Indeed, in a "perfect human being" powerful impulses and great energies are not abolished or overcome but, rather, serve as the indispensable raw materials of human excellence.[73] Strong passion is "the source from whence are generated the most passionate love of virtue, and the sternest self-control."[74] In the age of modern democracy, it is through the "cultivation" of moral and intellectual virtue, and their union in the discipline of individuality, "that society both does its duty and protects its interests."[75]

While Mill sometimes equates individuality with eccentricity, he does not thereby mean to champion an ideal that celebrates the infinite malleability of the human personality, nor does he intend to glorify arbitrary or aimless defiance of conventional opinion. He does not understand by eccentricity any sort of random or rebellious deviation from custom. Individuality, as Mill conceived it, has a certain structure, and it embodies the best of virtues from rival traditions, combining pagan self-assertion or modern self-development with the "Platonic and Christian ideal of self-government."[76] To be sure, this blend, especially in a free society, imposes a certain "compression," or restraint of the will, on "the stronger specimens of human nature," who must learn to respect the rights of others by complying with the rules that society lays down. But even this compression brings with it a benefit from the perspective of human excellence because it impels the man of strong impulses to cultivate "the social part of his nature," or what Mill subsequently calls the "social virtues."[77]

The distinction between social virtues and "self-regarding virtues" is a fifth point at which Mill's exposition of the principles of liberty leads him to discuss qualities of mind and character. Mill introduces the distinction between the social and the self-regarding virtues in his attempt in chapter 4 of *On Liberty* to specify some practical boundaries to the authority of society over the individual.[78] Self-regarding virtues govern that part of individual conduct which affects only the agent. Social virtues govern the conduct of human beings toward one another. Neither set of virtues arises spontaneously, and it "is equally the business of education to cultivate both."[79] The formation of character through education involves both persuasion and compulsion. Although the cultivation of character never ends, once adulthood has been reached an individual's character, so far as it touches himself alone, becomes his own business, and government may not use compulsion to regulate or interfere with his self-regarding conduct, however foolish or depraved. This is the more familiar implication of Mill's "one very simple principle."

The case, however, stands differently with regard to the social virtues, those qualities of mind and character which support the observance of the basic general rules of justice that make social life possible.[80] The social virtues, on which the preservation of collective life depends, are socially obligatory; one who, lacking them, infringes "the rules necessary for the protection of his fellow creatures" declares himself an enemy of society and is justly punished.[81] Since, however, the distinction between self-regarding and social virtues is at best imprecise and in any case must always be based on context-sensitive judgments, the effort to honor the distinction in practice will depend on public officials exercising wisdom and prudence.

A sixth point of intersection between the demands of liberty and the claim of virtue occurs in chapter 5, "Applications," where Mill suggests that government, consistent with respect for individual liberty, may sometimes take measures to foster good character in adults. Partly because of the complexity of moral and political life, partly because of the inevitability of "uncertain matters," it is practically impossible, Mill acknowledges, to draw a bright line between a purely self-regarding act and an act that does damage to the interests of another.[82] My weakness for drink, for example, may not only rot my liver and cost me my job but interfere with my ability to carry out my responsibility to provide for my family. And thus as a direct, if not quite immediate, result of my self-regarding habit of drinking myself into a stupor each evening, I may cause not only myself but my wife and children and perhaps my elderly parents to become dependent on the state. In fact, almost any act done in society is a social act in the sense that it has consequences for others and may injure the collective interests of society.[83]

Accordingly, Mill himself shows that his "one very simple principle," which he had introduced as a strictly inviolable rule, must in practice function instead as a strong presumption or rule of thumb. Where collective infringements on individual liberty are unavoidable, they should be well specified and as narrow as possible "for the sake of the greater good of human freedom."[84] For example, competitive examinations, commerce and trade, the sale of poisons and drugs, and public gambling establishments all involve activities concerning which respectable arguments can be made for both interference and noninterference by society.[85] The challenge is to devise laws that respect the distinction between self-regarding actions and those that damage the interests of others, while recognizing that interests (like pleasures) are complex and heterogeneous, and consequently in practice the most narrowly self-regarding actions can be shown to be entangled with the interests of others.[86]

Perhaps Mill's most revealing example of how laws can respect liberty while legitimately fostering self-regarding virtue comes in his discussion of the taxation of intoxicants. Taxing alcohol for the sole purpose of discouraging its use is in effect a prohibition on a pleasure or self-regarding act that the state has no business in supervising.[87] Yet other considerations are involved. To accomplish its legitimate ends, the state must tax to raise revenue even though taxes impose penalties by making some activities more costly. In the inevitable choices it must make to determine which commodities to tax, the state, Mill argues, may legitimately consider which items persons "can best spare," and which are injurious "beyond a very moderate quantity."[88] What can be spared and what is injurious, however, can be construed narrowly—in terms of physical harm—or more broadly—in terms of the "best interests of the agent." So long as the state is engaged in the unavoidable activity of raising basic revenues, it may, Mill holds, tax intoxicants or any other good that primarily relates to self-regarding activities with an eye to "the best interests of the agent." Such indirect but very real discouragement of self-regarding conduct by the state is "not only admissible, but to be approved of."[89] Of course, what part of taxation involves "basic revenues," and in what exactly "the best interests of the agent consist," will be matters of no small dispute. This does not imply that there is a flaw in Mill's principle. It means, rather, that even the restricted use of government power for the cultivation of character will require, on the part of public officials, restraint and delicacy of judgment.

A seventh instance of Mill's attention to virtue in his exposition of the principles of liberty concerns the institutions in a representative democracy that he thought would promote it. Mill was convinced that the primary source of the virtue on which liberty depended could not come from politics. This was not because he underestimated the importance of self-government, or because he denied that law must play some role in making men moral. Indeed, as I argue in the next section, in *Considerations on Representative Government* Mill affirms that one task of democratic self-government is to make men and women more virtuous. But politics could not be the chief source of virtue in the modern age because, as he observed in *The Subjection of Women* (1869), "citizenship fills only a small place in modern life, and does not come near the daily habits or inmost sentiments."[90]

More important than citizenship on Mill's account of the institutions that foster virtue were voluntary associations, the family, a state-supervised education, and even religion. Like Tocqueville, about whom he wrote with perception and admiration,[91] Mill saw associational life as rescuing individuals from the isolation and self-absorption fostered by modern democracy and the commercial spirit. Voluntary associations teach habits of cooperation and instill an enlightened concern with the public good.[92] But the most important institution, according to Mill, involved in the

157

preparation of individuals for the rigors of liberty in the age of modern democracy was the family. In *The Subjection of Women*, Mill argued that the family, as it was still constituted by law, was "a school of despotism in which the virtues of despotism, but also its vices, are largely nourished."[93] But "the family, justly constituted," that is, a family based on the legal equality of men and women, he also insisted, "would be the real school of the virtues of freedom."[94]

The state too had its role in fostering virtue. Active involvement of the state was necessary to correct the neglect of "one of the most sacred duties of parents," that of providing one's child with "an education fitting him to perform his part well in life towards others and towards himself."[95] It was "almost a self-evident axiom, that the state should require and compel the education, up to a certain standard, of every human being who is born its citizen."[96] Parents who failed to cultivate the moral and intellectual capacities of their child committed a "moral crime" that obliged the state to step in.[97] Mill did not want the state itself to be in the business of providing a universal education: he feared intractable controversies about the content of the curriculum; and in the event of agreement he feared a uniform education that cultivated nothing so much as uniformity of opinion. But he did want the state to enforce a universal standard of education through the administration of public examinations. Parents would be held legally responsible for ensuring that their children acquired a certain minimum of general knowledge. Parents who could not afford basic education for their children would receive payments from the state. In addition, the state would provide certification through examination in the higher branches of knowledge. To prevent the state from improperly influencing the formation of opinion, such examinations—in particular in the fields of morality, politics, and religion—would be confined to facts and to the opinions that had been held rather than to the truth or falsity of those opinions.[98]

But Mill's appeal to the virtue-fostering role of citizenship, voluntary association, the family, and education was not his last word on the sources that sustain virtue. It was to religion, or, better, religion rightly understood, that Mill assigned the task of perfecting the soul of modern man. In *Nature, The Utility of Religion,* and *Theism*—the first two written in the years leading up to the publication of *On Liberty* and *Utilitarianism,* the last written between 1868 and 1870, a decade or so after *On Liberty*—all of which were posthumously published under the title *Three Essays on Religion,* Mill argues for the need to promulgate a new religion to replace Christianity. More precisely, Mill wished to overcome organized Christianity, or the rituals, ceremonies, institutions, and dogmas through which Jesus' teachings have been handed down—and, in Mill's view, deformed. Mill conceded that in the past the virtues—courage, cleanliness, sympathy, self-control, veracity, justice, and even "the most elevated sentiments of which humanity is capable"—resulted from an "artificial discipline" and "artificial education" that was largely religious.[99] This, however, was due not to religion's "intrinsic force" but to the advantage that religion enjoyed from having at its disposal traditional authority, monopoly over early education, and the weight of public opinion.[100] Moreover, having lost its capacity to discipline or educate, Christianity, Mill argued, had lost its utility. Not only, in Mill's view, were its dogmas no longer believable, but its teachings, he judged, enfeebled the intellect, extirpated the passions, and made men selfish and weak.[101]

The new religion Mill envisaged, the "Religion of Humanity," would take its cue from Jesus, whom Mill regarded as a man of "sublime genius" and "the pattern of perfection for humanity."[102] Although the Religion of Humanity, as Mill expounded it, does not deny the existence of God, its teachings do render him all but irrelevant to the life of man.[103] For Mill, however, this secularization of religion represents not the negation of religion but its fulfillment. This is because "the essence of religion" is not, according to Mill, the idea of a supernatural creator or an all-knowing judge of human conduct and omnipotent dispenser of rewards and punishments after death; it is, rather, the promulgation of an image of human perfection, "the strong and earnest direction of the emotions and desires towards an ideal object, recognized as of the highest excellence, and as rightfully paramount over all selfish objects of desire."[104] The Religion of Humanity would, above all, teach individuals the virtue of selfless devotion to the welfare of fellow human beings. Uniting the heroic individuality he celebrates in *On Liberty* and the utilitarian principle of the greatest happiness of the greatest number, Mill envisaged a religion of humanity that would elevate man's intellect, harness strong passion, and summon individuals to a heroic devotion to the pursuit of the well-being of all.[105]

An eighth instance of the importance for liberty that Mill attaches to the formation of character can be seen in his brief examination at the end of *On Liberty* of reasons for limiting the activity of government in instances where interference with liberty is not immediately at issue. The main reason for governments to forbear and to permit citizens to take charge of the institutions and laws that directly affect them is "as a means to their [citizens'] own mental education—a mode of strengthening their active faculties, exercising their judgment, and giving them a familiar knowledge of the subjects with which they are thus left to deal."[106] Jury trials, vigorous local government, and various kinds of voluntary associations provide citizens with vital elements of civic or national education,

> taking them out of the narrow circle of personal and family selfishness, and accustoming them to the comprehension of joint interests, the management of joint concerns—habituating them to act from public or semi-public motives, and guide their conduct by aims which unite instead of isolating them from one another. Without these habits and powers a free constitution can neither be worked nor preserved. . . .[107]

Through the exercise of restraint and the giving of wide latitude to voluntary associations, the state strengthens itself by promoting institutions that foster qualities of mind and character appropriate to a free, self-governing people.

What form would a state capable of such forbearance take? What kind of government is best suited to preserve the social conditions of, and promote the qualities of mind and character that support, liberty? Mill provides the outline of such a regime in *Considerations on Representative Government*.

Virtue and Representative Government

Mill declares in the preface to *Considerations on Representative Government* (1861), his most systematic statement on fundamental political institutions, that while he introduces no new principles, he does weave old principles together in novel ways.[108] Consistent with his praise of the virtue of "many-sidedness," his insistence on the need to respect the principles animating both the "party of order" and the "party of progress," and his tributes of more than twenty years past to Bentham the scientific reformer and Coleridge the romantic conserver, Mill seeks to form a political doctrine out of what is true in the views of the two great parliamentary rivals, the Conservatives and the Liberals, but one that is free of their sectarian weaknesses.[109] Consistent with his understanding of the relation between liberty and the discipline of individuality, Mill's new political doctrine teaches that virtue is both a precondition for, and the aim of, good government. And good government in Mill's view is representative democracy, or what today is often called liberal democracy.

I shall call attention to three key theses about virtue that inform Mill's arguments on behalf of representative government: first, that virtue is a standard for judging actual regimes;[110] second, that the regime which in practice best takes advantage of and promotes virtue is popular government;[111] and third, that in a popular government suitable to modern conditions, representative institutions must be fashioned so as to bring to the fore individuals outstanding in terms of moral stature and intellectual excellence, while serving to increase the supply of virtue among the multitude of citizens.[112] All three theses reflect Mill's underlying argument that a representative democracy must take an active interest in virtue and may do so without infringing the legitimate claims of freedom and equality.

Virtue, Mill argues, forms a "foundation for a twofold division of the merit which any set of political institutions can possess."[113] The goodness of regimes

> consists partly of the degree in which they promote the general mental advancement of the community, including under that phrase advancement in intellect, in virtue, and in practical activity and efficiency; and partly of the degree of perfection with which they organize the moral, intellectual, and active worth already existing, so as to operate with the greatest effect on public affairs.[114]

Knowledge of the best regime and of human excellence is not an alternative to the empirical study of political institutions but, rather, forms the basis upon which a proper estimate of the strengths and weaknesses of any actual regime may be achieved.[115]

Mill's critique of despotism and his defense of popular government illustrate the use of virtue as a standard for the evaluation of regimes. The decisive argument against benevolent despotism, according to Mill, is not that most despots are tyrannical, nor is it that absolute power corrupts even wise and benevolent despots, nor again is it that despotism inherently violates individual rights. Rather, bringing to bear considerations that derive from that utilitarianism "in the largest sense" of which he spoke in *On Liberty*, Mill argues that even the most wise and benevolent despotism, one where the virtue of his subjects is the despot's chief concern, stultifies the moral and intellectual development of the people by depriving subjects of the discipline of mind and refinement of powers that come from the practice of self-government.[116]

Like his argument against benevolent despotism, Mill's brief on behalf of representative government as the "ideally best form of government"[117] is made in terms of "the permanent interests of man as a progressive being." Better than any other form of government, representative government improves the character of the citizens while drawing upon and enlisting in public service those persons outstanding in moral and intellectual virtue.[118] To be sure, the best arrangements are not always attainable, and so effective political institutions "must be adjusted to the capacities and qualities" of the people.[119] But those adjustments must be made in accordance with the goal of educating the people so as to make them capable of maintaining free and democratic institutions.

Good institutions, of course, are not good enough. Good government depends on "good institutions virtuously administered"[120] because even the best-designed laws and fairest procedures are of little value if they are not accurately implemented, honestly followed, and fairly applied. Or, as Mill states with exquisite clarity:

> Government consists of acts done by human beings; and if the agents, or those who choose the agents, or those to whom the agents are responsible, or the lookers-on whose opinion ought to influence and check all these, are mere masses of ignorance, stupidity, and baleful prejudice, every operation of government will go wrong: while, in proportion as the men rise above this standard, so will the government improve in quality. . . .[121]

The multitude of men and women are most likely to rise above ignorance, stupidity, and baleful prejudices, Mill contends, under what he calls popular government.

Popular government is one in which sovereignty is vested in the people, and in which every citizen, "at least occasionally, [is] called on to take an actual part in the government, by the personal discharge of some public function, local or general."[122] This is a government that is based on the principle of equality but is not in the thrall of it. For example, properly understood the principle of equality requires that all participate in government, but it does not demand that all participate in equal measure. Popular government, in Mill's view, promotes material prosperity and general well-being by making good use of the virtue already present in the polity, enlisting in the political decision-making process the collective strength and know-how of the people. It secures the rights and interests of individual citizens in part by making citizens themselves responsible for standing up for them. And it fosters "a better and higher form of national character,"[123] completing the education for liberty begun in the family, by creating a "school of public spirit" that arouses the passions, invigorates the mind, and enlarges and refines the sympathies.[124]

Historically, popular government had meant small, self-governing democracies. Adjustments had to be made, Mill saw, to adapt popular government to the size, diversity, and commercial character of modern society. In particular, participation in popular government must be mediated by the institution of representation. Representative government is that form of popular government in which "the whole people, or some numerous portion of them, exercise through deputies periodically elected by themselves, the ultimate controlling power, which, in every constitution, must reside somewhere."[125] Representative government has two characteristic weaknesses: mediocrity in the representatives and the people who choose them; and domination by the numerical majority and their class interests. These weaknesses, Mill was at pains to point out, derive not from the institution of representation but from its popular or democratic character.

To counteract those democratic tendencies of representative government that are detrimental to democracy, Mill discusses three major reform proposals which he had previously introduced in his political pamphlet *Thoughts on Parliamentary Reform* (1859): proportional representation, plural voting, and publicity in voting. It should be said straight out that the reforms, even when they were first advanced by Mill, were of dubious practical value. But much that can be said against them on practical grounds is beside the point inasmuch as Mill's proposals are meant not so much for immediate or direct implementation as to bring out what is involved in the idea, or perfected form, of representative government.[126] The impracticality or undesirability in practice of Mill's remedies need not obscure the seriousness of the dangers to democracy that they were designed to combat. Especially worth noting is the key supposition animating Mill's ideas for institutional reform: in democracies virtue is always necessary and, because of democracy's leveling tendencies, generally in short supply.

The idea of proportional representation is to secure a place in the legislature for minority groups.[127] So stated, the idea has a certain familiar ring to it, but the minority in whose name and the interest in behalf of which Mill introduces the need for proportional representation are rather foreign. In modern democracies, Mill points out, the numerical majority, representing the dominant class and its interests, gets in effect all the votes and all the representation. While the majority must prevail in a representative democracy, a democracy that is truly representative requires that the minority too have a hand in the formation and enactment of law. The details of the scheme Mill endorses—set forth in Thomas Hare's *Treatise on the Election of Representatives* (1859)—for insuring that minorities get their opinions heard in the representative body are of less importance than is the chief advantage Mill finds in Hare's scheme: the increased likelihood that the House of Commons will see representatives of a very particular minority, the men of national reputation, enlarged perspective, and independent thought, representatives of talent and character who, not beholden to local prejudices or interests, could raise the moral and intellectual standard in Parliament.

In other words, the disenfranchised minority that Mill wants to empower through the device of proportional representation is "the minority of instructed minds."[128] Since, in Mill's view, modern democracy promotes a collective mediocrity but depends on excellence in its legislatures, the state has an interest in adopting special measures to insure the presence in government of the voice of the "instructed minority." Mill's aim is thus quite different from that of contemporary proponents of proportional representation who seek to advance the private interests of disadvantaged groups that are thought to be underrepresented in government. By contrast, Mill wishes to advance the public interest by contriving to secure a place in the representative body for those whose private interest he believes most closely coincides with the public interest, and whose qualities of mind and character he believes will enable them to make government serve the "permanent interests of man as a progressive being."

Plural voting is the second remedy that Mill proposes to tap the available supply of virtue in representative democracy.[129] Mill firmly believed that gradual progress in the extension of suffrage produced one of the great benefits of representative democracy: the steadily increasing number of citizens who take an interest in public affairs. But the benefit of universal suffrage is accompanied by a cost: the tendency of representative democracy to be dominated by the passions and prejudices of the most poorly educated and least public-spirited among citizens. A preliminary step toward the elimination of this evil, Mill believed, was the understanding that while everyone has an equal right to participate in government, everyone does not have a right to participate equally. The opportunity to participate in government should be based on a principle of fundamental human equality. But the quality and extent of participation should be a function of competence or moral and intellectual virtue. Mill's idea is to give more votes to the more virtuous.

Mill begins from the supposition that basic literacy is a legitimate requirement for the privilege of suffrage since the very practice of voting presupposes the capacity to make informed judgments about public affairs. And Mill goes on to reason that voting well demands knowing more and caring more, from which he concludes that the public has an interest in assigning a larger number of votes to the more knowledgeable and public-spirited. But since moral and intellectual virtue is hard to measure, a proxy for it had to be found. Rejecting the traditional view that property is the best available sign or guarantee of political competence, Mill introduces the idea that more votes should be given to those who have attained higher levels of intellectual excellence.[130] In rejecting the oligarchic principle of property in favor of what he regarded as a more direct measure of virtue, Mill can be seen as agreeing with Thomas Jefferson on the need to diminish the role in democracy of an "artificial aristocracy, founded on wealth and birth," while welcoming within government a "natural aristocracy" grounded in "virtue and talents."[131] Although Mill acknowledges that intellectual attainment is an imperfect proxy and hard to measure, he does suggest "a system of general examination"; failing that, he proposes a hierarchy of occupations for determining how many votes each person should receive.[132] He envisages an ascending order moving from unskilled to skilled labor, rising to the liberal professions and from there to successful and well-established professionals. Those on higher rungs would receive more votes.

It is, of course, easy to ridicule Mill's contention that the better educated, as measured by professional and academic achievement, are more capable of sound political judgment.[133] But, as I have suggested, this is to miss Mill's larger point. Mill was aware that the test he proposed was an imperfect gauge of moral and intellectual virtue, and he understood that society was not yet, and might never be, ready for such devices as plural voting.[134] Criticism of the particular proxy he identified for determining moral and intellectual excellence does not dispose of—indeed, it arguably renders more acute—the problem that he uncovered: where moral and intellectual virtue is unevenly distributed, representative democracy must find means, compatible with its principles, for giving greater weight to the kinds of moral and intellectual excellence on which it depends.

In contrast to his first two remedies for the democratic excesses incident to representative democracy, Mill's third institutional remedy, publicity in voting, is not aimed at securing for the virtuous minority a greater role in government but, rather, seeks to raise the general level of the people's virtue.[135] The secret ballot, Mill believed, encouraged citizens to vote as they happened to be inclined, with a view only to their own private interest. It was Mill's hope that if the vote were made public, voters would be compelled to justify their choice; or at least, facing the possibility of having to justify their choice to fellow citizens, voters would be impelled to look beyond private advantage to considerations of the public good. Mill had originally favored a secret ballot on the grounds that publicity in voting could make the voter hostage to powerful individuals or interests in the community. But he believed that this had become much less of a threat in modern Europe than the danger of voters held hostage to their own private interest.[136] And so he concluded that the benefits which come from publicity in voting, in particular the formation of virtues that conduce to democratic self-government, outweigh the foreseeable costs.

In sum, his proposals for the reform and improvement of representative democracy show that unlike many contemporary liberals, Mill appreciates the political need for virtue and the need, within limits, for society and government to promote it. Because individuals are not equally capable of using freedom well, liberty creates opportunities for the bad as well as the good use of individual choice. If they are to respect individual choice by tolerating its misuses—within necessarily imprecise and elusive limits—even the most flexible and wise institutions must be administered by individuals capable of exercising what Mill is not embarrassed to call moral and intellectual virtue. Representative government, or what today is more commonly called liberal democracy, is from Mill's perspective the "ideally best form of government" because it gives moral and intellectual virtue—or the achievement Mill sometimes simply calls individuality—room in which to flourish, it contrives to bring those among the people who have achieved individuality into positions of political responsibility, and it seeks to make all the people more responsible.

Conclusion

In its emphasis on the discipline of individuality and the character that underlies good government, Mill's liberalism provides a strong warning and a timely corrective to the reigning forms of liberalism. Mill derives the essential importance of liberty, its right use and its proper social regulation, from reflections on what is good for human beings and the requirements of the preservation of a society that grants liberty to all. In contrast to many contemporary forms of liberalism, Mill's liberalism puts first neither markets nor procedures nor rights. Rather, his liberalism grows out of, and constantly returns to, questions of character and the ends of a human life. And in contrast to postmodern theorists who celebrate choice, diversity, and self-making in opposition to the very idea of discipline, Mill champions diversity and choice in terms of a particular discipline, the discipline of individuality, which is a conception of human excellence that is achieved through a rigorous moral and intellectual training. Where the discipline of individuality is lacking, the capacity for reasoned choice that in Mill's view made men and women truly human cannot in its fullness and vitality be present.

While certain of his isolated formulations may serve as slogans for the apotheosis of individual choice, Mill's defense of liberty never drifts far from an awareness of the social and political conditions that make liberty possible, and rarely loses sight of the ends for which liberty is rightly used. Where fundamental doubt about, or disbelief in, the very notion of human excellence has gained a foothold, and where education for liberty based on a demanding education rooted in the family and energetic democratic participation as an adult have become rare or unfeasible, liberalism, on Mill's view, must find itself lacking the resources necessary for its preservation.

✻ *Conclusion* ✻

For quite a while leading academic liberals and their best-known critics formed an unwitting alliance, promulgating the view that liberal political theory, on the one hand, and theories of politics that dealt with virtue, the common good, and the ends of political life, on the other hand, represented rival and incompatible frameworks. Despite the staying power of this view in many precincts of the academy, over the last decade innovative writings by a new generation of liberal thinkers have made clear that without violating, indeed in accordance with the dictates of, its own principles, liberalism may affirm that good government depends on the exercise of specific virtues by citizens and their representatives. Yet what appears as an innovation, when one focuses narrowly on the contemporary scene, comes into focus, when one takes the longer view, as an act of recovery as well.

In fact, broad agreement prevails among the makers of modern liberalism that a state based on the natural freedom and equality of human beings needs citizens able to exercise their rights responsibly and representatives capable of discharging the duties of office faithfully and effectively. Accordingly, it is not only in Aristotle's view that wherever functions can be performed poorly or properly, virtue is a decisive factor. On examination it turns out that Hobbes, Locke, Kant, and Mill, among the figures in the liberal tradition most widely reputed to have dispensed with virtue as a fundamental requirement of political life, do not imagine that politics can achieve its proper goals if those who govern and those who are governed lack the appropriate qualities of mind and character. To the contrary. Right from the start, and certainly in its classic moment, the makers of modern liberalism recognized the inseparable link between the practice of sound politics and the exercise of indispensable virtues. As I remarked at the outset, however, I do not wish to deny that the very idea of virtue in the liberal tradition is marked by basic and destabilizing tensions. What I do wish to affirm, though, is that the liberal tradition provides an illuminating and underappreciated source of instruction about the necessity of virtue where the natural freedom and equality of all is a principle on which the legitimacy of government is supposed to rest.

No controversial methodological assumptions or contentious ideological commitments are required to bring to light liberalism's fruitful reflections on virtue. What is needed is an approach to the history of liberal thought that attends to both text and context; that seeks the author's intention but recognizes that theories have a life of their own; that is alive to the ways in which the particularities of time and place determine linguistic resources and shape the fund of ideas available to a thinker, but is also supple enough to appreciate that through study and reflection upon experience particular individuals can bring into focus widely shared ideas and develop opinions in novel and illuminating ways. The serious question is how we have for so long managed to neglect or downplay the deep connection between virtue and liberalism, a connection that lies right before our eyes, not only in the texts of the makers of modern liberalism but also in the public and private demands that everyday experience places on citizens in liberal democracies.

The answer goes to the heart of the liberal predicament. The classic liberal tradition is neither silent about nor indifferent to the connection between virtue and politics, but leading liberal principles do set in motion a conceptual dynamic that all too easily induces silence about virtue and encourages indifference to questions about its cultivation. Whether it denies a greatest good, or views decisions about religious belief and worship as entirely between God and the individual, or understands morality in terms of universal forms of reason devoid of empirical content, or makes individual choice the touchstone of excellence, liberal ideas about human nature, metaphysical first principles, and the good work to shift focus away from a determinate set of excellences of character, moral and intellectual virtues that define a good human being. And liberal ideas about individual rights and human equality concentrate attention on the restraint of

171

government from legislating morals, or more recently on the expansion of government in the name of protecting the conditions of choice, at the expense of concern for what government legitimately may do in its circumscribed sphere with its restricted means to promote (or restrain itself from discouraging) the specific virtues necessary to society's preservation.

Although set in motion by liberal principles themselves, the neglect of virtue to which liberalism is prone is neither inevitable nor irreversible. It is, however, fueled by two conceptual confusions that must be cleared up if the process of neglect is to be arrested. First, as I have suggested in a variety of ways throughout this book, the rejection of the idea of a set of virtues defining human perfection must not be confused with the repudiation of the very idea of virtue. Instead, following Aristotle's lead—rather than the polemically charged distortions of Aristotle adduced and criticized by early modern thinkers and uncritically embraced by many contemporary scholars—we should allow virtue to refer to qualities of mind and character that serve a variety of ends, not only the ends that are most refined and elevated. This broader and more flexible view of virtue has several advantages: it is in harmony with ordinary experience, it brings into better focus familiar features of political life, and it calls attention to neglected dimensions and otherwise baffling aspects of the liberal tradition. I hasten to add that the view of virtue which I am recommending by no means excludes the idea of a greatest good or ultimate perfection. And it needs to be acknowledged that insofar as the link between the lesser virtues, which are exercised as a means to various ends, and the higher virtues or the virtues of human excellence, which are exercised for their own sake, is severed, virtue threatens to become a mercenary undertaking.

Second, the good liberal reasons for limiting government's role in supporting and supervising particular visions of human excellence has mistakenly come to be seen as prohibiting government's having any role in equipping citizens with the qualities of mind and character they need to live together in peace and prosperity. On the one hand, it needs to be better understood that the affirm-

172

ation that there is a greatest good for human beings does not entail (nor, of course, does it preclude the possibility) that it is government's business to promote the virtues which support it. On the other hand, the denial of a greatest good is compatible with the view that there are virtues government ought to promote. Limited government is not the same as neutral government, and neutrality in government actions, as Mill in effect observed more than a century ago, is impossible because, as he made clear in *On Liberty* in his discussion of taxing intoxicants to promote "the best interests of the agent," all government action imposes costs and benefits.[1] The principle of limited government does not require that government be bound and gagged: liberalism not only imposes limits on government but also limits the limitations on government. Owing to the variability of human circumstance, sudden emergencies, and the changing threats to freedom and equality, the principles for limiting government cannot specify in advance and for all situations the precise nature and extent of reasonable limits.

The liberal principles that shift focus away from human perfection and discourage government from engaging in the formation of citizens' character do not mean that formation of character is a matter of complete indifference to liberal regimes or a matter from which they must altogether abstain. There is a consensus in the classic liberal tradition, however, that the virtues necessary to sustain liberal political orders are to be principally sought in extraliberal or nongovernmental sources.

Times, however, change. Liberalism today no longer has easy access to the beliefs, practices, and institutions from which the makers of modern liberalism could once confidently draw to sustain virtue. Whether for the purpose of promoting virtue, or indeed for any other purpose, the absolute sovereign of protoliberal Thomas Hobbes is anathema. With more than half of all new marriages expected to end in divorce, with unwed mothers accounting for nearly 30 percent of all births, and with single-parent families becoming increasingly common, the family as Locke understood it cannot readily serve, as Locke thought it must, as a steady reservoir of the necessary virtues. Widespread skepticism about reason has cast doubt on Kant's appeal to reason's universal and necessary structure, as well as on his trust in nature's rational purpose working itself out in the progressive and morally improving movement of history. And the prolonged attack on classical learning in the universities, the changing character of civil society, government's remoteness from the lives of most people in liberal democracies today, and the breakdown of the family have seriously weakened the sources that Mill thought could foster the virtues appropriate to the demands of a life of liberty.

Liberalism itself, it must be acknowledged, bears no small responsibility for the stiff challenge it now faces. For the institution or actualization of liberal principles works to weaken the extraliberal or nongovernmental sources of virtue in liberal orders. No liberal can be sad to see Hobbes's sovereign diminished and disarmed by the liberal expansion of individual rights and the enlargement and fortification of limitations imposed on the use of governmental power. Yet the actualization of liberal principles does not always so clearly advance the long-term achievement of liberal purposes. Locke's family, depending on the confident exercise of parental authority, is weakened by the liberal antipathy, which Locke's philosophy encourages, to traditional authority; by individuals' tendency to make private conscience and subjective desire authoritative for their conduct; and indeed by Locke's own reinterpretation of children's duties to parents in terms of a calculus of costs and benefits. Spurred on by the Kantian injunction to question all authorities, Kant's successors become skeptical critics of Kant's own conception of universal reason as they turn to questioning the authority of reason itself. And realization of Mill's vision of a demanding education in philosophy, literature, and history given by parents to their children, combined with vigorous participation by adults in local affairs and representative government, is made increasingly rare through the exercise of the Millian freedom to choose, as people choose less demanding forms of education, private life over public affairs, and parents' interests over those of children. Thus the very actualization of liberal principles and exercise of liberal virtues can wither liberalism's roots and erode the soil on which liberal principles and virtues rely for their nourishment.

The anxious predicament in which liberalism finds itself today, a predicament in which liberalism has become the victim of its own successes and instigator of its own excesses, by no means reflects an infirmity exclusive to liberalism. Indeed, liberalism's predicament may very well embody an infirmity common to all regimes. So much is implied by the apparently conflicting but actually complementary observations that Plato and Aristotle offer about the fundamental relation between virtue and the regime.

In the *Politics*, Aristotle maintains that while human excellence has basically the same look everywhere, the dispositions and obligations of citizenship differ from regime to regime.[2] One tendency common to the different kinds of regime is to produce citizens in the regime's own image. Oligarchic regimes based on the principle of wealth tend to produce oligarchic citizens imbued with characteristics relative to oligarchies; democratic regimes devoted to the freedom and equality of all citizens tend to produce democratic citizens with qualities of mind and character relative to democracy. From Aristotle's view, it follows that liberal regimes grounded in the natural freedom and equality of all human beings tend to produce liberal citizens with dispositions relative to liberalism.

Like Aristotle in the *Politics*, Plato's Socrates in the *Republic* associates a particular character type with each kind of regime. But whereas Aristotle initially focuses on how regimes produce citizens in their own image, Socrates' account of regime change emphasizes how regimes produce a type of citizen at odds with the regime and directly responsible for the regime's downfall.[3] Oligarchic attachment to wealth produces citizens with a set of vices that hasten the slide into democracy. And democratic love for freedom and equality encourages character traits that open the door wide to tyranny. From Socrates' point of view, it would follow that liberalism produces citizens who prove the undoing of liberal regimes. And so Aristotle and Plato could seem to advance views that equally affirm an intimate relation between character and the regime, but which appear to lead them to diametrically opposed conclusions about the tendency of regimes to reproduce themselves through their influence on the formation of citizens' character.

In spite of the appearance of contradiction between the Aristotelian observation that regimes generally produce citizens in their own mold and the Platonic argument that regimes typically form citizens with traits which undermine the regime's principles and cause its destruction, Aristotle and Plato's Socrates are, in fact, in fundamental agreement about the basic relation between virtue and the regime. Indeed, in a discussion of the causes that preserve and destroy regimes in book 5 of the *Politics*, Aristotle illuminates the principle of reconciliation by making a Platonic point about the centrality of education to politics. The key is to understand that it is by counteracting through education the tendency to produce citizens in their own mold that regimes can avoid planting in citizens the seeds of the regimes' destruction:

> [T]he greatest of all the things that have been mentioned with a view to making regimes lasting—though it is now slighted by all—is education relative to the regimes. For there is no benefit in the most beneficial laws, even when these have been approved by all those engaging in politics, if they are not going to be habituated and educated in the regime—if the laws are popular, in a popular spirit, if oligarchic, in an oligarchic spirit. If lack of self-control exists in the case of an individual, it exists also in the case of a city. But to be educated relative to the regime is not to do the things that oligarchs or those who want democracy enjoy, but rather the things by which the former will be able to run an oligarchy and the latter to have a regime that is run democratically.[4]

Distinguishing between the pleasant and the necessary, Aristotle argues that whereas citizens naturally develop likes and dislikes typical of the regime under which they live, it is only through deliberate effort—through discipline and education—that regimes can produce citizens with habits and qualities necessary for the regime's preservation. One task of education, then, is to form citizens who in some measure oppose the regime's mold. Political education or education relative to the regime is typically an urgent matter because generally regimes imprint citizens more readily and distinctly with the regime's characteristic vices than with the virtues necessary to its preservation.

Indeed, exactly as Socrates had argued in the *Republic*,[5] Aristotle goes on to assert in the continuation of the passage just quoted that oligarchies decline by producing citizens who adore luxury too well, and democracies perish by forming citizens who love to an extreme the freedom to do as one pleases. Education relative to the regime, which Aristotle argued is the greatest preserver of regimes, must in significant measure cut against the dominant tendency of the regime, which is to form citizens with immoderate enthusiasm for its guiding principle.[6] For the guiding principle ceases to be an effective guide if it is allowed to become the regime's sole guide. Effective governance of oligarchies, for example, requires citizens who look beyond wealth and property to questions of honor and also to the claims of freedom and equality. And stability in democracies depends on citizens who can discipline the democratic inclination to do as one pleases so as to defer immediate gratification in the interest of longer-term benefits, and who can resist the democratic tendency to extend the idea of equality to absolutely all spheres of life in defiance of the legitimate claims of merit and human excellence.

What is true of oligarchies and democracies in their pure form is true as well of liberalism and mixed regimes such as liberal democracy. One cannot fault the makers of modern liberalism for having failed to see the necessity of virtue for the preservation of freedom and order, for this they saw with an impressive clarity superior, in many cases, to that of present-day liberals. The liberalism they made, however, has been left vulnerable because, having underestimated the vulnerability of liberalism's extraliberal and nongovernmental foundations to the actualization of the liberal regime and the triumph of the liberal spirit, the makers of modern liberalism failed to provide adequately for the sustenance of the virtues necessary to liberalism's preservation. A crucial task for future liberal theory is to determine how the virtues necessary to the preservation of liberalism may be sustained in a manner consistent with liberalism's fundamental premise, the natural freedom and equality of all, and in harmony with liberal scruples about limited government, but in moral and political circumstances very different from those in which modern liberalism was made.

LIBERALISM'S CHILDREN

Like Plato's oligarchic and democratic fathers, academic liberalism has produced descendants who endanger its preservation by taking its principles to an extreme. Such fashionable schools of political theory as deliberative democracy, feminism, and postmodernism are, despite frequent efforts to deny or disguise their lineage, liberalism's children. Each has a liberal root that leading proponents tend to suppress, each is marked by a dependence on virtue which these same proponents often fail to acknowledge, and each is oblivious to the vices generated by the principles it promotes.

Deliberative democrats, for example, can be understood as extending the liberal principle of consent, or the idea of freedom as the condition of living under laws one can be seen as having authorized or made, by imagining more robust forms of dialogue on a wider array of moral and political issues. But at the same time they tend to forget the qualities of character that responsible consent presupposes, and ignore the vices that preoccupation with dialogue can reasonably be expected to engender. Feminist theorists can be seen as expanding the liberal principle of natural equality and looking for more robust ways through which government can secure more comprehensive forms of equality between the sexes. But in so doing they tend to disregard the need to provide for the qualities of character that enable individuals—women and men—to respect equality and the limits of its claims in political life, and they themselves have often failed to respect the fears about human weakness and doubts about the competence of government that contribute to the case for limiting government's power in the quest to achieve even worthy ends. And postmodernists can be viewed as taking to new extremes the liberal principle of individuality, or the promotion of human development in its richest diversity. But in the meantime they tend to ignore that the exercise of individuality and development of one's capacities for new experiments in self-making require a demanding education that provides, among other things, what Mill called a "restraining discipline." Each of these contemporary schools is marked by a dialectic of extravagance and neglect, as a favored principle, enthusiastically carried to an extreme, works to obscure and sometimes undermine the preconditions for its actualization.

Consider, for example, deliberative democracy. Although deliberative democracy sometimes defines itself in opposition to liberalism, the principles for which deliberative democracy stands—wider and deeper participation, a more thoroughgoing popular legitimation of government, and heightened respect for one's fellow citizens expressed through richer and more robust dialogue in the public sphere—expand the political meaning of the liberal principle that government should be based on the consent of the governed.[7] In effect, deliberative democrats wish to extend consent beyond the basic political institutions or constitutional politics to an ever wider range of issues and practices. But in seeking broader, deeper, and more vigorous public discussion of laws and policy, deliberative democrats often put the cart before the horse. Principles of rational deliberation and ideal speech situations may capture appropriate standards for the judgment of the outcomes of actual deliberations. But such artificial and highly abstract constructions do little to illuminate, much less provide for, the qualities of mind and character that enable flesh-and-blood human beings, in many respects strangers to each other, who come together in living rooms and church basements, playgrounds and soccer fields, PTA meetings and union halls, campaign rallies and election headquarters, factory floors and office complexes, to make their own views known, to understand the views of others, to find common ground, and to learn to share it.[8]

In fact, deliberative democracy presupposes virtues whose origins outside of the practice of deliberation are too seldom considered, and readily fosters disreputable qualities of character that stymie public discussion, but whose origins in the act of public deliberation are often overlooked.[9] To deliberate well in public gatherings requires the ability to get one's point across, or the art of rhetoric; the capacity to appreciate another's point of view, or sympathetic understanding; and the scrupulousness to honor compromises, or integrity. But each of these virtues, like all virtues, has a shadow vice or extreme toward which it is constantly pulled by the very practice that depends on it. To get one's point across requires the art of rhetoric. But assemblies have a habit of rewarding smooth talkers, and the common desire for recognition in public life routinely induces a preference for victory through clever speech that overwhelms the cooperative search for mutual accommodation and the principled search for truth. To achieve a sympathetic understanding of another's view requires the patience to hear another out, a vigorous imagination, and a supple sense of proportion. But the obligation to publicly appreciate another's perspective easily induces a patronizing insistence on shared values, self-serving claims about the transparency of experience, and unseemly shows of compassion that exalt the giver and humiliate the recipient. To hit upon compromises in deliberation and honor them afterward requires self-restraint, toleration, and the capacity for long-term thinking. But the devotion to finding a middle way can also promote indifference to principle and shelter the cowardice of those who refuse to stand up for what they believe and the pusillanimity of those who shun worthy principles because of their stern demands.

To be sure, participation in the process does not only, or of necessity, produce vices inimical to deliberation with fellow citizens. Just as playing in a basketball game sharpens dribbling, passing, and shooting skills, engaging in deliberation can strengthen one's ability to persuade, to appreciate the viewpoint of another, and to achieve compromises and put them into effect. Yet while it is true that excellence in basketball culminates with one's performance on the court in the game, such excellence rests upon the acquisition of skills—and a host of qualities of mind and character—before the game and off the court as well as on. What is true of the achievement of excellence in basketball goes as well for the achievement of excellence—or indeed competence—in deliberation: skills and a host of qualities of mind and character—which to be sure must be honed through the actual practice of deliberation—must already be present and fairly well developed in deliberators if deliberation is to take place at all, and if its results are to have any lasting effect.

More than deliberative democracy, feminism has a tendency to define itself in opposition to liberalism, and yet as in deliberative democracy the principle at the center of feminism—equality—has a distinguished liberal lineage. This is not to deny that feminism embraces a diverse group of approaches, theories, and political movements but, rather, to stress that the core principle of most forms of feminism—equality for women[10]—can be seen as an implication made explicit of liberalism's core idea of human equality. Much of the disagreement among feminists revolves around the particular spheres in which men and women should be considered fundamentally equal, and the proper scope of the government's role in securing fundamental equality through law and public policy. Generally speaking, feminists want more equality in a wider range of spheres than liberalism has traditionally demanded, and seek more government intervention to attain this equality than liberal principles have been thought to support. The demand for equality, however, raises questions about the qualities of mind and character that are necessary to the securing and maintenance of a regime devoted to more comprehensive forms of equality, and the destructive dispositions such a regime, contrary to its own interests, may foster.

To make feminism's quest for more equality work, citizens must tolerate differences, must exercise moderation by accepting their fair share, and must act independently, not relying on government to secure all of that which they believe themselves to deserve. But the actualization of the principle of equality can encourage dispositions at war with these requirements. Preoccupation with equality can lead to intolerance of difference, because difference also implies difference in value, worth, or goodness. More equality can engender envy, resentment, and a hatred of excellence as one's fair share comes to be understood as no less (and no more) than anybody else's share. And extension of the principle of equality through public policy and intrusive legislation can promote a disabling dependence as individuals learn to rely on government to make equality prevail in more and more spheres of life. Consequently, if feminism is to work well, the principle of equality must be instituted in such a way that its tendency to promote intolerance, resentment, and dependence is curbed, and the toleration, moderation, and self-reliance which sustain a regime that can protect the equality of all are promoted.

Like deliberative democracy and feminism, postmodernism, despite its sometimes boastful insistence on its radical break with tradition and modernity, has deep liberal roots. The postmodern quest for freedom from arbitrary, oppressive, and often hidden hierarchies—even when those hierarchies are asserted to be rooted in the outlook of liberal modernity—represents in many cases a radicalization of the liberal principle of individuality or the demand for human development in its richest diversity. In the interest of human emancipation and the fostering of new experiments in self-creation, postmodern thinkers wish to encourage conflict and contestation, and indeed to politicize or open wide to question and revision ever new areas of public and private life.[11] But postmodernists too seldom pause to consider either the virtues citizens must exercise to contend productively with one another in so enlarged and enlivened an arena of contestation, or the qualities of mind and character, inimical to the goal of self-creation for all, that such intensified conflict and broadened contestation generate.

It would seem that to make postmodernism work, citizens must respect the public good by limiting their experiments in self-creation in such a way as to allow others a like opportunity for making and remaking themselves. In addition, citizens would need to cooperate with others, for the contest that generates new experiments in self-creation is a social affair and hence must be governed by shared values and acknowledged norms. And citizens would have to exercise the qualities of judgment that enable them to discriminate successful experiments in self-creation from self-indulgent exhibitions, destructive demonstrations, and squalid failures. Yet the virtues that support a postmodern politics can be difficult to acquire when individuality and the promotion of human development in its richest diversity are pushed to an extreme. For unqualified by other principles, choosing for oneself slides into the selfishness of choosing with only oneself in mind; development of one's own talents and abilities transforms cooperation with others into a mere means for satisfying the self's narcissism; and the ideal of self-creation, unconstrained by other considerations, encourages a chaotic free-for-all in which the only standards for the evaluation of experiments in self-creation become the self-serving inventions of the experimenting selves.[12] Accordingly, if postmodernism is to work well, the selfishness, narcissism, and anarchy that commitment to its principle readily engenders must be confronted and contained.

In deliberative democracy, feminism, and postmodernism a fundamental liberal principle is radicalized, while the contending principles and the practical necessities that led liberals to limit the scope and application of the principle in question are obscured. This combination serves to upset a delicate balance that the best of liberal theory seeks to maintain, to foster qualities that make the natural freedom and equality of all more difficult to recognize and respect, and to sanction imperatives that, if acted upon, would produce results which not only contravened liberal principles, but which also in many cases the partisans of deliberative democracy, feminism, and postmodernism would abhor. This is in part because many of the advocates of the supposed alternatives to liberalism remain wedded to a basically liberal sensibility. Without fully acknowledging its hold on them, many continue to embrace the fundamental premise of liberalism, the natural freedom and equality of all. And without really coming to grips with their debt to it, they still draw inspiration and sustenance from liberalism's governing moral impulse, which is defending the dignity of the individual. My contention is that if proponents of deliberative democracy, feminism, and postmodernism better appreciated both the virtues necessary to sustain their favored principle and the vices encouraged by it, they would find the temptation to the radicalization of their principle easier to resist, and they would discover good reason to respect the liberal tradition's effort to balance and limit the claims of consent, equality, and the free development of individuality.

By suggesting that a thoughtful concern for their own principles should lead deliberative democrats, feminists, and postmodernists to safeguard such principles and foster such virtues as would moderate their theories in the direction of liberalism, I do not mean to imply that all politics is liberal politics or claim that all regimes are strengthened by being moderated in the direction of a liberal mean. The larger point that my brief discussion of the extreme extensions of liberal principles is meant to illustrate—a point about the relation between virtue and the regime that has, as I have indicated, roots in the political philosophy of Plato and Aristotle—is that the preservation of a regime depends upon the exercise of specific virtues, but typically, through the influence of the principles it seeks to actualize, a regime more readily and forcefully engenders vices that subvert its purposes and threaten its preservation. The practical and pressing challenge faced by liberal democracies today is to discover not how to become a different or better kind of regime, but how to make themselves better at defending liberal principles and achieving the purposes for which liberal states are formed. This cause can be advanced by liberals who learn to take more responsibility for cultivating the qualities of mind and character whose necessity for the preservation of liberal states can be shown by theory, but whose existence, theory also suggests, cannot be presupposed by practice.

BRINGING VIRTUE BACK IN

Taking more responsibility for virtue—if only by refraining from the practices that subvert it—will require of liberal regimes forbearance as well as vigor. When it comes to particular cases, whether government should exercise restraint or in what way it should intervene will, of course, depend in part on the answers to complicated empirical questions about the actual effects of existing institutions on character and the likely consequence of proposed reforms on individual conduct. Theory has its uses, but its uses for politics are limited. One use of the sorts of theoretical considerations I have sketched in this book is to direct attention to questions about the proper ends that liberal regimes may pursue, the catalog of virtues that conduce to these ends, the range of beliefs, practices, and institutions that can, within the confines of a liberal state, foster virtue, and, not least, the vices that can be bred by the pursuit of liberal ends. Appreciation of these issues has become increasingly important as leading political theorists and social scientists have turned their attention to questions about the virtues and the institutions in American liberal democracy best suited to fostering them.

For example, a new appreciation of the family as a crucial institution for forming citizens has emerged among political theorists. Prominent among them, Susan Moller Okin has argued that the family as presently constituted disadvantages women; and in response she proposes reforms that she argues flow from liberal principles of justice.[13] One of her striking public policy recommendations is that in the case of a married employee with children, government require employers to pay half of the employee's wages to the employee and half directly to the employee's spouse.[14] In Okin's view, such a measure would bring many benefits: it would enhance the security and independence of married women who take primary responsibility for child rearing and domestic work; it would put such women on an equal footing in the family by eliminating the power that flows to men from control over financial resources; it would give public recognition to the importance of the unpaid labor involved in caring for children and maintaining the home; and in the event of divorce it would provide women who have stayed at home and have forgone professional development some financial independence and stability.[15]

In the pursuit of equality, however, Okin does not pause to consider the vices, characteristic of liberal democracies, that the measure she advocates is likely to exacerbate. After all, by design the liberal commitment to autonomy weakens the claims of inherited authorities; liberal preoccupation with individual rights and personal self-development very likely contributes to the experience of isolation felt by many today; and the democratic appetite for equality seems to encourage individuals to appeal to the strong arm of government to ensure more and more comprehensive forms of equality. Okin's measure plays into these tendencies. At a time when parental authority is challenged from many sides, Okin's proposal, by placing in government hands substantial responsibility for the supervision of family financial affairs, further undermines the authority of the family to manage its own affairs. At a time when husbands and wives already are inclined to view marriage as a business relationship made by parties whose interests have temporarily coincided, Okin's policy encourages spouses to think of themselves as separate individuals whose lives happen for the moment to have intersected. And at a time when government has taken over many traditional functions, Okin's legislation makes more expansive the realm in which government secures equality, and so contributes to the dangerous idea that every difference is the expression of an inequality that must be eradicated by law.

These objections do not deny that justice in the family is an important issue. Nor do they deny that as the structure of the economy and society undergo dislocating change, women are put at particular risk. Rather, they are meant to suggest that consideration of the tendencies and dispositions likely to be affected by Okin's proposal for state-supervised division of the paychecks of adults gives us reasons to prefer other sorts of measures which she also mentions. More generous divorce settlements and stricter enforcement of alimony payments and child support to ameliorate the real vulnerability of women in marriage today are preferable because they are more likely to secure a more just result without fostering vices detrimental to liberal democracy.[16]

In addition to the reform of the family, the revivification of civil society has come to be seen by a wide range of thinkers as a crucial means for fortifying liberal democracy in America.[17] Civil society consists of the host of voluntary associations and the various social networks that connect them. And what is today referred to as "the civil society argument" consists of three theses. The first is the very

Tocquevillian thesis that a vibrant civil society supports democracy in America by fostering certain essential habits of the heart and mind. The second thesis, based upon both casual observation and empirical study, is that for decades now civil society in America has been on the decline. The third thesis connects theory and empirical observation to policy, declaring that the well-being of democracy in America requires the revivification of civil society.[18]

Enthusiasts of the civil society argument tend to divide into left and right Tocquevillians. They differ over government's proper role in the project of revivifying civil society. Left Tocquevillians want government to play an active role by removing the social and economic forces that, they assert, have made people narrowly self-interested and isolated. They sometimes seem to believe that once government removes social and economic barriers, citizens will naturally join together in all sorts of common enterprises. By contrast, right Tocquevillians, informed by a kind of reverse Midas principle according to which everything that government touches turns to dross, think that the best thing that could be done for voluntary associations in America would be for government to do less, to withdraw and create more space for the exercise of personal initiative. They often appear to believe that the biggest institutional barrier to associational life in America is government itself, so that once it is removed, citizens will spontaneously seek out each other and cooperate for mutual advantage.

Things are not quite so simple, however, at least not from Tocqueville's own perspective. For Tocqueville did not think that voluntary associations were a panacea for the infirmities democracy fosters. Voluntary associations could not be a cure-all for democracy's disadvantages, in Tocqueville's view, because these associations themselves presupposed particular beliefs, practices, and institutions. Too little attention has been paid to the fact that Tocqueville conceived of associating as an "art," a "technique," and a "faculty and habit."[19] Accordingly, in order for associational life to improve democratic citizens, democratic citizens must bring to the creation and maintenance of associational life certain qualities of mind and character. Voluntary associations not only generate what Robert Putnam calls social capital—"features of social organization such as networks, norms, and social trust that facilitate coordination and cooperation for mutual benefit"[20]— but already presuppose a substantial accumulation of social capital for their effective functioning. Moreover, before there can be social capital, there must be—to put matters in terms both suggested and suppressed by Putnam's approach—moral capital.

Tocqueville envisaged in modern democracy a relationship of reciprocal influence between character and civil society: a vibrant civil society depends on good character, and good character depends on a vibrant civil society. One implication is that the capacity of democratic citizens to form and maintain voluntary associations—and thus to reap their benefits—is in part acquired outside of, or before entry into, civil society. In America, Tocqueville argued, within the family and through the discipline of religion occurred the formation of character that preceded civil society but was decisive for its vibrancy. Families and religion shaped mores, the fundamental and sometimes only half-articulate habits of the heart and mind, which, according to Tocqueville, were more important to democracy than good laws, because it was such habits or qualities of character that inclined and enabled citizens to respect, uphold, and fairly administer law. In bringing out the dependence of the political on the nongovernmental and the public on the private, Tocqueville found an intimate connection between realms whose integrity, he insisted, must be respected in order that each might benefit the other.

What may be done, consistent with the limitations on government imposed by liberal principles, to restore the means to forging the democratic dispositions, to producing the social and moral capital crucial to making liberal democracy in America work? In looking for ways to promote the "revivification of civil society"[21] and in the search for "strategies for building (or rebuilding) social capital,"[22] one must recognize that associational life can foster moral and intellectual virtue only if individuals endowed with a range of virtues are already in place forming and maintaining associations. Since human beings are not born with the self-reliance, discipline, rational understanding, and sympathetic imagination that the making of associations requires, such

188

individuals must themselves be made or educated. Accordingly, as I have suggested, associational life was but one of an integrated set of institutional mechanisms in nineteenth-century America, including the family and religion, that, Tocqueville argued, worked to counteract or moderate the envy, the restlessness, and the individualism that democracy engenders, and helped to prepare citizens to meet the demands of free and democratic self-government.

But that was then and this is now. In light of the democratization of the family, the movement of women out of the home into the marketplace, and the recent rise (or return) to national prominence of religiously inspired political movements, it is easy to mock Tocqueville's portrait of enlightened self-interest rooted in domestic bliss and simple and salutary religiosity. It is, however, more useful to understand the logic of Tocqueville's argument, and the links he illuminates between democracy, virtue, and the nongovernmental institutions that have in the past fostered the virtues on which the well-being of democracy still depends. What has changed since Tocqueville wrote is not the need of liberal democracy in America for the virtues that, according to his observations, were once fostered by associational life, family, and religious belief. What has changed is our capacity to satisfy that need.

THE EMBARRASSMENT OVER VIRTUE

When it comes to virtue, liberalism finds itself in a bind. At its core, liberalism is a doctrine that aims to secure the conditions of personal freedom for all through limited constitutional government. In the liberal tradition, personal freedom or individual liberty is originally understood in opposition to dependence on the arbitrary will of other human beings or submission to the rule of capricious laws. However, freedom on this understanding does not occur spontaneously or arise necessarily; it is created and maintained by human beings, and to actualize it, citizens and officeholders must exercise a range of basic virtues. Moreover, because of the limitations which liberalism places on the state, liberal regimes depend on virtues that they cannot, left to their own devices, summon easily or cultivate vigorously. Liberalism's dependence on even a modest degree of virtue can be embarrassing because liberalism must restrain itself from taking all the necessary steps to insure that citizens will develop the virtues necessary to sustain it. This embarrassment over virtue is less a virtue among liberals than the beginning of wisdom about the problem of character as it arises in liberalism.

Even as interest in virtue has grown in recent years, excesses on both the left and right within American political culture have worked to obscure the relation between politics and virtue in liberalism. On the left, a politics that in effect aims to impose a particular kind of character and a specific conception of the good life wants government to emancipate citizens from all kinds of oppression and all types of hierarchy. Ironically, by assigning the state responsibility for making life meaningful and guaranteeing that individuals become fully autonomous, this ambitious politics thrusts government back into the center of the business from which liberalism first sought to remove it, the business of caring for souls.

In reaction, some critics on the right have accepted the equation of liberalism with the activist ideal of human emancipation and have accordingly repudiated liberalism as a political ideology that fosters an intrusive state power while licensing personal irresponsibility and cultural decadence. This reaction on the right, however, is an overreaction, confusing the spirit of liberalism with one contemporary form of its debasement. The loud repudiation of liberalism in some conservative corners has been shortsighted, for many of the principles and practices that conservatives cherish can best be preserved in political societies where equality before the law and the protection of personal freedom, liberalism's core principles, are honored.

Today liberal democracy in America must learn to weave together elements that have not cohered well in contemporary politics and which much contemporary political thought, often in the sincere effort to be helpful, has unwisely split apart. To this end, many difficult questions will have to be asked. What impact do the

changing role of women, the increase of single-parent house-
holds, and the rise of same-sex marriages have on the function of
the family in developing the qualities of mind and character that
children will need to make their way in the world? How can
schools contribute better to liberalism's need for individuals who
can govern themselves well because they have learned, through
patient study, what needs to be changed in the present and preserved from the past? How can necessary social programs be designed so as to avoid fostering qualities that make their benefi-
ciaries less able to care for themselves and to contribute to public
life? What is to be done to defend our character and our communities against a commercial culture that is both an expression of
and a threat to our liberty?

In formulating these questions properly and pursuing answers
to them vigorously and responsibly, we will have to distinguish
between cultivation and coercion; between indirect and relatively
unobtrusive measures for fostering basic qualities of mind and
character—those required for good citizenship—and invasive
laws and regulations that foist on citizens state-sanctioned conceptions of human perfection; and between the necessary virtues, the
qualities of mind and character citizens must possess to keep liberal democracies running, and the noble virtues, the qualities citizens need to achieve the best of which human beings are capable.
This challenge will require steady nerves and the frequent exercise of prudent judgment on the part of those who govern, and
patience and self-discipline on the part of those who are governed. This is another way of saying that in order for a liberal
polity to economize on virtue, it will be necessary for its citizens,
both those who do and those who do not occupy political office,
to exercise virtue.

It is, finally, no flighty metaphysical impulse or self-indulgent
hankering for the transcendent, no sentimental yearning for
times past, no proud preoccupation with human perfection that
compels liberals and their friends to return to questions about the
virtues necessary to liberalism's preservation and to undertake inquiries into the beliefs, practices, and institutions that sustain
them. It is the logic of politics that makes virtue a permanent issue

for every regime; it is the logic of liberalism which ensures that the care for the necessary virtues in liberal democracies must be a delicate balancing act; and it is the logic of the peculiar situation in which American liberal democracy finds itself today that makes the recovery of the old sources of virtue or the development of new ones an urgent matter. Examination of the claims of virtue is an urgent matter, that is, for those who honor democratic equality, for those who cherish individual liberty, and for those who think regimes wise that, out of respect for both what is good and what is bad in human beings, push from the center of politics the enduring question of human excellence.

* *Notes* *

INTRODUCTION

1. "The Liberalism of Fear," in *Political Thought and Political Thinkers* (Chicago: University of Chicago Press, 1998), p. 3.

2. *Leviathan*, ed. Edwin Curley (Indianapolis: Hackett Publishing Company, 1994), chap. 15, p. 100.

3. See Judith Shklar, *Ordinary Vices* (Cambridge: Harvard University Press, 1984); and Stephen Macedo, *Liberal Virtues: Citizenship, Virtue, and Community in Liberal Constitutionalism* (New York: Oxford University Press, 1990). For a broader array of efforts to recover a substantive liberalism that in various ways recognizes the political significance of character, see Nathan Tarcov, *Locke's Education for Liberty* (Chicago: University of Chicago Press, 1984); Rogers M. Smith, *Liberalism and the American Constitution* (Cambridge: Harvard University Press, 1985); Joseph Raz, *The Morality of Freedom* (Oxford: Oxford University Press, 1986); *Liberalism and the Moral Life*, ed. Nancy Rosenblum (Cambridge: Harvard University Press, 1987); Nancy Rosenblum, *Another Liberalism* (Cambridge: Harvard University Press, 1987); Thomas L. Pangle, *The Spirit of Modern Republicanism* (Chicago: University of Chicago Press, 1988); Harvey C. Mansfield, Jr., *Taming the Prince: The Ambivalence of Modern Executive Power* (New York: Free Press, 1989); William A. Galston, *Liberal Purposes* (New York: Cambridge University Press, 1991); *Virtue: Nomos XXXIV*, ed. John W. Chapman and William A. Galston (New York: New York University Press, 1992); Jerry Z. Muller, *Adam Smith in His Time and Ours: Designing the Decent Society* (New York: Free Press, 1993); Yael Tamir, *Liberal Nationalism* (Princeton: Princeton University Press, 1993); Pierre Manent, *An Intellectual History of Liberalism*, trans. Rebecca Belinski (Princeton: Princeton University Press, 1994); Stephen Holmes, *Passions and Constraint: On the Theory of Liberal Democracy* (Chicago: University of Chicago Press, 1995); Steven B. Smith, *Spinoza, Liberalism, and Jewish Identity* (New Haven: Yale University Press, 1996); David Walsh, *The Growth of the Liberal Soul* (Columbia: University of Missouri Press, 1997); Charles Griswold, *Adam Smith and the Virtues of Enlightenment* (Cambridge: Cambridge University Press, 1998). For an interdisciplinary perspective, see *Seedbeds of Virtue*, ed. Mary Ann Glendon and David Blankenhorn (New York: Madison Books, 1995). For an account of the connection between the practice of law and the exercise of the virtue of practical wisdom, see Anthony T. Kronman, *The Lost Lawyer* (Cambridge: Harvard University Press, 1993).

4. For example, Michael Sandel's criticism of liberalism as a chief source of the ills that beset American political life is based on a sharp distinction between a liberalism that is devoted to individual rights and fair procedures, and a civic

republicanism that is concerned with freedom through self-government, democratic participation, and civic virtue. *Democracy's Discontent: America in Search of a Public Philosophy* (Cambridge: Harvard University Press, 1996), pp. 3–54, 321–323. At the same time, Stephen Holmes, in a vigorous defense of liberalism, goes out of his way to ridicule elements of Mill's political theory that stress the significance of moral and intellectual virtue, and implies that they are incompatible with Mill's liberalism. See "The Positive Constitutionalism of John Stuart Mill," in *Passions and Constraint*, pp. 188–193, 194–196. Ironically, Holmes joins forces with Sandel in advancing the dubious thesis that concern for virtue is foreign to, or incompatible with, the political theory of liberalism.

5. For works that illuminate the problem of virtue by examining the spirit and intellectual framework of liberal modernity, see Charles Taylor, *Sources of the Self: The Making of the Modern Identity* (Cambridge: Harvard University Press, 1989); Alasdair MacIntyre, *After Virtue*, 2d ed. (Notre Dame, Ind.: University of Notre Dame Press, 1984); and Leo Strauss, *Natural Right and History* (Chicago: University of Chicago Press, 1953).

6. *Leviathan*, chap. 4, pp. 30–31; John Locke, *An Essay Concerning Human Understanding*, ed. Peter H. Nidditch (Oxford: Oxford University Press, 1975), 1.3.1–27, pp. 65–84.

7. *Nicomachean Ethics* 1102a12–24.

8. See, for example, Locke's identification of the characteristically ancient understanding of virtue with the idea of "the highest Perfection of humane Nature." *An Essay Concerning Human Understanding* 1.3.5, p. 68. In his polemic against what he mockingly calls Aristotelity, Hobbes equates Aristotle's thought with the Christian Aristotelianism of the Scholastics and sees his conception of virtue as exclusively concerned with human perfection and grounded in a hopelessly implausible metaphysics. See *Leviathan*, chap. 46, pp. 453–468.

9. Plato, too, distinguishes between virtues relative to ends of differing dignity but more sharply distinguishes the idea of genuine virtue, which is relative to human perfection. See *Phaedo* 68b2–69c3, *Republic* 518d9–e3. In *On Duty*, Cicero examines two ends virtue may serve, the honorable and the beneficial or expedient, and denies any fundamental disjunction between them. *On Duty*, ed. M. T. Griffin and E. M. Atkins (Cambridge: Cambridge University Press, 1991), bk. 1, §§ 7–10, pp. 4–6; bk. 2, §§ 9–22, pp. 66–70; bk. 3, §§ 7–39, pp. 103–115.

10. *Ethics* 1102a15–21; *Rhetoric* 1360b20–21, 1361a2–3; 1361b3–34, 1362b14–18.

11. *Politics* 1260a5–8.

12. Ibid. 1260a10–1260b25; *Rhetoric* 1367a15–17.

13. *Ethics* 1102a12–27. Bernard Williams makes this mistake in his otherwise timely effort to make available Aristotle's account of the virtues for contemporary analytic philosophy. See *Ethics and the Limits of Philosophy* (Cambridge: Harvard University Press, 1985), pp. 35–40, 49–53, 153.

14. *Ethics* 1106b35–1107a26, and generally bks. 2–6.

15. Ibid. 1103a4–17, 1138b18–1145a13.

16. Ibid. 1178a15–20.

17. Ibid. 1106b15–25, 1109a25–30.

18. Ibid. 1138b20–1145a10.

19. Ibid. 1100b20–1102a1.

20. *Politics* 1274b30–1278b5.

21. See, for example, Sandel, *Democracy's Discontent,* p. 7. In appealing to Aristotle as a founder of the republican tradition in political theory, Sandel also routinely reduces the whole of virtue, including "human virtue" or "the virtues of the human soul," to civic virtue, or the virtues that govern participation in political life. *Democracy's Discontent,* pp. 26, 317–319, 350. This misrepresentation is critical to Sandel's accusation that the liberal tradition expels virtue from politics. A renewed appreciation of the internal articulations within Aristotle's account of virtue helps show that the tendency in the liberal tradition to which Sandel refers actually downplays one kind of virtue. Moreover, examination of Mill's *Considerations on Representative Government* reveals that it remains a serious exaggeration to argue that the liberal tradition has no enthusiasm or space for civic virtue.

22. In contrast to the tendency of contemporary liberals, Mill argues that for Aristotle politics was concerned with practices and institutions that "tend towards stability, rather than towards improvement." Mill goes on to add that with the possible exception of Plato "ancient politicians or philosophers" did not strive to perfect political society but concerned themselves with "guarding society against its natural tendency to degeneration." See "Grote's Aristotle," in *Essays on Philosophy and the Classics,* ed. J. M. Robson (Toronto: University of Toronto Press, 1978), p. 505.

23. *Ethics* 1102a7–25.

24. *Politics* 1309a32–1310a38.

25. *Ethics* 1094b10–25.

26. See the helpful account in T. H. Irwin, "The Metaphysical and Psychological Basis of Aristotle's Ethics," in *Essays on Aristotle's Ethics,* ed. Amélie Oksenberg Rorty (Berkeley and Los Angeles: University of California Press, 1980). See also Charles Taylor, "The Motivation behind a Procedural Ethics," in *Kant and Political Philosophy* (New Haven: Yale University Press, 1993), pp. 337–342; Stephen G. Salkever, *Finding the Mean* (Princeton: Princeton University Press, 1990), pp. 13–161; and Leo Strauss, *The City and Man* (Chicago: University of Chicago Press, 1964), p. 21.

27. See, for example, Aristotle's procedure for investigating the meaning of the term "happiness" in book 1 of the *Ethics.* See also Salkever, *Finding the Mean,* pp. 57–104.

28. Indeed, Aristotle can be seen as the first to censure the direct appeal to foundations in moral and political theory. In the first book of the *Ethics* Aristotle harshly criticizes the doctrine of a universal Good that he ascribes to his friend

and teacher Plato, arguing that knowledge of the Idea of the Good cannot serve as a practical guide in politics or the arts and sciences. But even here Aristotle does not assert that knowledge of the Good is therefore impossible or unimportant. It is, rather, the province of another kind of inquiry. See *Ethics* 1096a12–1097a12.

29. For an alternative and sharply opposed approach, one that defends liberalism by mocking and ridiculing liberalism's critics and which was greeted with enthusiasm by leading liberals in the academy, see Stephen Holmes, *The Anatomy of Antiliberalism* (Cambridge: Harvard University Press, 1993). I call attention to both Holmes's contribution to recovering neglected dimensions of the liberal tradition and the limits of that contribution which stem from his failure to appreciate the service to liberalism that its critics render, in "Liberal Zealotry," *Yale Law Journal* 103 (March 1994): 1363–1382.

30. Ibid., p. 39.

31. See, for example, Macedo, *Liberal Virtues*, pp. 13–17, 29–30; and Galston, *Liberal Purposes*, pp. 65–76. For the quoted passage, see MacIntyre, *After Virtue*, p. 263.

32. *After Virtue*, p. 243.

33. See in particular MacIntyre's discussion in *After Virtue* of Jane Austen, pp. 181–187, 239–243, and of William Cobbett, pp. 238–239.

34. *Sources of the Self: The Making of the Modern Identity*.

35. See, for example, "What Is Political Philosophy?" in *What Is Political Philosophy?* (Westport, Conn.: Greenwood Press, 1973), p. 40.

36. See, for example, preface to *Spinoza's Critique of Religion* (New York: Schocken, 1982), pp. 15–16, 30–31; *Natural Right and History*, pp. 78, 163–164, 167–169, 252–255, 294–296, 322–323; *Thoughts on Machiavelli* (Chicago: University of Chicago Press, 1958), pp. 288–289; "Notes on the Plan to Nietzsche's *Beyond Good and Evil*," in *Studies in Platonic Political Philosophy* (Chicago: University of Chicago Press, 1985), pp. 183, 190; and generally *The Political Philosophy of Hobbes* (Chicago: University of Chicago Press, 1952).

37. The remarks in this section have been adapted from my "Communitarian Criticisms and Liberal Lessons," *The Responsive Community*, Fall 1995, 54–64.

38. See, for example, the essays gathered together in *Liberalism and the Moral Life*, ed. Nancy Rosenblum (Cambridge: Harvard University Press, 1989).

39. See Ronald Dworkin, *Taking Rights Seriously* (London: Duckworth, 1977); and Bruce Ackerman, *Social Justice and the Liberal State* (New Haven: Yale University Press, 1980).

40. See Stephen Mulhall and Adam Swift, *Liberals and Communitarians* (Oxford: Blackwell, 1992). Charles Taylor takes a dimmer view of the utility of the liberal-communitarian debate, arguing that, owing to misunderstandings and confusions, it has largely been unproductive. Yet Taylor's own criticism of both sides provides an example of how the debate has opened up a more comprehen-

sive perspective. See "Cross Purposes: The Liberal-Communitarian Debate," in *Liberalism and the Moral Life*, pp. 159–182.

41. Rawls, *A Theory of Justice* (Cambridge: Harvard University Press, 1971), pp. 453–513. In his influential critique of Rawls, Michael Sandel scarcely acknowledges Rawls's view that liberalism depends on virtue, and takes little notice of Rawls's extended account of the development of moral virtues in the family, voluntary associations, and the public life of a liberal democracy. See *Liberalism and the Limits of Justice* (Cambridge: Cambridge University Press, 1982). Interestingly, in *Liberal Virtues*, his important reply to the communitarian critics of liberalism, Stephen Macedo also overlooks Rawls's account of the origins and function of the virtues in a just or liberal society.

42. Rawls, *A Theory of Justice*, p. 192; see also p. 436.

43. Ibid., pp. 497–498.

44. Ibid., pp. 462–467.

45. Ibid., pp. 467–472. In *Political Liberalism*, however, Rawls sees "basic political institutions" as playing the primary role in fostering the cooperative virtues. *Political Liberalism* (New York: Columbia University Press, 1993), p. 163.

46. Rawls, *A Theory of Justice*, pp. 472–479.

47. Ibid., p. 497.

48. Ibid., p. 461.

49. Ibid., p. 245.

50. From a different perspective Susan Moller Okin raises related questions about the idealization and sentimentalization of the family in Rawls's account and the incapacity of the family as presently constituted to perform the role in moral education that Rawls assigns to it. See *Justice, Gender, and the Family* (New York: Basic Books, 1989).

51. See, for example, Jean Bethke Elshtain, *Democracy on Trial* (New York: Basic Books, 1995); Robert Putnam, "Bowling Alone," *Journal of Democracy* 6, no. 1 (January 1995): 65–78; Frances Fukuyama, *Trust: The Social Virtues and the Creation of Prosperity* (New York: Free Press, 1995); and Nancy Rosenblum, *Membership and Morals: The Personal Uses of Pluralism in America* (Princeton: Princeton University Press, 1998).

52. It must be said that notwithstanding the logic of *A Theory of Justice*, which makes virtue a crucial precondition for the achievement of justice, Rawls seemed to lose interest in *Political Liberalism* in the question of virtue as he became increasingly consumed with abstract issues of justification and the form of legitimate argument in public debate.

53. See *The Morality of Freedom*, pp. 407–408, 412–429; also 372.

54. See ibid., p. 408.

55. See Macedo, *Liberal Virtues*, pp. 254–285; and Galston, *Liberal Purposes*, pp. 213–237.

56. Macedo, *Liberal Virtues*, pp. 271–272.

57. Ibid., p. 285.

58. Galston, *Liberal Purposes*, pp. 257–289.

59. *Ordinary Vices* (Cambridge: Harvard University Press, 1984).

60. Ibid., pp. 1–44.

61. Ibid., pp. 87–137.

62. Shklar's evident embarrassment over virtue and the limits of her liberal strategy for speaking about character are thrown into even sharper relief in "The Liberalism of Fear," her most focused exposition of her distinctive brand of liberalism. On the one hand, Shklar attempts to distance herself from Hobbes, maintaining that while there are many types of liberalism, Hobbes is no liberal because he is not a defender of the principle of toleration, and because he endows the sovereign with the unconditional right to impose beliefs and even vocabulary on citizens (p. 6). On the other hand, just like Hobbes, Shklar rejects the idea of a summum bonum; and again like Hobbes, "begin[s] with a *summum malum*, which all of us know and would avoid if only we could. That evil is cruelty and the fear it inspires . . ." (pp. 10–11). And still again like Hobbes, Shklar understands this fear as a primal fear, not as a fear of disappointment or physical pain per se but, rather, as fear "of pain inflicted by others to kill and maim us" (p. 11). Shklar's liberalism thus seems to be based on a minimalist core conception of moral personhood with striking affinities to the core of Hobbes's moral and political theory. It is therefore worth noting that one of the limitations of Shklar's strategy for bypassing virtue in her investigation of character is suggested by the fact that even Hobbes himself, as I shall discuss at length in chapter 1, finds it necessary in his political theory to give pride of place in his account of the preconditions for maintaining political society to such moral virtues as "*justice, gratitude, modesty, equity*, [and] *mercy*." Hobbes, *Leviathan*, chap. 15, p. 100.

63. Shklar, "The Liberalism of Fear," p. 15. With this argument, Shklar presents herself as following George Kateb, "Remarks on the Procedures of Constitutional Democracy," in *Constitutionalism: Nomos XX*, ed. J. Roland Pennock and John Chapman (New York: New York University Press, 1979), pp. 215–237.

64. Shklar, "The Liberalism of Fear," p. 15.

65. Ibid.

66. Ibid.

67. Ibid.

CHAPTER 1
HOBBES: POLITICS AND THE VIRTUES OF A LESSER ORDER

1. See G.A.J. Rogers, "Hobbes's Hidden Influence," in *Perspectives on Thomas Hobbes*, ed. G.A.J. Rogers and Alan Ryan (New York: Oxford University Press, 1990), p. 189, and introduction, pp. 3–4; Richard Tuck, *Hobbes* (Oxford: Oxford University Press, 1989), pp. 27–39.

2. See, for example, Roberto Mangabeira Unger, *Knowledge and Politics* (New

York: Free Press, 1975), pp. 29–103; John Gray, review of John Rawls's *Political Liberalism* in *New York Times Book Review*, 16 May 1993, p. 35.

3. See, for example, Judith Shklar, "The Liberalism of Fear," in *Political Thought and Political Thinkers*, ed. Stanley Hoffmann (Chicago: University of Chicago Press, 1998), p. 6. In a letter to the *New York Times* responding to John Gray's dismissive review of *Political Liberalism*, a review in which Gray compared the liberalisms of Hobbes and Rawls to Rawls's disadvantage, Thomas Nagel declared that "anyone who can describe Hobbes, that great opponent of all limitations on government power, as a liberal has a very poor grasp of the fundamentals of political theory." *New York Times Book Review*, 6 June 1993, p. 58.

4. Although he denies that Hobbes is a liberal, Alan Ryan stresses that, in fact, Hobbes's doctrine can be viewed as one of limited government, and in so doing Ryan brings out a certain continuity linking Hobbes to the liberal tradition. Placing the limitations that Hobbes imposes on the sovereign in historical perspective, Ryan argues that these limitations were seen by some of Hobbes's contemporaries as "tantamount to denying the sovereign's authority altogether." To the proponents of sovereignty from divine right, that is, those whose views Hobbes was writing against, "the sovereign's power has strict and easily recognized limits." See "Hobbes and Individualism," in *Perspectives on Thomas Hobbes*, p. 99.

5. See Michael Oakeshott, "Introduction to *Leviathan*," in *Rationalism in Politics and Other Essays*, foreword by Timothy Fuller, new and expanded ed. (Indianapolis: Liberty Press, 1991), pp. 282–283; Leo Strauss, *Natural Right and History* (Chicago: University of Chicago Press, 1953), pp. 181–182; John Gray, *Liberalism: Second Edition* (Minneapolis: University of Minnesota Press, 1995), p. 10; and Tuck, *Hobbes*, pp. 72–74, 97.

6. *Leviathan*, ed. Edwin Curley (Indianapolis: Hackett Publishing Company, 1994), chap. 13, pp. 74–78; chap. 14, pp. 82, 84–85, 87; chap. 15, p. 97; chap. 21, pp. 144–145; chap. 27, pp. 191, 198. See also *De Cive*, in *Man and Citizen*, ed. Bernard Gert (Indianapolis: Hackett Publishing Company, 1991), 2.18–19, pp. 130–131.

7. *Leviathan*, chap. 15, pp. 97–99; chap. 18, p. 114; chap. 46, pp. 465–466; and in general chapters 26–30. See also Norberto Bobbio, *Thomas Hobbes and the Natural Law Tradition*, trans. Daniela Gobetti (Chicago: University of Chicago Press, 1993), p. 213.

8. *Leviathan*, chap. 19, p. 120.

9. Ibid., chap. 21, p. 138.

10. Ibid., chap. 30, p. 228; see also chap. 24, pp. 161–162.

11. Ibid., chap. 42, pp. 338–339; chap. 46, p. 466.

12. Ibid., chap. 47, pp. 481–482; See also *The Elements of Law*, in *Human Nature and De Corpore Politico*, ed. J.C.A. Gaskin (Oxford: Oxford University Press, 1994), 2.25.3, p. 142, hereafter noted as *Elements*.

13. *Leviathan*, chaps. 16–18, pp. 101–118; chap. 24, pp. 161–162; chap. 21, pp. 136–138; *Elements* 2.25.12, p. 153. For a critical perspective on the relationship

between Hobbes and Enlightenment thought, see Robert P. Kraynak, *History and Modernity in Hobbes* (Ithaca: Cornell University Press, 1990), chap. 8, esp. pp. 203–216.

14. While conceding that one can find "some features typical of liberalism in Hobbes's thought," Norberto Bobbio contends that Hobbes "was neither a liberal writer, nor a precursor of liberal ideas" because "the ideal for which he fights is authority, not liberty." This, however, is not quite right. After all, Hobbes is compelled to justify authority in terms of natural liberty. Bobbio rightly points out that "Hobbes would never dare to say, as Hegel would, that 'true' liberty consists of obedience to the laws." But Hobbes did dare to affirm repeatedly that the obligation to obey even those laws one finds onerous comes from each individual's having originally authorized all the sovereign's acts and having consented to the sovereign's sweeping authority. See Bobbio, *Thomas Hobbes and the Natural Law Tradition*, pp. 69–70.

15. There are several notable exceptions to the tendency to neglect the importance of virtue to Hobbes's political theory. One is R. E. Ewin's fine book, to which my own analysis is much in debt. See Ewin, *Virtue and Rights: The Moral Philosophy of Thomas Hobbes* (Boulder, Colo.: Westview Press, 1991). For another recent full-length account, see David Boonin-Vail, *Thomas Hobbes and the Science of Moral Virtue* (New York: Cambridge University Press, 1994). Bernard Gert offers a brief and incisive discussion in his introduction to *Man and Citizen*, ed. Bernard Gert (Indianapolis: Hackett Publishing Company, 1991), pp. 16–18. For classic accounts that shed light on the problem of virtue in Hobbes, see Michael Oakeshott, "The Moral Life in the Writings of Thomas Hobbes," in *Rationalism in Politics and Other Essays*, pp. 295–350; and Leo Strauss, *The Political Philosophy of Hobbes: Its Basis and Its Genesis*, trans. Elsa M. Sinclair (Chicago: University of Chicago Press, 1936, 1952), esp. pp. 44–58, 108–128; and *Natural Right and History*, pp. 166–202, esp. 186–189.

In a new book, Quentin Skinner argues, among other things, "that Hobbes is essentially a theorist of the virtues." See *Reason and Rhetoric in the Philosophy of Hobbes* (Cambridge: Cambridge University Press, 1996), pp. 11, 316–326. Oddly, however, in stressing how his thesis—won, he claims, by the historical and contextual approach he has long championed—contrasts with the conventional views of Hobbes "as the creator of an egoistic or a contractarian type of moral theory," Skinner does not mention that Leo Strauss, largely on the basis of a textual approach, had already sixty years ago identified the centrality of virtue to Hobbes's political theory. See Skinner, p. 11. Nor does Skinner acknowledge Oakeshott's subtle treatment of virtue in Hobbes. What especially distinguishes my account from Skinner's instructive discussion, which focuses on Hobbes's claim to have transformed the study of virtue and vice into a science, is the emphasis that I lay on Hobbes's inability to account for all the virtue that his science of politics requires.

16. *Leviathan*, chap. 11, p. 57.

17. Ibid., chap. 46, p. 458.

18. Ibid., chap. 15, p. 100; see also *Elements* 1.17.12, p. 97; and *De Cive* 3.33, p. 152.

19. *Leviathan*, chap. 16, p. 100. This forthright statement from the most detailed exposition of the laws of nature in Hobbes's writings, in which the laws of nature are equated with the moral virtues, far from being an aberration in Hobbes's thought, is affirmed just as clearly elsewhere in *Leviathan*, as well as in the *Elements of Law* and *De Cive*. See *Leviathan*, chap. 26, pp. 172–173, 180–181, and chap. 31, p. 237. See also *Elements* 1.17.10–15, pp. 96–99; and *De Cive* 3.29–33, pp. 149–152, and 15.8, p. 295.

20. *Elements*, "Epistle Dedicatory," pp. 19–20; *Leviathan*, "A Review and Conclusion," pp. 496–497; *De Cive*, preface, in *Man and Citizen*, pp. 95–98, 104. On the way in which a work such as *Leviathan* reveals "the universal predicament in the local and transitory mischief," see Oakeshott, "Introduction to *Leviathan*," p. 227.

21. *Leviathan*, chap. 31, pp. 243–244.

22. Ibid., "Epistle Dedicatory," p. 1; "A Review and Conclusion," pp. 489–490.

23. Ibid., "Epistle Dedicatory," pp. 1–2.

24. Ibid., chap. 4, pp. 21–22.

25. Ibid., chap. 6, pp. 27–35.

26. Ibid., chap. 11, pp. 57, 58–63.

27. See Richard Tuck, *Natural Rights Theories: Their Origin and Development* (Cambridge: Cambridge University Press, 1997), pp. 174–177.

28. See Strauss, *The Political Philosophy of Hobbes*, pp. 30–43. See also David Johnston, *The Rhetoric of Leviathan* (Princeton: Princeton University Press, 1984); and Skinner, *Reason and Rhetoric in the Philosophy of Hobbes*.

29. *Leviathan*, chap. 46, p. 457.

30. Ibid., pp. 456, 457–461.

31. Ibid., p. 460.

32. Ibid.

33. Ibid..

34. Ibid..

35. Ibid., p. 456. See also *De Cive* 3.32, pp. 151–152.

36. *Leviathan*, chap. 15, p. 100.

37. Ibid. See also *De Cive* 3.31, pp. 150–151; *De Homine*, in *Man and Citizen*, 11.6, p. 48; and Ewin, *Virtue and Rights*, pp. 150–154.

38. *Elements* 1.17.14–15, pp. 98–99.

39. See, for example, *Leviathan*, chap. 5, pp. 25–26; chap. 9, p. 48.

40. Tom Sorell, "The Science in Hobbes's Politics," in *Perspectives on Thomas Hobbes*, p. 69.

41. Leo Strauss makes a powerful case that "the real basis" of Hobbes's political philosophy was not modern science but "Hobbes's 'pre-scientific' thought on 'men and manners.'" See *The Political Philosophy of Hobbes*, p. ix; also pp. 27–29.

Norberto Bobbio emphasizes that Hobbes was "mainly a political philosopher," in "Hobbes's Political Theory," in *Thomas Hobbes and the Natural Law Tradition.* On how Hobbes understood the term "science" and the mistake of seeing his civil philosophy as a deduction from his natural philosophy, see also Oakeshott, "Introduction to *Leviathan,*" pp. 235–248; and Ewin, *Virtue and Rights,* pp. 7–25.

42. *Elements* 1.6.4, p. 41; also "Epistle Dedicatory," p. 19.

43. *De Cive,* "The Author's Preface to the Reader," p. 103; also pp. 98–99.

44. *Leviathan,* introduction, pp. 4–5

45. *De Corpore,* in *Human Nature and Politics* 1.9, p. 192.

46. *Leviathan,* chap. 5, pp. 25–26; chap. 9, pp. 47–49; *De Cive,* "The Author's Preface to the Reader," pp. 95–103.

47. *Leviathan,* introduction, p. 3.

48. Ibid., pp. 4–5; also *De Corpore* 6.7, pp. 199–200. See also Strauss, *The Political Philosophy of Hobbes,* pp. 6–7.

49. *Leviathan,* introduction, p. 4.

50. Ibid., p. 5.

51. The trouble, in Hobbes's theory, of accounting for the production of the moral virtues on which civil society depends can be seen as a variation on a classic criticism of Hobbes's political philosophy. Rousseau famously argued that Hobbes's account of man in the condition of mere nature covertly presupposed civil society. According to Rousseau, in the search for natural man Hobbes saddled man in the state of nature with selfish passions that actually were acquired only in civil society. Many variations on this Rousseauian theme have been put forward in criticism of Hobbes. One can, for example, place the accent on language, stressing that the compact by which men leave the condition of war presupposes the existence of a common language, and a common language presupposes the existence not of war but of political society. But the essence of the Rousseauian criticism is that Hobbes's attempt to describe man outside of political society fails because in a variety of ways it presupposes men who are constituted, and already corrupted, by social and political life.

Some of the force of the Rousseauian criticism is lost once it is appreciated that the condition of mere nature was meant by Hobbes to describe in the first place not a primitive prepolitical condition but more generally a condition without politics, a condition, therefore, that also included socialized men in the anarchy created by the breakdown of civil society. In fact, Hobbes's account of the condition of war, or the natural condition of mankind, not only allows for but invites the inference that if the inconveniences of the condition of mere nature are to be escaped, practices and institutions that reflect the stamp of society must already be present in the men who are establishing or reestablishing peace. The variation on the Rousseauian criticism which I have sought to introduce is that Hobbes's account of the escape from the condition of war presupposes moral virtues in the combatants which could be the product only of a discipline and cultivation that occurs in social and political life. See *Second Discourse,* in *The First and Second Discourses Together with the Replies to Critics and Essay on the Origins of Language,* trans. Victor Gourevitch (New York: Harper & Row, 1986), 1.35, pp. 159–160.

52. Indeed, Hobbes openly doubts that the condition of war was ever universal, and explicitly indicates that one good way to determine the quality of life in the condition of war is to look at what becomes of men whose peaceful government has deteriorated, and who have, as a consequence, found themselves locked in civil war. *Leviathan,* chap. 13, pp. 76–78.

53. Ibid., p. 77.

54. Ibid., chap. 14, p. 79.

55. *De Cive* 1.9–11, pp. 116–117; 7.18, pp. 203–204; 10.1, p. 221, 15.1, pp. 289–290.

56. *Leviathan,* chap. 13, p. 76.

57. Ibid., pp. 76–77.

58. See Stephen Holmes, "Hobbes's Irrational Man," in *Passions and Constraint* (Chicago: University of Chicago Press, 1995), pp. 69–99. Holmes effectively brings out Hobbes's opinion that political order is constantly threatened by the human propensity to irrational behavior, but Holmes overlooks the role Hobbes assigns to virtue in his solution to the problem. In contrast, Leo Strauss provides an interpretation of Hobbes that both identifies "irrational striving after power" as man's distinguishing characteristic and explains why such a view requires the overthrowing of aristocratic virtue and its replacement by bourgeois virtue. See *The Political Philosophy of Hobbes,* pp. 11, 44–58, 108–128.

59. *De Cive* 1.2, pp. 112–113.

60. *Leviathan,* chap. 13, p. 74.

61. Ibid., chap. 14, pp. 87–88; also p. 81.

62. Ibid., p. 88.

63. Ibid., chap. 13, p. 78; see also *De Cive,* "Epistle Dedicatory," p. 90.

64. *Leviathan,* chap. 13, p. 78; chap. 14, pp. 79–80.

65. Ibid., chap. 19, p. 120; see also *De Cive* 3.32, p. 151.

66. It follows from what I have said that the creation of political society depends on virtue both in the case of what Hobbes calls a "commonwealth by institutions," in which men bring a commonwealth into existence and choose a sovereign because they fear each other, and also in that of a "commonwealth by acquisition," in which an established commonwealth is conquered and men submit to a sovereign because they fear not each other but the new sovereign himself. *Leviathan,* chap. 20, p. 127. Moreover, Hobbes is, as many "game theorists" have noted, keenly interested in the logic of cooperation. See David Gauthier, *The Logic of Leviathan* (Oxford: Oxford University Press, 1969). And it is therefore useful to clarify how Hobbes's understanding of the logic of cooperation depends, according to its own terms but in a way often missed by game theoretical analyses, on the exercise of the moral virtues that discipline passion and make desire submit to reason.

NOTES TO CHAPTER 1

67. The same peculiarity is true of Hobbes's account of the laws of nature in chapters 16 and 17 of *Elements of Law* and chapters 2 and 3 of *De Cive*. For a subtle exploration of the theoretical status of the laws of nature, see Oakeshott, "Introduction to *Leviathan*," pp. 268–269; and "The Moral Life in the Writings of Thomas Hobbes," pp. 309–312, 321–322, 332–344.

68. *Leviathan*, chap. 14, p. 79.

69. Ibid., chap. 26, p. 173; also *De Cive* 14.1–3, pp. 271–274, 14.13, p. 279, 14.19, p. 284.

70. *Leviathan*, chap. 15, p. 100; see also *Elements* 1.17.12, p. 97; and *De Cive* 3.33, p. 152. See also Bobbio, *Hobbes and the Natural Law Tradition*, pp. 114–148, esp. p. 145.

71. See Bobbio, *Hobbes and the Natural Law Tradition*, pp. 44–46, 158–159.

72. *Leviathan*, chap. 15, p. 100; see also *Elements* 1.17.12, p. 97.

73. *Leviathan*, chap. 12, pp. 63–65; chap. 3, p. 15; chap. 11, pp. 62–63. See also *Elements* 1.11.2, pp. 64–65; *De Cive* 15.14, pp. 298–300. In his discussion of Hobbes's views on religion, Tuck emphasizes that Hobbes "never advanced the view (which some modern scholars have attributed to him) that the *reason* for doing what the laws prescribe is that they are commands of God." See Tuck, *Natural Rights Theories*, p. 79. But in arguing that the fact that God commands something is not for Hobbes a reason for doing it, Tuck glosses over the more fundamental difficulty: Hobbes repeatedly advances a view which implies that God cannot properly be conceived of as issuing commands. That is, as incomprehensible, God cannot be understood to be "progenitor of the laws of nature" or, for that matter, the author of any other act.

74. *Leviathan*, chap. 15, p. 100. See also chap. 26, pp. 174–175, 180–181; and chap. 31, p. 237.

75. Ibid., chap. 15, p. 100; also chap. 6, pp. 28–29.

76. Ibid., chap. 15, pp. 99–100, chap. 26, p. 181; also *De Cive* 3.29, p. 149.

77. *Leviathan*, chap. 11, p. 57.

78. Ibid., chap. 6, pp. 34–35.

79. The term is borrowed from Rawls, who defines "primary goods" as "things that every rational man is presumed to want." See *A Theory of Justice* (Cambridge: Harvard University Press, 1971), p. 62.

80. *De Homine* 13.9, p. 69.

81. *Leviathan*, chap. 15, p. 100; *Elements* 1.17.15, p. 99.

82. *Leviathan*, chap. 15, p. 99; also *Leviathan*, chap. 14, pp. 980–981, chap. 26, p. 177; *Elements* 1.17.9, p. 96; *De Cive* 3.26, p. 148.

83. *Politics* 1269a20–22. In *The Elements of Law* Hobbes refers to justice as "that habit by which we stand to covenants." 1.17.14, p. 98.

84. *Leviathan*, chaps. 14–15. For related enumerations, see also *Elements* 1.16–17, and *De Cive* 1–2.

85. *Leviathan*, chap. 15, p. 100.

86. Ibid., chap. 14, p. 80.

87. Ibid., chap. 15, p. 99; also *Elements* 1.17.10, pp. 96–97, and *De Cive* 3.27–28, pp. 148–149.

88. *Leviathan*, chap. 15, p. 89.

89. Ibid., p. 90 .

90. Ibid., pp. 90–93, chap. 27, pp. 194–195; see also *Behemoth; or, The Long Parliament*, ed. Ferdinand Tönnies (Chicago: University of Chicago Press, 1990), p. 44.

91. *Leviathan*, chap. 15, p. 93.

92. Ibid., chap. 14, pp. 87–88; also p. 81.

93. Ibid., p. 88.

94. Ibid., chap. 6, p. 30.

95. Ibid., chap. 8, pp. 38–41. See also Aristotle, *Nicomachean Ethics* 1144b17–1145a11, 1142a14–1142a21.

96. Aristotle, *Ethics* 1144b17–1145a11, 1142a14–1142a21.

97. *Leviathan*, chap. 15, p. 95.

98. Ibid., p. 97.

99. Ibid.

100. Ibid., chap. 18, pp. 115–116.

101. Ibid., chap. 19, pp. 118–119; also *De Cive* 7.2–3, pp. 192–194.

102. *Leviathan*, chap. 19, p. 120; and chap. 30, pp. 226–228; also *De Cive* 13.2, pp. 258–259. See also Hobbes's prefatory letter to Sir William Cavendish in *The Pelopennesian War*, trans. Thomas Hobbes, ed. David Grene (Chicago: University of Chicago Press, 1989), pp. xix–xx, and Albert O. Hirschman, *The Passions and the Interests* (Princeton: Princeton University Press, 1977), pp. 97–98.

103. Stephen Holmes notes the implausibility of Hobbes's claim that private interest all but compels a monarch to advance the public interest, and points out that in *Behemoth* Hobbes more realistically argues that monarchs often undermine their authority through misgovernment. But in defending Hobbes against the charge that he failed to appreciate the possibility that kings can be corrupt, Holmes overlooks the core problem: Hobbes's political theory relies on virtues for which it fails to furnish a persuasive explanation. See *Passions and Constraint*, p. 93.

104. Interestingly, in the preface to *De Cive*, Hobbes says of his proposition that "monarchy is the most commodious government" that it is the "one thing alone I confess in this whole book not to be demonstrated, but only probably stated." *De Cive*, p. 104. The tenuousness of Hobbes's argument is reflected in the fact that Spinoza defends democracy as the best regime on the very ground that Hobbes adduces in favor of monarchy: in democracy, Spinoza argues, the private advantage of the ruler most closely coincides with the common good. See *Theologico-Political Treatise*, trans. R.H.M. Elwes (New York: Dover, 1951), chap. 16, pp. 205–206.

105. *Leviathan*, chap. 19, p. 120.

106. Ibid.

107. Hobbes acknowledges that it is a "great and inevitable inconvenience" that a monarch has the power to enrich himself, his family, and his friends at the expense of subjects, but insists that this grievance, which can be leveled at all governments, is actually more of a problem in democracy because the greater number of representatives means more rulers, friends, and families to enrich. See ibid., p. 121; also *De Cive* 10.6, pp. 225–226. Hobbes does not consider, though, that the sort of representative democracy he envisages could be designed so that "ambition ... be made to counteract ambition," with the effect that the competing efforts of the many rulers to enrich themselves and their favorites would balance one another out. See *The Federalist* (New York: New American Library, 1961), no. 51, p. 322.

108. The very difficulty Hobbes glosses over in the case of the sovereign monarch is brought into focus in the *Hiero*, a dialogue by the ancient Greek author Xenophon on the burdens and benefits of tyranny. The *Hiero* records a conversation in which the poet Simonides counsels the tyrant Hiero to rule as a beneficent monarch, the better to satisfy his dominant desires. In the first part of the dialogue, Hiero complains to Simonides that the tyrant's lot is supremely miserable. According to Hiero, the tyrant is by necessity the most unhappy man in the city because he has no friends but countless flatterers; the people either envy or hate him; ministers constantly plot his death; and consequently the tyrant is little better than a despised prisoner in his own palace. In the second part of the dialogue, Simonides seeks to persuade Hiero that he is potentially the happiest man in the city. According to Simonides, the tyrant is best positioned to achieve the very thing that Hiero, like all men, most truly craves. By benefiting rather than plundering his city, by working to make his subjects happy and prosperous, a tyrant such as Hiero can achieve wealth, power, and even what he desires above all, honor, or the love of human beings.

In other words, Simonides tries to persuade the tyrant Hiero of the truth that Hobbes assumes monarchs will understand without any effort: that the monarch's actual private interest, understood in terms of wealth, power, and honor, coincides with the public interest understood in terms of the security and material prosperity of his subjects. But Xenophon's dialogue brings out that even thoughtful and persuadable tyrants—or, to use the term Hobbes prefers, monarchs—do not, to put it mildly, automatically recognize how they can satisfy their private interest by ruling for the sake of the public good. By showing that even thoughtful tyrants need to be artfully persuaded to rule in terms of their own actual or enlightened self-interest, Xenophon's dialogue brings into focus the fundamental problem suppressed by Hobbes: how monarchs are to be educated so that they will be capable of exploiting their office to satisfy their long-term and considered private interest and thereby benefit the commonwealth as a whole. See *Hiero or Tyrannicus*, in *On Tyranny*, ed. Victor Gourevitch and Michael S. Roth (New York: Free Press, 1991), pp. 3–21.

109. *Leviathan*, chap. 23, p. 157.

110. Ibid., chap. 42, pp. 338–339; chap. 46, p. 466.

111. Ibid., chap. 18, p. 113; see also *Elements* 2.28.8, pp. 176–177, and *De Cive* 6.11, p. 179, 17.27, p. 365. For a list of opinions Hobbes regarded as arousing passions hostile to peace, see *De Cive* 12.1–8, pp. 243–251.

112. *Leviathan*, chap. 42, pp. 366–367; chap. 18, pp. 113–114.

113. Ibid., chap. 11, pp. 61–63; chap. 12, pp. 63–67; also chap. 6, p. 31.

114. Ibid., chap. 8, p. 38.

115. Ibid., chap. 2, p. 11.

116. Ibid., chap. 12, p. 71.

117. Ibid., p. 67.

118. Ibid., chap. 1, pp. 4–5; chap. 29, pp. 215–216; chap. 46, pp. 458–467. See also *Behemoth*, pp. 20, 23, 58, 62, 73, 114–119.

119. *Leviathan*, chap. 30, pp. 225–226.

120. Ibid., "A Review and Conclusion," p. 496; chap. 30, pp. 225–226; also *De Cive* 13.9, pp. 262–263.

121. *Leviathan*, "A Review and Conclusion," pp. 496–497.

122. Ibid., chap. 20, p. 135.

123. G.W.F. Hegel, *Hegel's Lectures on the History of Philosophy*, vol. 3, trans. E. S. Haldane and Frances H. Simson (New York: Humanities Press, 1974), p. 316.

124. See Richard Tuck, *Philosophy and Government 1572–1651* (Cambridge University Press, 1993), pp. 338–340.

125. Richard Ashcraft, "Hobbes's Natural Man: A Study in Ideology Formation," *Journal of Politics* 33 (1971): 1078 and, generally, pp. 1077–1086.

126. *Leviathan*, chap. 15, p. 100; *De Cive* 2.1–3, pp. 121–124; *Elements* 1.14.14, p. 81; 1.15.1, pp. 81–82.

127. *Leviathan*, chap. 26, p. 174. See also *De Cive* 3.29–31, pp. 149–151, 15.8, p. 295.

CHAPTER 2
LOCKE: PRIVATE VIRTUE AND THE PUBLIC GOOD

1. C. B. Macpherson, *The Political Theory of Possessive Individualism* (Oxford: Clarendon Press, 1962).

2. Leo Strauss, *Natural Right and History* (Chicago: University of Chicago Press, 1953), pp. 231–251.

3. Robert Nozick, *Anarchy, State, and Utopia* (New York: Basic Books, 1974); Richard Epstein, *Takings* (Cambridge: Harvard University Press, 1985).

4. Harvey C. Mansfield, Jr., *Taming the Prince: The Ambivalence of Modern Executive Power* (New York: Free Press, 1989), pp. 181–211.

5. *Locke* (Oxford: Oxford University Press, 1984), p. 2.

6. *Locke's Education for Liberty* (Chicago: University of Chicago Press, 1984).

7. *Sources of the Self: The Making of the Modern Identity* (Cambridge: Harvard University Press, 1989), pp. 159–176.

8. *An Essay Concerning Human Understanding*, ed. Peter H. Nidditch (Oxford: Oxford University Press, 1975), "Epistle to the Reader," p. 6; hereafter noted as *Essay*. Citations will include book, chapter, paragraph, and page numbers. I have in a few instances modernized spelling.

9. *The Reasonableness of Christianity*, ed. I. T. Ramsey (Stanford: Stanford University Press, 1958), § 245, p. 70.

10. Ibid. For a criticism of Christianity for transforming the virtuous life into an essentially selfish and self-regarding life, see J. S. Mill, *On Liberty*, in *Essays on Politics and Society*, ed. J. M. Robson (Toronto: University of Toronto Press, 1977), pp. 254–256. For a view that lends support to Locke's interpretation of Christianity by arguing "that interest is the chief means used by religions themselves to guide men," see Alexis de Tocqueville, *Democracy in America*, trans. George Lawrence (Garden City, N.Y.: Doubleday & Company, 1969), bk. 2, pt. 2, chap. 9, p. 529.

11. *The Political Thought of John Locke: An Historical Account of the Argument of the "Two Treatises of Government"* (Cambridge: Cambridge University Press, 1969), pp. x–xi, 266–267.

12. *Essay*, p. 6.

13. Ibid. 1.1.1, p. 43.

14. Ibid.

15. Ibid.

16. Ibid. 1.1.5, p. 45.

17. Ibid. 1.1.5, p. 46.

18. Ibid. 1.2.1, p. 48.

19. Ibid. 1.2.2–5, pp. 49–51.

20. Ibid. 1.3.1, p. 65.

21. Ibid. 1.3.2, p. 66.

22. Ibid. 1.3.3, p. 67.

23. Ibid.

24. Ibid. 1.3.4, p. 68.

25. Ibid.

26. Ibid. Cf. Hobbes, *Leviathan*, ed. Edwin Curley (Indianapolis: Hackett Publishing Company, 1994), chap. 14, p. 80; chap. 15, p. 99.

27. *Essay* 3.11.16, p. 516; 4.3.18, p. 549; 4.12.8, p. 643.

28. Ibid. 2.21.51, p. 266.

29. Ibid. 2.21.52, pp. 266–267.

30. Ibid. 2.21.58–63, pp. 272–276. See also 2.21.35–57, pp. 252–272, and 2.21.64–70, pp. 276–282.

31. Cf. Spinoza, *A Theologico-Political Treatise*, trans. R.H.M. Elwes (New York: Dover, 1951), chap. 5, pp. 73–74.

32. *Some Thoughts Concerning Education*, in *Some Thoughts Concerning Education and Of the Conduct of the Understanding*, ed. Ruth W. Grant and Nathan Tarcov

(Indianapolis: Hackett Publishing Company, 1996), § 33, p. 25; § 38, p. 29; § 45, pp. 32–33; § 52, p. 34; hereafter noted as *Education*.

33. *Essay* 1.3.5, p. 68. Cf. Rawls's discussion of how an overlapping consensus is possible, in *Political Liberalism* (New York: Columbia University Press, 1993), pp. 144–150.

34. *Essay* 1.3.6, pp. 68–69.

35. Ibid., p. 69. See also 2.28.8, p. 352; and *Education* § 61, p. 38.

36. In his *Letter Concerning Toleration*, Locke does assert that atheists are not to be tolerated because, lacking fear of the ultimate consequences of their conduct, they cannot be trusted to keep their oaths and promises. *Letter Concerning Toleration*, ed. John Horton and Susan Mendus (New York: Routledge, 1991), p. 47; hereafter noted as *LT*. But one can retain Locke's principle—that only those capable of honoring promises deserve toleration—and reject his denial of toleration to atheists, by showing that atheists can have their own powerful reasons for keeping oaths and promises. This indeed is the line of argument suggested by Locke's own analysis in the *Essay*, where the rules necessary for the preservation of social life are arrived at from a variety of starting points, including those of the heathen and criminal. See *Essay* 1.3.2–5, pp. 66–68. See also Mill's argument for trusting the promises of atheists in *On Liberty*, pp. 239–240.

37. *Essay* 1.3.6, p. 69.

38. Ibid. 1.3.17, p. 78. Cf. Hobbes, *Leviathan*, chap. 4, pp. 21–22.

39. *Essay* 1.3.18, p. 78.

40. Nathan Tarcov has called attention to a suggestive passage in a minor work on education in which Locke himself articulates a fundamental distinction between two kinds of political inquiries: "Politics contains two parts very different the one from the other, the one containing the original of societies and the rise and extent of political power, the other, the art of governing men in society." "Some Thoughts concerning Reading and Study for a Gentleman," in *The Educational Writings of John Locke*, ed. James L. Axtell (Cambridge: Cambridge University Press, 1968), p. 400. For illuminating discussions of this passage, see Tarcov, *Locke's Education for Liberty*, pp. 4–8; and Ruth Grant, *John Locke's Liberalism* (Chicago: University of Chicago Press, 1987), pp. 21–26. Moreover, in the preface to the book that Locke called *Two Treatises of Government*, which contains the *First Treatise* as well as the *Second Treatise*, Locke himself indicates the essential incompleteness of the account of politics he is offering by stating that it contains the beginning and end but not the middle of a "Discourse concerning Government." *Two Treatises of Government*, ed. Peter Laslett (Cambridge: Cambridge University Press, 1988), preface, p. 137.

41. *Second Treatise*, in *Two Treatises of Government*, §§ 54–63, pp. 304–309; hereafter noted as *ST*.

42. Ibid., §§ 4, 54, 57.

43. Ibid., § 6, pp. 270–271.

44. While emphasizing the theoretical point that Locke's conception "of free-dom rests upon fundamental moral duties we have to one another," Charles Larmore does mention virtue but slights its significance in Locke's understand-ing of the right use of freedom. Granting a bit too much to the "civic republican" school, Larmore speaks in this context only of "the virtue of active citizenship" that is involved in the maintenance of the rule of law. See *The Morals of Modernity* (Cambridge: Cambridge University Press, 1995), pp. 124–125. But this is not what Locke stresses. What Larmore fails to mention, though it is crucial in Locke's view to the maintenance of the rule of law, is the individual's exercise of virtue in the family, in looking after personal property, and in holding public office.

45. *ST*, § 128, p. 352.

46. Ibid., § 7, p. 271.

47. Ibid., § 8, p. 272.

48. Ibid., § 9, p. 273.

49. Ibid., § 16, p. 278; §§ 17–21, pp. 279–282; § 101, p. 334; §§ 123–127, pp. 350–352; and § 131, p. 353.

50. Ibid., §§ 17–21, pp. 279–282; § 101, p. 334; §§ 123–127, pp. 350–352; and § 131, p. 353.

51. Ibid., § 25, pp. 285–286.

52. Ibid., §§ 27–30, pp. 287–290; §§ 39–40, p. 296; § 44, pp. 298–299.

53. Ibid., § 26, p. 286; § 31, p. 290; § 46, pp. 299–300.

54. Ibid., § 34, p. 291.

55. Ibid.

56. Ibid., §§ 36–37, pp. 292–295.

57. Ibid., § 36, pp. 292–293; § 51, p. 302.

58. Ibid., § 37, p. 294; § 49, p. 301.

59. Ibid., § 48, p. 301.

60. Ibid., § 42, p. 297.

61. Ibid., pp. 297–298.

62. Ibid., §§ 104–106, pp. 336–338.

63. John Rawls, *A Theory of Justice* (Cambridge: Harvard University Press, 1971), pp. 467–472; *Political Liberalism*, p. 163.

64. Jean Bethke Elshtain, *Democracy on Trial* (New York: Basic Books, 1995), p. 2.

65. *ST*, § 3, p. 268.

66. Ibid., § 111, pp. 342–343.

67. Ibid., §§ 145–148, pp. 365–366.

68. Ibid., § 147, p. 366.

69. Ibid., § 160, p. 375.

70. For an elaboration of this theme, see Mansfield, *Taming the Prince*, pp. 181–211.

71. *ST*, § 232, p. 419.

72. Ibid., § 87, p. 324. Cf. *Leviathan*, chap. 17, pp. 109–111; chap. 29, p. 212.

73. See, for example, *Leviathan*, chap. 14, pp. 82, 87; chap. 27, p. 191.

74. *ST*, § 223, p. 414.

75. For an elaboration of this theme, see John Dunn, "Trust and Political Agency," in *Interpreting Political Responsibility* (Cambridge: Cambridge University Press, 1990).

76. *LT*, p. 47.

77. Ibid., p. 19.

78. Ibid., p. 22.

79. Ibid., p. 16.

80. Ibid., p. 45.

81. Ibid., p. 53.

82. Ibid., p. 45.

83. *ST*, §§2–55, pp. 303–304.

84. Ibid., § 56, p. 305.

85. Ibid., § 61, p. 308. For a development of this idea and application to constitutional theory, see Rogers M. Smith, *Liberalism and American Constitutional Law* (Cambridge: Harvard University Press, 1985).

86. *ST*, § 63, p. 309; § 67, p. 312.

87. Ibid., § 59, p. 307.

88. As for gender, Locke mentions that since his remarks are designed for "a young Gentleman," they "will not so perfectly suit the Education of *Daughters*." At the same time, he indicates that the inconvenience will be slight because the education for sons and daughters is similar enough that it will be easy to determine when different approaches are required. *Education*, § 6, p. 12.

89. Ibid., § 70, p. 47. The leading study of the *Education* is Tarcov, *Locke's Education for Liberty*. For an interpretation which provides a subtle account of the formation of character that Locke envisaged, and which suggests that the formation involved was a kind of deformation, see James Tully, "Governing Conduct: Locke on the Reform of Thought and Behaviour," in *An Approach to Political Philosophy: Locke in Contexts* (Cambridge: Cambridge University Press, 1993), pp. 179–241. For a critique of Tully's interpretation, see J. M. Dunn, "'Bright Enough for All Our Purposes': John Locke's Conception of a Civilized Society," in *Notes and Records of the Royal Society of London* 43, no. 2 (July 1989): 133–153.

90. *Education*, dedication, p. 7.

91. Ibid., p. 8.

92. Ibid., § 1, p. 10; also § 32, p. 25.

93. Ibid., §§ 32–33, p. 25; § 70, pp. 45–50; § 94, pp. 66–72; § 135, p. 102; § 147, pp. 112–113; § 200, pp. 152–153.

94. Where he does discuss religion, he tends to refer to it in very general terms. See, for example, *Education*, § 61, p. 38; § 116, pp. 90–91; §§ 136–137, pp. 102–103. Cf. *Essay* 1.3.6, p. 69.

95. *Education*, § 122, p. 95.

96. *Of the Conduct of the Understanding*, in *Some Thoughts concerning Education and Of the Conduct of the Understanding*, § 6, p. 179; § 12, p. 187; § 28, pp. 203–204; §§ 38–39, pp. 215–217.

97. *Education*, § 94, pp. 70–71; also § 198, p. 151.

98. Ibid., § 7, pp. 12–14; § 18, p. 19.

99. Ibid., § 42, p. 32.

100. Ibid., § 7, pp. 12–14; § 18, p. 19; § 64, pp. 39–40; § 82, pp. 58–59.

101. Ibid., §§ 64–66, pp. 39–43.

102. Ibid., § 82, p. 59; see also § 64, p. 39.

103. Ibid., § 110, p. 83.

104. Ibid., §§ 88–94, pp. 62–72.

105. Ibid., § 90, p. 63; see also § 39, p. 30.

106. Ibid., §§ 90–92, pp. 63–64.

107. This is also a doctrine central to Aristotle's account of the virtues of the soul. See *Nicomachean Ethics* 1104b10–1105a15, 1172a20–30. A crucial difference between Locke and Aristotle concerns the relevant objects of pleasure and pain.

108. *Education*, § 33, p. 25; also § 38, p. 29; § 45, pp. 32–33; § 52, p. 34.

109. Ibid., § 36, p. 27.

110. Ibid., § 38, pp. 29–30.

111. Ibid., § 46, p. 33.

112. Ibid., § 86, p. 61.

113. Ibid., § 87, p. 61.

114. Ibid., §§ 54–61, pp. 35–38; also § 48, p. 33; § 53, p. 55.

115. Ibid., § 56, p. 36. Cf. *Essay* 2.28.10–12, pp. 353–357.

116. *Education*, § 61, p. 38. Earlier in the *Education* Locke distinguishes the love of virtue from the love of reputation. See § 42, p. 31.

117. *Reasonableness of Christianity*, § 245, p. 70.

118. *Education*, § 78, pp. 54–55.

119. Ibid., § 103, p. 76.

120. Ibid., §§ 104–105, pp. 76–77.

121. Ibid., § 110, pp. 81–83.

122. Ibid., § 110, p. 82.

123. Ibid., § 115, pp. 85–90.

124. *Ethics* 1115a25–1115b5. Aristotle, however, does recognize qualified senses of courage; see 1115a4–1117b22.

125. *Education*, § 115, p. 86.

126. Ibid., § 143, p. 107.

127. Ibid.

128. For an attempt by a leading contemporary liberal theorist to wrestle with the implications for liberalism of the breakdown of the family, see William Galston, *Liberal Purposes* (Cambridge: Cambridge University Press, 1991), pp. 283–287.

CHAPTER 3
KANT: VIRTUE WITHIN THE LIMITS OF REASON ALONE

1. See Onora O'Neill, "Kant after Virtue," in *Constructions of Reason: Explorations of Kant's Practical Philosophy* (Cambridge: Cambridge University Press, 1989), pp. 148–149. For Hegel's classic criticism, see *The Philosophy of Right*, trans. T. M. Knox (Oxford: Oxford University Press, 1980), §§ 105–140, pp. 75–103; and *Phenomonology of Spirit*, trans. A. V. Miller (Oxford: Oxford University Press, 1980), §§ 419–437, pp. 252–262. For contemporary versions of the classic criticism, see Bernard Williams, *Ethics and the Limits of Philosophy* (Cambridge: Harvard University Press, 1985), pp. 54–70; Alasdair MacIntyre, *After Virtue*, 2d ed. (Notre Dame, Ind.: University of Notre Dame Press, 1984), pp. 43–47; Michael Sandel, *Liberalism and the Limits of Justice* (Cambridge: Cambridge University Press, 1982), pp. 1–65, 104–122, 166–168, 175–183; Charles Taylor, *Hegel and Modern Society* (Cambridge: Cambridge University Press, 1979), pp. 76–84; and Roberto Unger, *Knowledge and Politics* (New York: Free Press, 1975), pp. 50–51, 53–55.

2. See, for example O'Neill, *Constructions of Reason*, esp. pp. 145–164; Richard L. Velkley, *Freedom and the End of Reason: On the Moral Foundation of Kant's Critical Philosophy* (Chicago: University of Chicago Press, 1989); Henry E. Allison, *Kant's Theory of Freedom* (Cambridge: Cambridge University Press, 1990), pp. 180–198; Barbara Herman, *The Practice of Moral Judgment* (Cambridge: Harvard University Press, 1993); and Susan Shell, *The Embodiment of Reason: Kant on Spirit, Generation, and Community* (Chicago: University of Chicago Press, 1996). See also Jürgen Habermas, "Morality and Ethical Life: Does Hegel's Critique of Kant Apply to Discourse Ethics?" in *Kant and Political Philosophy* (New Haven: Yale University Press, 1993), pp. 320–336. For special emphasis on Kant's political theory, see Patrick Riley, *Kant's Political Philosophy* (Totowa, N.J.: Rowman and Littlefield, 1982).

3. For Rawls's interpretation of the Kantianism of his approach, see *A Theory of Justice* (Cambridge: Harvard University Press, 1971), chap. 40, "The Kantian Interpretation of Justice as Fairness," pp. 251–258; "Kantian Constructivism in Moral Theory," *Journal of Philosophy* 77 (1980): 515–572.

4. *A Theory of Justice*, pp. 453–479.

5. *Ordinary Vices* (Cambridge: Harvard University Press, 1984), p. 232.

6. Ibid.

7. Ibid., pp. 232–233.

8. "The Liberalism of Fear," in *Political Thought and Political Thinkers*, ed. Stanley Hoffmann (Chicago: University of Chicago Press, 1998), p. 15.

9. *Critique of Pure Reason*, trans. Norman Kemp Smith (New York: St. Martin's Press, 1965), A540/B568, A550/B578; hereafter noted as *CPR*.

10. *Groundwork of the Metaphysic of Morals*, trans. H. J. Paton (New York: Harper & Row, 1964), pp. 397–399 (hereafter noted as *Groundwork*; page numbers are

those found in the margins of Paton's translation and refer to the standard edition issued by the Prussian Academy of the Sciences).

11. *Perpetual Peace*, in *Kant's Political Writings*, ed. Hans Reiss (Cambridge: Cambridge University Press, 1970), pp. 112–113.

12. Similarly, while he acknowledges that there is much in the letter of Kant's thought that downplays the moral and political significance of virtue, William Galston suggests that the spirit of Kant's practical philosophy points firmly to the importance of virtue and the sources that sustain it. See "What Is Living and What Is Dead in Kant's Practical Philosophy," in *Kant and Political Philosophy*, pp. 207–223.

13. Christine Korsgaard draws attention to the relation between Kantian autonomy and the social contract tradition, and in particular to the thought of Kant's successor John Rawls and his predecessor Rousseau. See "Kant," in *Ethics in the History of Western Philosophy*, ed. James P. Sterba, Robert J. Cavalier, and James Gouinlock (New York: St. Martin's Press, 1989), pp. 219–221, and see also p. 237 n. 30 and pp. 237–238 n. 31.

14. *Leviathan*, ed. Edwin Curley (Indianapolis: Hackett Publishing Company, 1994), chaps. 16–18, pp. 101–118.

15. *Second Treatise*, in *Two Treatises of Government*, ed. Peter Laslett (Cambridge: Cambridge University Press, 1988), § 4, p. 269; §§ 87–88, pp. 323–325.

16. Hobbes, *Leviathan*, chap. 21, pp. 136–138; Locke, *Second Treatise*, § 4, p. 269.

17. *Groundwork*, p. 452. See also *Critique of Practical Reason*, trans. Lewis White Beck (New York: MacMillan, 1956), pp. 94–97 (hereafter noted as *CPrR*; page numbers are those found in brackets at the top of the page of Beck's translation and refer to the standard edition issued by the Prussian Academy of the Sciences), and *CPR* A444-A451/B472–479. In the *Critique of Pure Reason*, Kant distinguishes between the determination of desires and the decision whether or not to act upon a desire. We can, he allows, choose which of the many desires to act upon for prudential or other reasons. See *CPR* A802/B830. It remains the case, however, that the achievement of true freedom for Kant consists not in choosing among desires but in respecting the moral law.

18. For a more detailed treatment, see Charles Taylor, "Kant's Theory of Freedom," in *Philosophy and the Human Sciences: Philosophical Papers* (Cambridge: Cambridge University Press, 1985), esp. pp. 318–325, 335–337.

19. *Doctrine of Right*, in *The Metaphysics of Morals*, trans. Mary Gregor (Cambridge: Cambridge University Press, 1991), pp. 213–214 (page numbers are those found in the margins of Gregor's translation and refer to the standard edition issued by the Prussian Academy of the Sciences).

20. *Groundwork*, p. 389. See also *On the Common Saying: "This May Be True in Theory, but It Does Not Apply in Practice"*, in *Kant's Political Writings*, p. 61.

21. *Groundwork*, pp. 411–412. See also the *Doctrine of Right*, pp. 216–221. Kant's argument as to why practical anthropology is an irreducible part of ethics shows

how little Kantian-inspired contemporary schools such as deliberative democracy—including the "discourse ethics" of Jürgen Habermas, who regards himself as a "postmetaphysical Kantian"—can do without exploration of the qualities of mind and character that make the social activity of deliberation possible and enable individuals to act consistently in accordance with its results.

22. *Groundwork*, p. 393.

23. Ibid., p. 398.

24. For a more relaxed use of the term "virtue," one that seems to allow the term to be used also in reference to qualities of mind and character that stem from an impure source, see *Religion within the Limits of Reason Alone*, trans. Theodore M. Greene and Hoyt H. Hudson (New York: Harper & Row, 1960), pp. 12–13, 42–43.

25. *Groundwork*, pp. 392, 397, 445.

26. Ibid., p. 396.

27. Ibid., p. 400.

28. Ibid., pp. 402–403.

29. Ibid., pp. 403–404.

30. Ibid., pp. 404–405.

31. Ibid., p. 407. See also the *Doctrine of Virtue*, in *The Metaphysics of Morals*, pp. 392–393.

32. *Groundwork*, p. 426. See also the *Doctrine of Virtue*, pp. 482–483.

33. *Groundwork*, p. 435.

34. Ibid., pp. 435–436.

35. *Religion within the Limits of Reason Alone*, pp. 15–39.

36. *Groundwork*, p. 435.

37. Ibid., p. 423.

38. Ibid. See also the *Doctrine of Virtue*, pp. 391–393, 444–445; *CPrR*, p. 93.

39. *Doctrine of Virtue*, p. 379.

40. Ibid., pp. 405–406; also pp. 380, 394. In addition, see *Anthropology from a Pragmatic Point of View*, trans. Victor Lyle Dowdell, ed. Hans H. Rudnick (The Hague: Martinus Nijhoff, 1974), § 12, p. 147 (page numbers are those found in the margins of Dowdell's translation and refer to the standard edition issued by the Prussian Academy of the Sciences).

41. *Doctrine of Virtue*, pp. 383–384. On this point J. B. Schneewind exaggerates the difference between Kant and Aristotle. While virtue, as Schneewind argues, may always be a struggle for Kant and must become a kind of second nature for Aristotle, the principle, in Kant's view, that informs one's act must be settled and firmly held. See Schneewind, "The Misfortunes of Virtue," in *Ethics* 101, no. 1 (October 1990): 61.

42. *Ethics* 1138b18–30.

43. *Doctrine of Virtue*, pp. 397, 399; also pp. 399–403; cf. Aristotle, *Ethics* 1103a24–25.

44. See Christine Korsgaard, "Morality as Freedom," in *Kant's Practical Philos-*

ophy Reconsidered, ed. Yirmiyahu Yovel (Dordrecht: Kluwer Academic Publishers, 1989), pp. 42–43.

45. *Doctrine of Virtue*, pp. 385–386, 392; also p. 419.

46. Ibid., pp. 419, 421–428.

47. Ibid., pp. 387, 392.

48. Ibid., pp. 380, 425–428.

49. See "An Answer to the Question: 'What Is Enlightenment?'" in *Kant's Political Writings*, p. 54. Cf. *Anthropology from a Pragmatic Point of View*, § 77, p. 257.

50. *Doctrine of Virtue*, pp. 424–428.

51. Ibid., pp. 420, 429–437.

52. Ibid., p. 438.

53. Ibid., pp. 452–461.

54. Ibid., p. 458.

55. Ibid., p. 462.

56. Ibid., pp. 465–468.

57. Ibid., pp. 469–473. While he holds that there is only one best form of friendship, Aristotle, in contrast to Kant, emphasizes the continuities between friendship based on virtue and a shared conception of the good with friendships based on pleasure and those based on utility. See the *Ethics* 1155b15–1157b4.

58. *Doctrine of Virtue*, pp. 473–474. See also *Anthropology from a Pragmatic Point of View*, § 14, pp. 151–153.

59. Jean-Jacques Rousseau, "Discourse on the Sciences and the Arts," in *Discourses and Essay on the Origin of Languages*, ed. and trans. Victor Gourevitch (New York: Harper & Row, 1986), pp. 4–7.

60. See *Doctrine of Virtue*, pp. 477–484. In the *Critique of Practical Reason*, Kant argues that education for virtue primarily consists in the practice of moral reasoning. See "Methodology of Pure Practical Reason," in *CPrR*, pp. 150–161. In his *Lectures on Ethics* Kant declares that the end of mankind is moral perfection, and the only hope for its achievement is education. But even here Kant is concerned with the highest moral perfection, and while appealing to education, he offers little guidance as to its content or instruction as to its institutionalization in a free society. See *Lectures on Ethics*, trans. Louis Infield (Indianapolis: Hackett Publishing Company, 1963), pp. 252–253.

61. See *Doctrine of Virtue*, p. 376.

62. *CPR* A316/B373, p. 312; cf. Kant's exposition of "the Universal Principle of Right," in *Doctrine of Right*, pp. 230–233.

63. *Perpetual Peace*, p. 112.

64. Ibid., pp. 112–113.

65. Tocqueville, who cannot be accused of ignoring the place of virtue in liberal democracy, is largely in agreement with Kant that lawmaking must neither depend on true virtue nor take chief responsibility for fostering it. He observed, generally approvingly, that "American legislation appeals mainly to private interest; that is the great principle which one finds again and again when

one studies the laws of the United States. American legislators show little confidence in human honesty, but they always assume that men are intelligent." However, Tocqueville does make clear, as Kant does not, that the doctrine of "self-interest rightly understood" crucially depends on a variety of beliefs, practices, and associations. *Democracy in America*, ed. J. P. Mayer, trans. George Lawrence (Garden City, N.Y.: Doubleday & Company, 1969), vol. 1, pt. 1, chap. 5, p. 79; vol. 2, pt. 2, chap. 8, pp. 525–528.

66. See, for example, Michael Sandel, *Democracy's Discontent* (Cambridge: Harvard University Press, 1996), pp. 321–322. Interestingly, Judith Shklar makes the same mistake. With reference to Kant's devils she notes, "Why crass self-interest should be enough for representative republican institutions is, however, not so obvious." *Ordinary Vices*, p. 234. Shklar, like Sandel, is right to doubt that *crass* self-interest is enough to sustain representative institutions, but they are both wrong to attribute this proposition to Kant, whose notion of intelligent devils suggests the need for self-interest that has been enlightened and disciplined.

67. Even the interpretation that I have suggested may not go far enough. For Kant's republic of devils, though it does not legislate morals and does presuppose the absence of purity of moral intention in citizens, may well still require actions that depend on the exercise of virtue that is more closely related to nobility and moral excellence. After all, a nation of intelligent devils, it may be presumed, will face foreign threats and so will require citizens to engage in military service, which in turn depends upon actions that express courage. See Aristotle *Ethics* 1129b15–25.

68. *Perpetual Peace*, p. 113; see also pp. 124–125.

69. Ibid., p. 122. Similarly, Kant argues that whereas the legislator must retain a right of judgment about the justice of particular laws, subjects must always obey. And therefore, until such time as perpetual peace is achieved, politics will depend upon the virtue of rulers. See the conclusion to *On the Common Saying: "This May Be True in Theory, but It Does Not Apply in Practice"*, in *Kant's Political Writings*, pp. 87–88.

70. *Idea for a Universal History with a Cosmopolitan Purpose*, in *Kant's Political Writings*, pp. 41–42.

71. Ibid., p. 44.

72. Ibid., pp. 44–45. See also *Critique of Judgment*, trans. Werner S. Pluhar (Indianapolis: Hackett Publishing Company, 1987), pp. 430–434 (page numbers are those found in the margins of Pluhar's translation and refer to the standard edition issued by the Prussian Academy of the Sciences).

73. See also *Perpetual Peace*, pp. 108–114.

74. Hans-Georg Gadamer argues that Kant does not fully appreciate Aristotle's doctrine that human beings are made open to arguments about ethics based on reason by an education that begins with "reward and punishment, praise and reproach, model and emulation, and the foundation of solidarity, sympathy, and love on which their effect rests. . . ." Gadamer thereby suggests a

path of rapprochement between Kantian and Aristotelian ethics. See "On the Possibility of a Philosophical Ethics," in *Kant and Political Philosophy*, pp. 371–372.

75. *Ordinary Vices*, p. 232.

Chapter 4
Mill: Liberty, Virtue, and the Discipline of Individuality

1. *On Liberty*, in *Essays on Politics and Society*, ed. J. M. Robson (Toronto: University of Toronto Press, 1977), chap. 2, p. 247; hereafter noted as *OL*.

2. For an extended account of the centrality of virtue to Mill's life and thought, see Bernard Semmel, *John Stuart Mill and the Pursuit of Virtue* (New Haven: Yale University Press, 1984).

3. For the view that free societies require *more* virtue than others, see also *Federalist*, no. 55, in *The Federalist Papers*, ed. Clinton Rossiter (New York: New American Library, 1961), pp. 345–346; and Montesquieu, *The Spirit of the Laws*, ed. Anne Cohler, Basia Miller, and Harold Stone (Cambridge: Cambridge University Press, 1989), 1.3, pp. 22–24.

4. *Autobiography*, in *Autobiography and Literary Essays*, ed. J. M. Robson and J. Stillinger (Toronto: University of Toronto Press, 1981), chap. 1, p. 15. See also "Grote's Aristotle," in *Essays on Philosophy and the Classics*, ed. J. M. Robson (Toronto: University of Toronto Press, 1978), pp. 504–505.

5. Sir Isaiah Berlin maintained that Mill defended the cause of individual liberty as the indispensable condition for the attainment of the highest ends of a human life. But Berlin also saw that Mill's defense of individual liberty did not preclude his appreciating the importance of self-restraint and the need for the exercise of coercive state power to promote education for a life of liberty. See "John Stuart Mill and the Ends of Life," in *Four Essays on Liberty* (Oxford: Oxford University Press, 1969), pp. 178–180, 190–192. In arguing for the existence of two Mills, Gertrude Himmelfarb criticizes *On Liberty* as a relentless celebration of individual choice. Her criticism of the Mill who wished to understand all of moral and political life in terms of "one very simple principle" is delivered in light of the "other Mill," the less famous but in Himmelfarb's estimation more representative Mill, who sought to protect and elevate modern liberty by limiting and directing it through prudent legislation and well-designed political institutions. See *On Liberty and Liberalism: The Case of John Stuart Mill* (New York: Alfred A. Knopf, 1974). For a criticism of the "two Mills" thesis, not on the grounds that there are not two Mills but on the basis of the claim that both, contrary to Himmelfarb, are present in *On Liberty*, see Joseph Hamburger, "Individuality and Moral Reform: The Rhetoric of Liberty and the Reality of Restraint in Mill's *On Liberty*," *Political Science Reviewer* 24 (1995): 7–70.

6. *Autobiography*, chap. 1, p. 5.

7. "Bentham," in *Essays on Ethics, Religion, and Society*, ed. J. M. Robson (Toronto: University of Toronto Press, 1969), p. 77.

8. *Autobiography*, chap. 1, pp. 23–25. For Mill's affirmation of the importance of the study of the classics to "liberal education" in the universities, see "Inaugural Address Delivered to the University of St. Andrews," in *Essays on Equality, Law, and Education*, ed. J. M. Robson (Toronto: University of Toronto Press, 1984), esp. pp. 225–233.

9. *Autobiography*, chap. 1, p. 25.

10. Ibid., chap. 4, p. 115; also chap. 2, p. 49. In addition, see Mill's discussion of the Gorgias in *Essays on Philosophy and the Classics*, p. 150.

11. *Autobiography*, chap. 1, p. 25. See also "Inaugural Address," pp. 229–230; *OL*, pp. 251–252; "Grote's Plato," in *Essays on Philosophy and the Classics*, pp. 382–383; and "Nature," in *Essays on Ethics, Religion, and Society*, pp. 373–374. For what came to be a canonical statement of the view that Plato was a dogmatist, see Friedrich Nietzsche, preface to *Beyond Good and Evil* (New York: Vintage, 1966). For a perspective different from that of Mill but which in effect makes common cause with Mill against the view that Plato's aim was to teach "certain dogmatical conclusions," see Leo Strauss, "On Plato's *Republic*," in *The City and Man* (Chicago: University of Chicago Press, 1964), pp. 50–138.

12. *Autobiography*, chap. 5, p. 141.

13. Ibid., p. 147.

14. "Inaugural Address," pp. 217–218, 220, 234, 243, 247–248, 256–257.

15. "Bentham," p. 78; "Coleridge," in *Essays on Ethics, Religion, and Society*, p. 119.

16. "Bentham," p. 78, emphasis in the original.

17. "Coleridge," p. 119.

18. Ibid., p. 120.

19. "Bentham," pp. 83–88.

20. Ibid., p. 89.

21. Ibid., pp. 95–96.

22. Ibid., pp. 90–91.

23. Ibid., pp. 91–92.

24. "Coleridge," p. 133.

25. Ibid., pp. 133–134.

26. Ibid., pp. 134–135.

27. Ibid., p. 136.

28. *OL*, chap. 1, p. 217.

29. Ibid.

30. Ibid., pp. 219–220.

31. Mill quoting Wilhelm von Humboldt, *Spheres and Duties of Government*, in ibid., p. 215.

32. Ibid., p. 223.

33. Ibid.

34. For a summary, see John Gray, *Mill on Liberty: A Defense* (New York: Routledge, 1981), pp. 1–21.

35. See also *Principles of Political Economy: With Some of Their Applications to Social Philosophy*, ed. J. M. Robson (Toronto: University of Toronto Press, 1965), bk. 5, chap. 1, §§ 1–2, pp. 799–804.

36. *OL*, chap. 1, p. 224.

37. Richard Flathman asserts a fundamental conflict between liberal education and the freedom to create oneself: "Education, however liberal, is unavoidably in tension with self-making." See "Liberalism versus Civic, Republican, Democratic, and Other Vocational Educations," *Political Theory* 24 (February 1996): 7. Flathman, of course, is in a sense correct. If by self-making he has in mind an ideal so severe and demanding that it requires human beings to become in every way entirely responsible for absolutely every one of their acts and achievements, then education, insofar as it contributes to making us who we are, is incompatible with the idea of a completely self-made self. Suffice it to say that such a super-human being, as Nietzsche recognized, would have to be self-caused, his own first principle—in short, a god. See, for example, *Beyond Good and Evil*, sec. 9. So long as you do not raise self-making to a metaphysical level and make the extravagant demand that human beings make themselves the absolute authors of their existence, there is no fatal tension in seeing self-making as an art that, like all arts, requires training and discipline.

38. *OL*, chap. 1, p. 224.

39. See, for example, ibid., chap. 2, p. 257; chap. 3, pp. 265–267. See also *Utilitarianism*, in *Essays on Ethics, Religion, and Society*, chap. 2, pp. 210–216.

40. *OL*, chap. 2, p. 235.

41. *U*, p. 210.

42. "Bentham," pp. 94–99.

43. *U*, pp. 210–211.

44. Ibid., pp. 211–212.

45. Ibid., pp. 215, 218–219, 227, 230–232.

46. Ibid., pp. 234–239.

47. Berlin, "John Stuart Mill and the Ends of Life," p. 181.

48. *OL*, chap. 2, p. 231.

49. Ibid.

50. *Discourse on Inequality*, in *Discourses and Essay on the Origin of Languages*, ed. and trans. Victor Gourevitch (New York: Harper & Row, 1986), pt. 1, § 17, pp. 148–149.

51. *OL*, chap. 2, p. 232.

52. Ibid., p. 235.

53. Ibid.

54. Ibid.

55. Ibid., p. 237.

56. Ibid., pp. 229–243.

57. Ibid., pp. 243–252.

58. Ibid., pp. 252–257.

59. Ibid., p. 244.

60. Ibid., p. 250.

61. Ibid., p. 254.

62. Ibid., pp. 244–246, 251.

63. Ibid., p. 252; and *Autobiography*, chap. 5, p. 171. See also "Inaugural Address," p. 219, and generally pp. 248–250.

64. *OL*, chap. 2, pp. 253–254. See also p. 245; and *Considerations on Representative Government*, in *Essays on Politics and Society*, chap. 2, pp. 383–389; hereafter noted as *CRG*.

65. *OL*, chap. 2, p. 251.

66. Ibid., p. 259.

67. Ibid., p. 257.

68. *U*, chap. 2, p. 216.

69. Alexis de Tocqueville, *Democracy in America*, ed. J. P. Mayer, trans. George Lawrence (Garden City, N.Y.: Doubleday & Company, 1969), vol. 2, pt. 2, chap. 2, p. 508.

70. *OL*, chap. 3, p. 262.

71. Ibid.

72. Ibid., p. 263.

73. Ibid.

74. Ibid., p. 264. See also *The Subjection of Women*, in *Essays on Equality, Law, and Education*, chap. 3, pp. 308–309. Some, with Rousseau's view in mind (that "the most sublime virtues" come from the education of "grand and strong passion"), may be tempted to dismiss Mill's praise of passion as mere romanticism. See *Émile, or On Education*, trans. Allan Bloom (New York: Basic Books, 1979), p. 312. It is therefore worth noting that Locke entertains a similar appreciation that passion is a ground of greatness: "extravagant young fellows that have liveliness and spirit come sometimes to be set right, and so make able and great men; but *dejected* minds, timorous and tame, and *low spirits* are hardly ever to be raised and very seldom attain to anything." See *Some Thoughts concerning Education* in *Some Thoughts concerning Education and Of the Conduct of the Understanding*, ed. Ruth W. Grant and Nathan Tarcov (Indianapolis: Hackett Publishing Company, 1996), § 46, p. 33.

75. *OL*, chap. 3, p. 264.

76. Ibid., p. 266.

77. Ibid., chap. 4, pp. 276–277. Stephen Holmes rightly observes that in *On Liberty* Mill understood good character to consist in choosing a way of life in accordance with one's nature, but then Holmes asserts without argument that "[e]lsewhere, in a brilliant essay, Mill demolished the fallacious belief that 'nature' can serve as a moral standard." *Passions and Constraint: On the Theory of Liberal Democracy* (Chicago: University of Chicago Press, 1995), p. 195. Holmes's characterization of Mill's accomplishment cannot withstand scrutiny. The essay to which Holmes refers, *Nature*, written during the same period as *On Liberty*,

actually embodies a far more interesting and ambiguous view about nature as a moral standard than Holmes recognizes, one that is consistent with the view Mill puts forward in *On Liberty*. Mill's arguments against nature as a moral standard are actually directed against two particular conceptions of nature. First, he criticizes the use of nature as a moral standard where nature is understood, following natural science, as physical nature, that is, in terms of matter in motion. Second, he criticizes the use of nature as a moral standard where nature is understood, following some romantics, as untutored human impulses and instincts. Neither conception of nature, Mill argues, is compatible with a defense of the virtues. In Mill's view, such undoubted moral virtues as courage, cleanliness, self-control, veracity, and justice do not receive support from the teachings of natural science and, contrary to the romantic celebration of impulse, require the mastery of instinct and feeling. See *Nature*, in *Essays on Ethics, Religion, and Society*, pp. 373–402, esp. 393–402. But these conceptions do not exhaust the meanings that nature as a moral standard can have. Human excellence, for Mill, is an achievement, the cultivation of certain virtues whose goodness is not a matter of choice, but whose necessity as a precondition for making good choices can be established if one thinks through a human being's fundamental qualities and the "permanent interests of man as a progressive being." Moreover, in *Utilitarianism* Mill affirms that the capacity to reason, to cooperate, and to exercise "the moral faculty" are parts of our nature, or "a natural outgrowth from it," but only if cultivated can these capacities reach a "high degree of development." *Utilitarianism*, p. 283. In fact, the relation between nature and human excellence that Mill puts forward in *On Liberty*, *Nature*, and *Utilitarianism* bears a striking resemblance to Aristotle's view that "virtues arise in us neither by nature nor contrary to nature; but by nature we can receive them and perfect them by habituation." See *Nicomachean Ethics* 1103a24–25. For Mill himself writes: "If it be said, that there must be the germs of all these virtues in human nature, otherwise mankind would be incapable of acquiring them, I am ready with a certain amount of explanation, to admit the fact." Mill's explanation consists in acknowledging that the "beneficent germs" of virtue in human nature are threatened by "weeds." And, in a manner consistent with the spirit of Aristotle's understanding of nature, Mill argues that the "fostering" of the "good germs" is the only way to overcome these "rankly luxuriant growths" and so form virtuous human beings. See *Nature*, p. 396.

78. *OL*, chap. 4, p. 277. See also *Nature*, pp. 394–395.

79. *OL*, chap. 14, p. 277.

80. For an elaboration, under the rubric of justice, of the general rules that make social life possible, see *Utilitarianism*, chap. 5, pp. 255–259. See also *Nature*, p. 396.

81. *OL*, chap. 4, p. 280.

82. Ibid., chap. 5, p. 292.

83. Ibid., pp. 292–293.

84. Ibid., chap. 4, p. 282.

85. Ibid., chap. 5, pp. 292–297.

86. Ibid., pp. 297–298.

87. Ibid.

88. Ibid., p. 298.

89. Ibid.

90. *The Subjection of Women*, chap. 2, p. 295.

91. See "Tocqueville on Democracy in America, vol. I," and "Tocqueville on Democracy in America, vol. II," in *Essays on Politics and Society*.

92. *OL*, chap. 5, p. 305.

93. *The Subjection of Women*, chap. 5, pp. 294–295.

94. Ibid., p. 295. See also "Inaugural Address," pp. 247–249. To attain legal equality for women, society would have to, Mill believed, overcome "social condition" and "custom" that conspire to "place women in social and political subjection to men." *The Subjection of Women*, chap. 1, pp. 270–272; also chap. 3, pp. 307–309. Although he did not connect it to virtue, Kant also insisted on the legal equality of men and women in marriage. See *The Doctrine of Right* in *The Metaphysics of Morals*, trans. Mary Gregor (Cambridge: Cambridge University Press, p. 278 (the page number is found in the margins of Gregor's translation and refers to the standard edition issued by the Prussian Academy of the Sciences). Locke too. See the *Second Treatise*, in *Two Treatises of Government*, ed. Peter Laslett (Cambridge: Cambridge University Press, 1988), §§ 52–53, pp. 303–304.

95. *OL*, chap. 5, pp. 301–302.

96. Ibid., p. 301.

97. Ibid., p. 302.

98. Ibid., pp. 302–304.

99. *Nature*, pp. 393–397; *The Utility of Religion*, in *Essays on Ethics, Religion, and Society*, pp. 407–410.

100. *Utility of Religion*, pp. 410–411.

101. Ibid., pp. 403–404, 422; *OL*, chap. 1, pp. 226–227, chap. 2, p. 255.

102. *Theism*, in *Essays on Ethics, Religion, and Society*, pt. 5, pp. 487–488. See also *OL*, chap. 2, pp. 235–236, 255–257.

103. *Utility of Religion*, pp. 419–420, 426; *Theism*, pp. 429–489.

104. *Utility of Religion*, p. 422.

105. For a trenchant critique of the use of the Religion of Humanity to form character, a critique that brings out the illiberal and intolerant side of Mill's liberalism, see Joseph Hamburger, "Religion and *On Liberty*," in *A Cultivated Mind—Essays in Honor of J. M. Robson*, ed. M. Laine (Toronto: University of Toronto Press, 1991), pp. 139–181, esp. p. 166.

106. *OL*, chap. 5, p. 305. For the argument that government must limit its interventions in economy and society in order to give citizens the opportunity to develop their "intelligence and virtue," see also *Principles of Political Economy*, bk. 5, chap. 11, § 6, pp. 943–944.

107. *OL*, chap. 5, p. 305.

108. *CRG*, preface, p. 373.

109. Ibid.; *OL*, chap. 2, pp. 252–253.

110. *CRG*, chap. 2, pp. 385–386, 390–392.

111. Ibid., chap. 3, pp. 403–404, 406–412.

112. Ibid., chap. 2, p. 392.

113. Ibid.

114. Ibid.; also p. 404.

115. Mill's view that virtue is a standard for the judgment of actual regimes, and that knowledge of virtue is indispensable for empirical political science, provides another connection between his political science and that of Aristotle. See *Politics* 1288b10–1289a25, 1323a14–23.

116. *CRG*, chap. 3, pp. 399–412.

117. Ibid., p. 399.

118. In a compact study of Mill's *Considerations on Representative Government*, Dennis Thompson emphasizes two constitutive principles of representative government—the principle of participation and the principle of competence. Although he displays a distinctly un-Millian aversion to the word "virtue," Thompson's analysis sheds light on the variety of ways in which Mill connects character to good government, and, though Thompson does not pursue the point, to the blend of democratic participation and aristocratic excellence that Mill's political science reveals to be at the heart of effective representative democracy. See *John Stuart Mill and Representative Government* (Princeton: Princeton University Press, 1976).

119. *CRG*, chap. 1, p. 376.

120. Ibid., chap. 2, p. 388.

121. Ibid., p. 390.

122. Ibid., chap. 3, p. 404.

123. Ibid.

124. Ibid., p. 412.

125. Ibid., chap. 5, p. 422.

126. Ibid., chap. 2, pp. 397–398; "Thoughts on Parliamentary Reform," in *Essays on Politics and Society*, pp. 321–322.

127. *CRG*, chap. 7, pp. 455–460.

128. Ibid., p. 457.

129. Ibid., chap. 8, pp. 473–479.

130. Ibid., pp. 474–475.

131. Letter from Thomas Jefferson to John Adams (28 October 1813), in *The Portable Thomas Jefferson*, ed. Merrill D. Peterson (New York: Viking Press, 1975), p. 533.

132. *CRG*, chap. 8, p. 475.

133. As Stephen Holmes demonstrates. See *Passions and Constraint*, p. 189.

134. *CRG*, chap. 8, p. 476. In the *Autobiography*, Mill states that his proposal

that a plurality of votes be given to those who could demonstrate "superiority of education" did not appear to find favor with anybody. He adds that the very institution which could make it an attractive proposition, a system of national education, might also render it unnecessary. See *Autobiography*, pp. 261–262.

135. *CRG*, chap. 10, pp. 488–495.

136. Ibid., pp. 490–495.

Conclusion

1. *On Liberty, in Essays on Politics and Society*, ed. J. M. Robson (Toronto: University of Toronto Press, 1977), chap. 5, pp. 297–299. Too often neutrality and toleration are confused. But in contrast to the principle of neutrality, which, at least in the case of government action, demands a nonjudgmental stance that is impossible to attain, toleration implies a distinction between what we admire and that with which we are obliged to live.

2. *Politics* 1276b15–1277b30.

3. *Republic* 543a–576d.

4. *Politics* 1310a12–17.

5. *Republic* 555b–566a.

6. In the *Rhetoric* Aristotle observes that in theory democracies can take their principle to an extreme either by extending it too widely or by applying it too narrowly. *Rhetoric* 1360a.

7. See, for example, Amy Gutmann and Dennis Thompson, *Democracy and Disagreement* (Cambridge: Harvard University Press, 1996); *Democracy and Difference*, ed. Seyla Benhabib (Princeton: Princeton University Press, 1996); Michael Sandel, *Democracy's Discontent* (Cambridge: Harvard University Press, 1996). Sandel may appear to be the odd man out here as he defends a communitarian or civic republican political theory, but since the most important part of politics, according to his version of republicanism, is talking about fundamental moral principles in the public sphere, he too can be seen as engaged in the project of radicalizing the liberal idea of consent. Indeed, in a review of John Rawls's *Political Liberalism*, Sandel goes so far as to call his conception "deliberative." See *Harvard Law Review* 107 (May 1994): 1765–1794, p. 1794. And in his own book, Sandel reveals in his final chapter that the "civic conception of freedom" which he favors is (like deliberative democracy) formal and procedural: "It offers a way of conducting political argument, not transcending it." See *Democracy's Discontent*, p. 320.

8. This point is quite different from the view Michael Sandel puts forward in his critique of Rawls's *Political Liberalism*, in the *Harvard Law Review* 107 (May 1994): 1765–1794 and in *Democracy's Discontent*, pp. 320, 338, 349–351. Sandel favors an enlarged and enlivened public conversation in which citizens proclaim their basic beliefs in the public square, showing their respect for fellow citizens by participating in public debates in which they engage each other's first princi-

ples and fundamental moral convictions. What Sandel overlooks is that in a liberal society marked by widespread and deep-seated disagreement about the good, reticence and restraint may be the practicable and appropriate expressions of respect. By neither asking citizens to defend what they hold as most sacred nor seeking to persuade them to alter their cherished beliefs, but, rather, by looking for a common ground in spite of sharp disagreements about God and the Good, one can show respect for individuals and for the differences of principle that create distances among fellow citizens. Moreover, the ambition to open wide the public square to debate on fundamental beliefs itself runs the risk of trivializing religious faith by treating it as subject to bargaining and negotiation, and not, as many believers hold faith to be, the kind of thing for which one fights and dies. As Sir Isaiah Berlin has observed, it is out of respect for the power of principle and the passions that underlie deep conviction that liberals call for toleration rather than demanding from each respect for all beliefs. See Isaiah Berlin, "John Stuart Mill and the Ends of Life," in *Four Essays on Liberty* (Oxford: Oxford University Press, 1969), p. 184; see also John Stuart Mill, *Autobiography*, in *Autobiography and Literary Essays*, ed. J. M. Robson and J. Stillinger (Toronto: University of Toronto Press, 1981), chap. 2, pp. 52–53. A public philosophy that deliberately focuses debate on the opinions which most divide citizens may well be a recipe for derailing public deliberation and disuniting the regime.

9. I explore this issue in "The Debating Society," a review of *Democracy and Disagreement* by Amy Gutmann and Dennis Thompson, in the *New Republic*, November 25, 1996, pp. 36–42.

10. See, for example, Simone de Beauvoir, *The Second Sex* (New York: Vintage, 1952, 1989), pp. xxvi, 169–170, 694, 724–732; Betty Friedan, *The Feminine Mystique* (New York: Dell Publishing, 1963; reprint, 1983), p. x; Susan Moller Okin, *Justice, Gender, and the Family* (New York: Basic Books, 1989), pp. 14–17; and Catharine A. MacKinnon *Toward a Feminist Theory of the State* (Cambridge: Harvard University Press, 1989), p. xii.

11. See, for example, Jean-François Lyotard, *The Postmodern Condition: A Report on Knowledge*, trans. Geoff Bennington and Brian Massumi, foreword by Fredric Jameson (Minneapolis: University of Minnesota Press, 1984); Roberto Mangabeira Unger, *The Critical Legal Studies Movement* (Cambridge: Harvard University Press, 1986), and *Politics, a Work in Constructive Social Theory* (New York: Cambridge University Press, 1987); Richard Rorty, *Contingency, Irony, and Solidarity* (Cambridge: Cambridge University Press, 1989); and William Connolly, *Identity\ Difference: Democratic Negotiations of Political Paradox* (Ithaca: Cornell University Press, 1991).

12. Charles Taylor pursues this line of argument in *The Ethics of Authenticity* (Cambridge: Harvard University Press, 1993).

13. *Justice, Gender, and the Family.*

14. Ibid., pp. 180–181.

15. Ibid.

16. Mill went so far as to argue that "if, either from idleness or from any other avoidable cause, a man fails to perform his legal duties to others, as for instance to support his children, it is no tyranny to force him to fulfil that obligation, by compulsory labour, if no other means are available." *On Liberty*, chap. 5, p. 295.

17. My remarks on the civil society argument are drawn from "The Art of Association," *New Republic*, 24 June 1996, pp. 44–49.

18. Political theorist Jean Bethke Elshtain speaks for many when she notes an alarming discrepancy between the qualities of character that American political life presupposes (ability to cooperate, readiness to compromise, respect for principle, and individual responsibility) and the dispositions that American political culture is producing (selfishness, cynicism, and despair). *Democracy on Trial* (New York: Basic Books, 1995), p. 2. And building on *Making Democracy Work*, his influential study of how recent successes in democratic government in Italy have been a function of a vibrant civil society, political scientist Robert Putnam has assembled striking empirical evidence to show a dramatic weakening over the past several decades of civil society in America. Precipitous decline in voter turnout, drop in trust of government, falloff in churchgoing, significant decrease in participation in the PTA, and decline in labor union membership and involvement in fraternal organizations are, according to Putnam, all signs of erosion of what he calls "social capital." See "Bowling Alone: America's Declining Social Capital," *Journal of Democracy* 6, no. 1 (January 1995): 65–78. For a critique of Putnam and the counterclaim that civil society in America is, in fact, vibrant, see *The Public Perspective* 7, no. 4 (June/July 1996): 1–46.

19. *Democracy in America*, ed. J. P. Mayer, trans. George Lawrence (Garden City, N.Y.: Doubleday & Company, 1969), vol. 2, pt. 2, chap. 7, pp. 520–524.

20. Putnam, "Bowling Alone," p. 67.

21. Elshtain, *Democracy on Trial*, p. 16.

22. Robert Putnam, "The Prosperous Community: Social Capital and Public Life," *The American Prospect*, Spring 1993, p. 42.

NEW FORUM BOOKS

New Forum Books makes available to general readers outstanding original interdisciplinary scholarship with a special focus on the juncture of culture, law, and politics. New Forum Books is guided by the conviction that law and politics not only reflect culture, but help to shape it. Authors include leading political scientists, sociologists, legal scholars, philosophers, theologians, historians, and economists writing for nonspecialist readers and scholars across a range of fields. Looking at questions such as political equality, the concept of rights, the problem of virtue in liberal politics, crime and punishment, population, poverty, economic development, and the international legal and political order, New Forum Books seeks to explain—not explain away—the difficult issues we face today.

Paul Edward Gottfried, *After Liberalism: Mass Democracy in the Managerial State*

Peter Berkowitz, *Virtue and the Making of Modern Liberalism*

John E. Coons and Patrick M. Brennan, *By Nature Equal: The Anatomy of a Western Insight*